ROBERT BURNS

Robert Burns. Miniature by Alexander Reid. *Courtesy of the National Galleries of Scotland.*

ROBERT BURNS

RICHARD HINDLE FOWLER

ROUTLEDGE

First published in 1988 by
Routledge
11 New Fetter Lane, London EC4P 4EE

© Richard H. Fowler 1988

Typesetting by Columns of Reading
Printed in Great Britain by
T.J. Press, Padstow, Cornwall.

British Library Cataloguing in Publication Data
Fowler, Richard Hindle
Robert Burns.
1. Poetry in English, Burns, Robert,
1759–1796 – Biographies
I. Title
821'.6

ISBN 0–415–00169–2

To the memory of my parents,
and of longer-departed Mull
and Lanarkshire forebears.

Such welcome and unwelcome things at once
'Tis hard to reconcile.
>   (*Macbeth* IV. 3, 138–9)

But what is truth? 'twas Pilate's question, put
To Truth itself, that deign'd him no reply.
>   (Cowper: *The Task* III, 270)

CONTENTS

ILLUSTRATIONS

ILLUSTRATIONS

Endpapers
Craigieburn: A Burn's landscape, from *The Card of Burns* by David Octavius Hill.

ACKNOWLEDGMENTS

In offering this work I acknowledge a debt and express thanks to many persons and institutions. High on the list is Ian Bowman of Torrance who procured reference items and put me in touch with others who assisted. Prominent among the latter is Cyril J. Bown of the West of Scotland Agricultural College, who filled gaps in my knowledge of the Burns farms. My thanks also go to George A. Dixon of Edinburgh for seeking out contemporary records of eighteenth-century climate and the economy. For reference material and expressed opinions I thank Professors Robert Fitzhugh of New York and Derek Bryce-Smith of Reading; Dr J.E. Phillips of the Royal (Dick) School of Veterinary Studies; Professors Kenneth Russell and Norman Beischer of Melbourne; Mr W.H. Dunlop of the Burns Cottage; Mr A.E. Truckell and Mr D. Lockwood of the Dumfries Museum and Mr Eric Freeman and Mr Robin Price of the Wellcome Institute for the History of Medicine. The staff of Glasgow's famed Mitchell Library dealt with numerous inquiries with patience and efficiency, and the National Galleries of Scotland generously supplied photographs. Nearer home, essential aid was provided by the staff and stacks of the Victorian State Library and Melbourne University's Baillieu, Brownless, Agriculture and Earth Sciences Libraries. I thank the Australian National University Press and *The Bulletin* (Sydney) for permission to use published texts. I am grateful to fellow members of the Robert Burns Club of Melbourne for encouragement and material assistance, and, through that club, a path to the important resources of the Burns Federation. Final – but very valuable – assistance was given generously by Dr William J. Murray of La Trobe University in his critical reading of my manuscript.

R.H. Fowler

Kelvin Grove, Ashburton,
Victoria 3147, Australia.

ABBREVIATIONS

Extensive reference has been made to two resources that have become virtually essential for writers on Burns. These are *The Letters of Robert Burns*, ed. J. De Lancey Ferguson, and *The Poems and Songs of Robert Burns*, 3 volumes, ed. James Kinsley (both Oxford University Press). The prefix 'L' and serial number indicate a reference to the former and the prefix 'K' and serial number a reference to the latter. It may be noted that the chapter titles, all quoted from the words of Burns, are so identified. For the works of Hogarth, the prefix 'B&C' with serial number used by Burke and Caldwell in their volume *Hogarth: The Complete Engravings* furnish identification.

INTRODUCTION

A penetrative study of the life and works of the Scottish poet Robert Burns (1759–96) has to be more than a study of the life and works of Robert Burns. His life was short, but it spanned almost four critical decades of Scottish history: decades of dawning agrarian enlightenment, of simmering theological divisiveness, of divergent moral standards, of stormy politics, of medical groping. All those issues intruded into the stressed life of Burns, and by his world-handling genius he left us a graphic read-out of his reactions to them. The most reliable core record of the life of Burns was written by Burns – in verse, letters and diaries – but a full grasp of that record demands collateral study of the *milieu*. One objective of this book is to further that study.

One famed component of the Burns virtuosity – conversational brilliance – remains out of reach, as Burns had no Boswell at hand with pen at the ready, but we can 'tak the lave' because his ever-frank and every-busy pen went some way to make Burns his own Boswell in the recording of events and impressions. Inevitably, gaps remain. Drawn by such a celebrated subject, biographers were not slow to move in: there have been scores of them since 1796, and for missing pieces the temptation to set down the superficial interpretation as *fact* has not always been resisted. The tendentious option, confidently presented as determinate fact, has no place in responsible biography.

A second objective of the book is to weigh in the balance some of the dubious conclusions implanted in the Burns story. Of special significance is a re-examination of the poet's health record and final decline – a dialectic leading to the rejection of the entrenched Crichton-Browne account and its later modifications, without reinstating the older alcohol version.

Additionally, Burns enthusiasts will find points of interest that have escaped the attention of the most meticulous writers. For instance, for the first time are now brought forward the key influence of the philosopher John Locke on the bard's religious course, the startling presence of two of his close friends on the jury for the scandalous trial of one of Scotland's political martyrs of

1794, a critical review of the farming performance of the Burns men in the light of twentieth-century science, and the spirited wrangle that raged for months in 1897 and 1898 in the pages of the Sydney *Bulletin* on the topic of Burns as a plagiarist poet.

The opening chapter takes the form of a birth-to-death outline account; one which, in the main, will be familiar to students of the life of Burns. However, the reader will find pauses in the general flow for the elaboration of some specific topics, such as the political stresses that engulfed Burns in his earlier Dumfries years and the money problems that plagued him later. Some major separable issues, too complex and pervasive for biographical dispatch *en passant*, are picked up afresh for discussion in depth in the chapters and appendices that follow on.

Chapter One

SANDS O' LIFE

(K.453)

PREAMBLE

Robert Burns, Scotland's celebrated poet of 'splendour among shadows', like many men who had both achieved major successes and suffered reverses, was moved to set down the details of his life. But the autobiographical end-product, unlike most autobiographies written with conscious design late in life, is not a single book. Rather it is a succession of revealing letters, set in time from adolescence until the march of the poet's eventful years was halted. More than seven hundred of those letters have been assembled for our perusal in a published collection.[1] A high proportion of them give the impression that they were written with one eye on their preservation for posterity – in fact of many the writer laboriously had made fair copies, clearly to that end. He would have stayed his hand with some others had he any inkling that some day a critical world would find and publicize them. One very long lettter, written by Burns in 1787, stands out as the major component of this diffuse autobiography, the addressee being Dr John Moore, a London physician whom he never met. Two Common Place Books, tour diaries and many poems provide extensive amplification. While it all offers an abundance of source material for the follow-up biographers, a recurrent problem of interpretation can be very demanding. One thing at least is clear. Burns, a true son of the Scottish Enlightenment, has an image set to be revivified annually, as it already has been over years which stretch back well into the nineteenth century. That image has prompted the upraise of many statues and much oratory from their plinths, and clubs by the hundred honour the poet's name all over the world. The enchantment born of his poems and song lyrics has been amplified by his stance against political injustice, unearned privilege and repressive religious discipline. Even his erotic excesses have been euphemized, by some almost to a degree suggestive of admiration. What follows is a new look at the 'standard' Burns biography, with

3

a few important amendments offered to those not simply content to
march to old drum-beats.

TO ADOLESCENCE

Robert Burn's paternal forebears had long been farmers on the
estates of the Earl Marischal in Kincardineshire, and if Robert
Burnes (or Burness), grandfather of the poet-to-be, did not actually
participate in the 1715 Jacobite rising he was certainly grievously
involved in its aftermath. After the rising was crushed the estates of
the leaders became forfeit to the Crown and were sold off by
appointed commissioners, and the Jacobite tenth Earl Marischal's
did not escape that fate. The political turmoil added much to the
prevailing misery of the peasants, some of whom had barely
escaped starvation in the bad seasons of 1695 to 1702 – the 'King
William years' – and later the disastrous Darien scheme had
magnified the general poverty of Scotland. Grandfather Burnes
found the going tough but he battled on as best he could. The
fateful last straw was the 1745 Jacobite rising, so much bigger and
bloodier than the 'Fifteen', and more economically devastating in
the north. Soon Burnes could no longer meet his rent commitments
and his tenancy was terminated, and his three sons, now grown
men, decided that they must make a fresh start elsewhere. Our
interest from now on centres on the third son, William, who,
possessed of some skill as a gardener, went south to Edinburgh,
and a few years later to Ayrshire.

William Burnes enjoyed several periods of employment as a
gardener in Ayrshire but eventually decided to develop a small
property in his own right. He acquired in feu some seven acres in
Alloway from Dr Fergusson of Doonholm, building on that land a
clay and stone cottage, and soon afterwards marrying Agnes
Brown. To the couple the first child, a boy, was born on
25 January 1759, and this is where the story really starts. The boy
was given the name Robert after his paternal grandfather in the
tradition of the times. Six more children were to be added to the
family – Gilbert in 1761, Agnes in 1762, Annabella in 1764,
William in 1767, John in 1769 and Isabella in 1771. The date of
the shortening of the family name from Burnes to Burns is
uncertain, but the entry of Robert's birth in the parish register uses
the shortened version.

The birthplace of Burns: Alloway, in the early nineteenth century. From *National Edition of the Works of Robert Burns*, ed William Wallace, London 1866.

Robert had a brief period of schooling, when aged six, at the parish school at Alloway Mill. This school closed when the master left to take a new post in Ayr, and William Burnes, an ardent believer in the value of education, pooled his slender resources with some neighbours to employ an independent teacher. They selected John Murdoch, who was only eighteen years old at the time. This young man, if only to be judged by the results he achieved, must have been a competent teacher, with his task made all the more rewarding through the innate aptitude of Robert and Gilbert who generally stayed at the top of the class. But then, as now, parental collaboration after school hours was a vital component of the process of learning and character development, and this collaboration was there in the Burns family in full measure. Both teacher and father implanted a love of reading in the boys, who quickly mastered grammar and learnt to appreciate poetry and prose literature. The daughters evidently gained the benefit of this communal home instruction, as indicated by the later letters of Isobel which are characterized by a graceful ease of expression.[2] Agnes the mother was adept at singing the old songs of her land

and undoubtedly she created an early love for them in Robert. The ability to sing the metrical version of the psalms had long been regarded as an essential part of the rearing of children in Scotland, and Murdoch gave due attention to this requirement, but he was later to write that 'Robert's ear, in particular, was remarkably dull, and his voice untunable'.

In November 1765 William took the lease of the Mount Oliphant farm, about two miles south-east of Alloway and also owned by Dr Fergusson of Doonholm. The soil was sour, stony, weed-infested and ill-drained, but Mount Oliphant's seventy acres and a primitive steading were to be the home and support of the Burns family for the following twelve years. Robert and Gilbert continued their schooling under Murdoch for a while, but before long Murdoch departed and the Alloway school closed. William Burnes continued to encourage the boys in home study, and to that end he maintained a supply of books – mostly borrowed from friends. There was intermittent contact with Murdoch again from 1772 when he took a teaching post at Ayr. He would often visit the home bearing books and ever ready for profitable discussion.

As a young teenager, Robert became his father's right-hand man for all the arduous labour demanded by the farm, and Gilbert, eighteenth months junior to Robert, was able to contribute his share as he grew older and stronger. But the farm was steadily failing as an economic proposition, and to add to the misery of unremitting drudgery the lenient landlord Fergusson died. The routine control of his estate was passed to the hands of a factor who, for another eight years, proved to be a pragmatic individual whose main preoccupation was seeing that the rent of the farm was paid on the due dates. Both Robert and Gilbert wrote bitterly, in later years, of the trials of the Mount Oliphant period. Robert, when aged sixteen, enjoyed a brief respite when his father sent him to a Kirkoswald school to learn surveying, but that interlude achieved little apart from some broadening of outlook and a transient infatuation with a lass named Peggy Thomson. Around that period he also went to a country dancing school, thereby occasioning some distress to his devout Presbyterian father. In 1777 the Mount Oliphant lease was terminated and the farm vacated by the Burns family. They moved to Lochlea, a larger property which presented better prospects.

LOCHLEA AND MOSSGIEL

Lochlea was in the parish of Tarbolton, about half way between
the town of that name and Mauchline. Maclure the landlord
collaborated in soil improvement but charged a rental which was
to become onerous. The Lochlea period appears to have been one
of initial enthusiasm and progress, with planting diversified to
include flax. The proximity to Tarbolton brought welcome social
contacts for Robert, and he became prominent in the debating
bouts of the Tarbolton Bachelors' Club. When first introduced into
the Tarbolton circle, eighteen-year-old Robert was, in his own
words, 'perhaps the most ungainly, awkward boy in the parish'
(L.125), but that image was to change rapidly. His special joy was
the new-found access to books in abundance, and their influence on
him was profound. At Mount Oliphant his reading had been
limited mainly to books that Murdoch had been able to bring and
to some that his father had been able to borrow. The devout
William appears to have given priority to various religious works,
and Murdoch had been able to add some Shakespeare, English
Augustan poetry, some French language study, and, with inconsequential results, some Latin. The reading field broadened at
Lochlea. There Robert gained ready access to the *Spectator*, more
Shakespeare, John Locke's *Essay Concerning Human Understanding*,
John Taylor's somewhat heterodox *The Scripture Doctrine of Original Sin*,
Boyle's Lecture Sermons, Allan Ramsay's poetry, *A Select Collection
of English Songs*, Tull's and Dickson's works (both on agricultural
improvement), and, later, Thomson's and Shenstone's poems,
Sterne's *Tristram Shandy*, Mackenzie's *Man of Feeling*, and various
other works. During the early Lochlea years young Burns often
tried his hand at writing poetry, with the undistinguished results to
be expected of a youthful beginner. Most of those early poems are
lost.

The linen industry had been growing in importance in Scotland
from the early years of the century, and Robert, aged twenty-two,
went to Irvine to learn the craft of flax-dressing. The whole venture
was a fiasco. At Irvine he suffered a bout of crippling depressive
illness ('my hypochondriac complaint') which lasted for three
months, and the flax-dressing project terminated unceremoniously
when the premises burnt to the ground on New Year's Eve, 1781.
It was in Irvine that he formed a friendship with Richard Brown, a

7

merchant seaman, and enjoyed his stimulating company. Robert later blamed Brown – rightly or wrongly – for leading him astray in his sexual ethics – 'his friendship did me a mischief' (L.125). It could have been around this same period that he came across the poetry of Robert Fergusson, much of which was written in Lowlands vernacular, and this inspired him to press on with his own poetry in the same style – 'I strung anew my wildly sounding lyre with emulating vigour' (L.125). In July 1781 he joined the Freemasons in Tarbolton, to make lasting friendships there and pave the way to more in later life.

In 1783, a very troubled year for the Burns family, Robert commenced the writing of his first Common Place Book, and this remains today as a revealing and valuable source of information on its author.[3] Keeping a Common Place Book was a popular diversion for the cultured classes of those times, serving as a repository of philosophical reflections, poetic efforts and the like. It is clear from this book that by 1783 Burns had made his debut as a poet of noteworthy potential. He also recorded in it his ambition to do some poetic service to the rich history of the 'Bailieries' of Ayrshire – Carrick, Kyle and Cunningham. He also set down significant medical information – his susceptibility to depression – 'that most dreadful distemper, a hypochondria, or confirmed melancholy'.

The year 1783 could hardly have been worse for William Burnes and his family. The winter had been a severe one and the crops were poor. William was in failing health, almost certainly through pulmonary tuberculosis, and to make matters worse a financial crisis was fast approaching as a dispute with the landlord, concerning expenditure on improvements, strung on. Protracted and costly legal action was to be terminated only by the death of the unhappy tenant farmer in February 1784. Other members of the family had been able to avoid serious involvement in the litigation by arranging to be recorded as servants of the father, and even retained some assets as creditors of the estate. Robert and Gilbert had already taken the lease of another farm, Mossgiel, late in 1783, and the whole family made it their new home after William Burnes's death.

Mossgiel, about two miles south-east of Lochlea, has become more notable for Robert Burns's poetical and sexual enterprises, both productive, than for his farming, which was not. The revealed pregnancy of the servant girl Lizzie Paton resulted in a humiliating public rebuke in the kirk, to be followed by the writing of the cleverly defiant *Epistle to J. Rankine* (K.47). The subsequent birth of an infant girl (on 28 May 1785) inspired the writing of two more poems: the famous *A Poet's Welcome to his Love-begotten Daughter* (K.60), and the long-suppressed bawdy poem *The Fornicator* (K.61). It also meant that Agnes Burns who had reared six children was landed with yet another to look after. In that same year Robert's youngest brother John died from an unidentified illness.

Entries in the Common Place Book ceased around October 1785, evidently beause its author had become more and more diverted to other matters. He was devoting much of his time to the writing of poetry; in fact the Mossgiel period was to become by far the most productive of his poetic life, accounting for such masterpieces as *The Vision, To a Mouse, The Twa Dogs, The Cotter's Saturday Night, Halloween, Address to the Deil, To a Louse, The Jolly Beggars, To a Mountain Daisy* and some notable *Epistles,* It was also the main period of Burns's sequence of satires on the kirk and its dignitaries. In this category are *Address to the Unco Guid, The Holy Tulzie, Holy Willie's Prayer, Epistle to John Goldie, To the Rev. John M'Math* and *The Holy Fair.* Social situations, class distinction and politics were critical themes in *The Ronalds of the Bennals, Death and Doctor Hornbook, Scotch Drink, The Author's Earnest Cry and Prayer, Address of Beelzebub, A Dream* and others. Up to the close of the Mossgiel period he had written about thirty song lyrics, only three of which are really popular today: *Corn Rigs, Green Grow the Rashes O* and *Mary Morison.*

The pre-printing subscription procedure, minimizing the financial risk, was often used by authors and artists to facilitate the publication of books in the eighteenth century, and it persists as an appropriate procedure in special circumstances to this day. Robert Burns distributed his printed proposal for the publication of his first book of poems in April 1786, and later he made it clear in his long letter to Dr Moore (L.125) that he was keen to ensure its release prior to going to the West Indies. And why go to the West Indies? We can point to a likely contributory reason – his involvement with two girls; one certainly pregnant and the other almost certainly also pregnant.

The story of Jean Armour is well documented. Her condition became obvious in March 1786 and her enraged parents forbade further contact with Robert despite a written mutual declaration of marriage; legal and binding then under Scots law. When James Armour, Jean's father, discovered that the book of poems was in production he issued a writ against the young Bard to cover the maintenance of an expected child. Robert avoided accepting service of the writ by going into hiding with the connivance of friends. He also executed a deed making over his assets, including the copyright of his forthcoming book, in favour of Liz Paton's daughter (his 'Dear-bought Bess') with Gilbert as trustee. For reasons not clear to us, Armour did not proceed further with his writ. In the style of the day, Jean and Robert were both obliged to make their confession of guilt before the kirk congregation. Robert, still rejected by the Armours, repeated the marriage formality with Mary Campbell. Documentation is sparse, but there is little doubt that Mary was pregnant well before the stated date of exchanging inscribed Bibles – the second Sunday in May – 'After a pretty long tract of the most ardent reciprocal attachment'.[4] Tragedy lay ahead for Mary. Robert received word that she had died late in October from a feverish infection: it could well have been from the then direful coincidence of feverish infection and pregnancy. No longer was the Bard to be haunted by a possible bigamy accusation, but his conscience was not to escape a more baneful haunting for the rest of his life. The more fortunate Jean Armour safely gave birth to twins – a boy and a girl – early in September.

The book of poems came off the press in August 1786. Printed by John Wilson of Kilmarnock, the agreed-upon issue was six hundred copies. The forty-four poems it contained covered a broad thematic range, from the mock-serious *The Death and Dying Words of Poor Mailie* and *To a Louse* to the gloom of *Despondency* and *Man Was Made to Mourn*. The depicting of eighteenth-century farm life in *The Cotter's Saturday Night* and *The Vision* has added materially to the historical record. Only the mildest of political comment was included, as in *A Dream* – an imagined appearance at the King's Birthday Levee – and *The Author's Earnest Cry and Prayer*, which was an appeal to Parliament for a better deal for Scottish whisky distillers after the Scotch Distillery Act of 1786 equalized the taxation on the English and Scottish products. Burns at this time had accumulated a stock of satires against the kirk but he included only the mildly satirical *Address to the Deil* and *The Holy Fair*. His more forthright satires on the kirk such as *The Holy Tulzie* and *Holy*

Willie's Prayer were only to appear in print posthumously, although he freely circulated hand-written copies among his friends. The '1786', or, as it is more commonly called today, the 'Kilmarnock' edition, sold out very quickly and it returned to its author about twenty pounds. That sum would represent more than a year's wages for a skilled artisan – not a bad return for the first publishing venture of a poet whose name had never yet graced a rejection slip.

EDINBURGH

A friend of Robert Burns had passed on a copy of the 'Kilmarnock' to Dr Blacklock in Edinburgh, and he responded with a highly commendatory letter to the poet, expressing in it his hopes for the issue of a reprint. But Wilson refused to risk a new edition without a very substantial subsidy, so Robert decided to go to Edinburgh in person to find another publisher. The journey, on a borrowed pony, took two days. In the weeks ensuing, Edinburgh and London reviews were appearing, the most famous of them being Henry Mackenzie's in *The Lounger*. Mackenzie, author of *The Man of Feeling* (which had already become a favourite book of Robert's), was at that time the acknowledged front-runner of the Edinburgh *literati* and his review was highly influential. In the fashion of the day he expressed misgivings on the poet's use of the Lowlands dialect – asserting that it made the poems difficult for Scots to follow, and impossible for English readers. But he declared that readers ' . . . will perceive with what uncommon penetration and sagacity this Heaven-taught ploughman, from his humble and unlettered station, has looked upon men and manners'. The 'Heaven-taught' portrayal was no more than a follow-up from the impression Burns deliberately projected in his Preface. Although incorrect, for Burns through his own passion for reading and study was anything but unlettered, the idea fascinated Edinburgh society. The gentry, top academics and law lords all wanted to meet him and he was plied with invitations, but, surprisingly to his numerous hosts, confidence and conversational power quickly gave the impression that the poet was no fish out of water in fashionable drawing-rooms. (In a second Common Place Book, commenced in April 1787, Burns recorded his impressions of many persons he met during his Edinburgh period.[5])

11

The Earl of Glencairn, a distinguished figure in Scottish society, was probably the first of that set to read the Kilmarnock volume, having been shown a copy by Mr Dalziel, the factor of his Ayrshire estate. He befriended Burns and introduced him to the leading publisher William Creech, who agreed to bring out a new edition of the poems. Notices inviting subscriptions were being circulated before Christmas 1786. Creech drove a hard bargain and his slowness in paying up tried his client's patience. In subsequent letters to friends Burns referred to Creech as a 'scoundrel', but after the final settlement he admitted that he had been treated fairly. Creech was canny but honest – the sort of business man from whom one could have bought a used sedan chair with some confidence. Later in the chapter we encounter his political stance as a juror.

The year 1786 had witnessed the progress to term of two pregnancies, one doubly productive and one tragic, plans for emigration to Jamaica made and dropped, the issue of a legal writ and the signing away of all the poet's assets in a trusteeship deed, the publication of a book of verse which was to bring immortal fame, a horse-back ride to Edinburgh and a heady reception there. It had been quite a year for Rab Mossgiel.

In terms of results accruing, the most significant championing of Burns in the early weeks of the Edinburgh visit was undoubtedly by the Earl of Glencairn. He and the Countess subscribed for twenty-four copies of the new edition and successfully prompted the Caledonian Hunt gentry to subscribe for a hundred more. On opening a copy of the '1787' today one is struck by the inclusion of thirty-eight preliminary pages, in small typeface, listing the names of around 1,500 subscribers, many for more than one copy. (The Duchess of Gordon, admittedly smitten by the attractive young poet, took twenty-one.) Such listing, aimed at patronage, was not uncommon in eighteenth-century publication. The Dedication is to the Caledonian Hunt, and in it the poet again fostered the image of his humble origins: 'The Poetic Genius of my Country found me as the prophetic bard Elijah did Elisha – at the plough; and threw her inspiring mantle over me.' It is also clear that Robert's temerity was increasing by his inclusion of some sensitive poems held back from the Kilmarnock volume. In this category are the satirical *Death and Doctor Hornbook* (K.55) which is a lampoon on a Tarbolton school teacher who was running a small medical practice – without formal qualifications – as a side line. The victim, John Wilson, appears not to have been offended, nor adversely affected, by the poem. Also appeared the witty *Green Grow the Rashes*, a cleaned-up, but still mildly erotic, version of an old bawdy song. More boldly he included *The Ordination* – a topical satire on the likely consequences of an Auld Licht minister being admitted to second charge of the Laigh Kirk, Kilmarnock, under a New Licht. Out of range of censorious glares back home he cheekily included *Address to the Unco Guid* – a mildly picaresque masterpiece which has become a favourite of Burns reciters with its well-expressed admonitions. The witty *Address to a Haggis* carried no risk of evoking disparagement, except perhaps in those not disposed towards the eating of 'thairm' (intestine).

Burns was to spend two winters with Edinburgh as his base, this long sojourn being enforced by the slowness of negotiations with Creech. Between business sessions, however, he found ample time to make quite extensive tours. The first of these, on horseback in the company of his friend Ainslie, was through the Borders with a return route through Carlisle, Dumfries and Ayrshire. On arrival back at Mossgiel he found Gilbert in financial difficulties and advanced him £180 out of the interim proceeds on his first Edinburgh book of poems. Now quite famous and relatively affluent, he found the Armour parents seeing him with a very different eye. They were friendly and receptive. He also found their daughter Jean receptive in a more specific sense, with the predictable consequence – her second pregnancy. He resumed his wanderings, going first to Glasgow and on to West Argyll, alone, returning to Mossgiel in August 1787. Around that time he settled a maintenance claim made by May Cameron who was expecting to give birth, or had given birth, to the next of his 'bastart weans'. He was back in Edinburgh in August for more negotiation with Creech and the planning of an extensive tour of the Highlands with William Nicol, a rather irascible Latin teacher with whom he had formed a close friendship.

The Highlands tour, by coach, was important to Burns for several reasons. It provided the long-awaited opportunity to visit historic places, such as Bannockburn and Stirling Castle. Moved by the sight of the ruins of the latter he wrote, using a diamond stylus he had been given, a poem on the glass window of the Stirling inn – a poem that was viciously anti-Hanoverian and pro-

His fpindle fhank a guid whip-lafh,
    His nieve a nit;
Thro' bluidy flood or field to dafh,
    O how unfit !

    But mark the Ruftic, *haggis-fed*,
The trembling earth refounds his tread,
Clap in his walie nieve a blade,
    He'll mak it whifsle;
An' legs, an' arms, an' heads will fned,
    Like taps o' thrifsle.

    Ye Pow'rs wha mak mankind your care,
And difh them out their bill o' fare,
Auld Scotland wants nae ftinking ware
    That jaups in luggies;
But, if ye wifh her gratefu' pray'r,
    Gie her a *haggis!*

The 1787 misprint in *To a Haggis*. 'skinking' is wrongly set as 'stinking'.
Poems, Chiefly in the Scottish Dialect, by Robert Burns, Edinburgh 1787.

Stuart and one that was to bring him bad reactions at a later date. From Stirling he went on to Harvieston and Blair Atholl. He enjoyed the hospitality of the Duke and Duchess of Athole and met Josiah Walker, whose later reminiscences have contributed to Burns's biography. But more important as an influence in later life was his meeting, at Athole House, with Robert Graham, twelfth Laird of Fintry, one of the Commissioners for the Excise in Scotland. Continuing his journey, he visited Culloden Moor and Nairn and enjoyed the hospitality of the Duke and Duchess of Gordon at Fochabers. Proceeding next to Aberdeen and Montrose he met two elderly aunts and his cousins before returning through Dundee, Perth and Kinross.

Another short tour was made by Burns in October 1787, this time with another friend, Dr James McKitterick Adair, a relation of Mrs Dunlop, a lady who had written to Burns after reading the Kilmarnock poems. The destination was Harvieston, where the pair spent eight days in the company of Charlotte Hamilton (half-sister of Gavin Hamilton of Mauchline) and Margaret Chalmers, a young lady who combined the attractions of good looks, poise and cultural accomplishments. Later correspondence reveals that Burns unsuccessfully proposed marriage to Margaret. On that occasion the doctor evidently had more winning ways than had the poet, Charlotte becoming Mrs Adair in the following year. On the way home from this visit Burns performed a second fruitless exercise. He returned to the Stirling inn and smashed the window pane still displaying the disloyal verses he had inscribed on his earlier tour, but, as events were to prove, he had left his action too late. Many travellers must have taken note of the verses and the Jacobite sympathies of the writer during the weeks of their open display. Lines 7 to 11 ran:

> The injur'd Stewart-line are gone,
> A Race outlandish fill their throne;
> An idiot race, to honor lost;
> Who know them best despise them most.

> (K.166)

The lionizing of Burns by Edinburgh society was soon to wane, and he turned to clubs and taverns for his diversions. These were meeting places for plenty of very interesting people. A club called the Crochallan Fencibles was a favourite, numbering among its members the law lords Monboddo and Hailes, and less exalted lawyers such as Alexander Cunningham who became a lifelong friend of Burns. The Crochallan was famed as an arena for bawdy verse and song, and Burns's talents in that art form were exercised there with enthusiasm. Another club of prominence was the Cape Club, numbering amongst its members David Herd, famed for collecting Scottish folk poetry and lyrics, Deacon Brodie (hanged for burglary in October 1788) and Henry Raeburn the artist. A member who had died in 1774 was Robert Fergusson, the poet of beloved memory to Burns. He was the forgotten man of Scottish dialect poetry and Burns successfully sought permission to place a commemorative stone over the grave at his own expense.

One of the really good things Edinburgh did for Burns was to make possible his meeting with James Johnson, a fellow-Fencible. Johnson was an engraver who had set himself the task of collecting and publishing the folk-songs of Scotland, with the prevailing style of musical notation (melody line plus figured bass), in a series of volumes to which he gave the name *The Scots Musical Museum*. Poorly educated, and with little technical knowledge of music, he had enlisted the aid of the organist Stephen Clarke. Burns immediately joined forces with Johnson with tremendous enthusiasm, and so began a collaboration which the poet was to find artistically rewarding for the rest of his life. However, rendering honorary assistance in a worthy cause is a very different matter to earning a living. Even prior to his first visit to Edinburgh the Bard had been considering the possibility of an appointment to the Excise service and had mentioned it in a letter to his lawyer friend Aiken (L.53). Against that, the offer of a lease of a farm on Patrick Miller's Dalswinton estate in Dumfriesshire was to engage his attention before he left Edinburgh. He had called to see the farm site, upstream from Dumfries on the Nith, on the way home from his tour of the Borders.

The closing months of 1787 were bringing new complications into Robert's life. In October his baby daughter, one of Jean Armour's twins, died. In December in Edinburgh he met Agnes M'Lehose, the attractive twenty-nine-year-old wife of an absentee husband of bad repute. She was talented and vivacious, and had a flair for poetical composition in a small way. A quite torrid love affair developed, although it would seem that her strong Calvinist convictions debarred any sexual union. The flowery grandiloquent

16

correspondence between the lovers, for which they adopted the pseudonyms Clarinda and Sylvander, suggests a passionate mutual involvement. Sylvander found an alternative release for his coercive libido with a serving-wench, Jenny Clow, who was to bear him a son in consequence.

In February 1788 a final settlement with Creech was reached and Burns left Edinburgh. He estimated his net return from the 1787 edition of his poems to be in the vicinity of £500, but the advance to Gilbert and his Edinburgh spending left him with only about half that amount for his future needs. Before going back to Mauchline he detoured to Glasgow for a reunion with his sailor friend Richard Brown. Returning *via* Stewarton he called on Mrs Dunlop of Dunlop, the well-connected landed lady who had initiated a correspondence with him after reading the Kilmarnock poems. This correspondence was to continue until the end of 1794. Mrs Dunlop was soon his chief confidante and confessor, and the preserved letters remain as an important source of biographical information.[6] On his return to Mauchline, Burns found Jean Armour well advanced in her second pregnancy and rejected in disgrace by her parents, but that did not debar another sexual performance with her. The boastful and very explicit letter he wrote describing the encounter, to his friend and fellow-fornicator Robert Ainslie on 3 March 1788, remains as a source of acute embarrassment to those Burns admirers who like to cling to the notion that he was the paradigmatic romantic lover. A mere nine or ten days after the described event, Jean gave birth to her second pair of twins, but the infants failed to survive more than a few days. Burns was soon back in Edinburgh, and his high-flown, sentimental correspondence with his Clarinda was soon on again with renewed intensity.

Early in 1788 Burns was facing up to the realization that a major decision about his future livelihood had to be made. Would he revert to farming, or press on with plans to secure an appointment in the Excise service? He made his decision – a bad one. He decided to try both.

At Burns's invitation, John Tennant of Glenconner, who was an experienced farmer, accompanied him on a visit of inspection of the Dalswinton farms on offer by Patrick Miller. He decided that the Ellisland farm was the one he wanted, and the lease was signed in Edinburgh on 13 March 1788. He also realized that a farmer getting started with limited funds would need a farmer's wife – to cook meals, to tend fowls, to milk cows, and to see to sundry other essentials like churning and cheese-making. Who was it to be? Hardly petite, soft-fingered Clarinda, even though she may have been harbouring the hope that her worthless husband might die in Jamaica and free her. Margaret Chalmers would certainly have graced the drawing-room of Scotland's greatest poet, but not his kitchen and byre. It just had to be long-suffering, compliant Jean Armour. They were quietly married, and the husband proceeded to write to friends in higher stations praising her many qualities, but his rationalizing of her lack of education is evident in some of the letters. Nothing is known about the precise date or style of the marriage, apart from it later costing the groom a fine for its irregularity. Clarinda received the news by a roundabout route – through Ainslie – and she responded by calling her Sylvander 'villain'. After a calming-off period the correspondence was resumed in lower key, with the term of address by Burns no longer 'Dear partner of my soul' or 'My dearest angel' – simply 'Madam'. Included with a letter dated 27 December 1791, Burns sent the lady the song lyric masterpiece *Ae Fond Kiss*. Posterity might well consider that the chagrin of unhappy Agnes M'Lehose was a trivial purchase price for that beautiful song of farewell. Whether Agnes M'Lehose shared that view is another matter.

TO ELLISLAND AND THE EXCISE

Early in 1788, after a short course of instruction in Excise procedure, Burns made a written request to Commissioner Graham to be considered for appointment. In the meantime he took possession at Ellisland, committed to a lease which provided for an initial grant of £300 for improvements, a rental of £50 per annum for three years and £70 thereafter.[7] The grant was to cover the cost of a new house and farm buildings, and the required dykes to make six enclosures, with any residue to be used by the tenant for unspecified improvements. As the only accommodation was in the nearby hovel of the ageing David Cullie, the former tenant of Ellisland farm, Jean and the baby boy stayed in Mauchline and Robert rode back to see them every week or two. There was a long frustrating wait for the completion of the house – from June 1788 to May 1789 – but Robert was able to get temporary use of a better house in December 1788 and the family joined him. Cullie had sown a field of corn in the spring of 1788 and this was harvested under difficult weather conditions late in September. In November, Major Andrew Dunlop, who was managing his mother's estate, gave Robert 'the finest Quey (two-year-old cow) in Ayrshire' to augment his herd. But as labour had to be hired for harvesting, equipment and stock bought, and rent payments had to be met, he became concerned about his dwindling funds. He saw the Excise as the solution and again approached his influential friend Graham of Fintry, Commissioner of Excise, and to speed things up suggested to Fintry that as one Leonard Smith, exciseman for the local Divison, had acquired private means and didn't really need the job, he should be given Smith's position. This dubious move, which would be scandalous in today's Civil Service, succeeded. It sheds light on the style of eighteenth-century oligarchic administration, shot through with patronage dispensed by an influential coterie. Burns received his appointment on 10 October 1789, carrying a salary of £50 per annum plus liberal commissions on goods seized and smuggler arrests. The job was centred on Dumfries but the circuit involved extensive riding – up to 200 miles weekly over four or five days – and book work had to be done at home. From now on the farm took second place, with farm hands almost wholly unsupervised and eating up the profits and Jean's food. It is no wonder that on 11 January 1790 Burns despairingly told Gilbert: 'It is a ruinous affair on all hands. But let it go to hell! I'll fight it out and be off with it' (L.381).

Neither is it any wonder that his depression returned. To Clarinda he complained of 'an incessant head-ache, depression of spirits, and all the truly miserable consequences of a deranged nervous system' (L.388). It is a fair assumption that at that time he had still not shaken off the long-term effects of a severe infection which had struck several months earlier – an infection he described as 'malignant squinancy' but which was almost certainly diphtheria. In March he told Mrs Dunlop that the farm was 'a ruinous bargain' and that the Excise 'is indeed my sole dependance', and further on – 'So much for farming. Would to God I had never engaged in it' (L.396).

Despite financial and medical stresses, nothing could lessen Burns's determination to mix with old friends and make new ones. Nor did the drive to write song lyrics for James Johnson in

Edinburgh, and poems for others on appropriate occasions, diminish. Nor did another ever-pressing urge abate. Anna Park, a blonde barmaid at the Globe Inn at Dumfries, bore him a daughter on 31 March 1791, and for good measure, his own Jean bore him another son nine days later. Jean took Anna's baby to her own breast to keep company with her new baby boy, and Anna faded into obscurity. How is that ultra-maternal act to be regarded? Was it dull-minded deference to an erring husband's urging, or was it an irresistible act of compassion? It was probably the latter. Jean was not *that* compliant, as was revealed by her husband's complaints to correspondents Peter Hill (L.387) and Robert Ainslie (L.482) about her upbraidings and scolding.

Mutual interests encouraged a neighbour, Robert Riddell, to extend his hospitality to the poet, even to the extent of giving him unrestricted use of the hermitage on his estate, Friars Carse. Riddell was well educated, with diverse interests which included farmland improvement, music, poetry, literature and antiquities,

'Gathering her brows like gathering storm,
Nursing her with wrath to keep it warm.'
(*Tam O' Shanter*: 11–12). L. Stocks, after John Faed. 1855

'Auld Ayr, wham ne'er a town surpasses,
For honest men and bonny lasses.'
(*Tam O' Shanter*: 15–16). W. Miller, after John Faed. *Tam O' Shanter*
published for the Royal Association for the Promotion of Fine Arts in
Scotland, 1855.

and a warm friendship was quickly forged. One consequence of poetical importance for posterity was the introduction of a visitor, Francis Grose, to Burns. Grose was on a tour of Scotland studying antiquities, and during discussions on Alloway, Robert agreed to furnish traditional witch stories associated with Alloway Kirk. He did much more with one such. He turned it into the long poetic tale *Tam o' Shanter*. This hilarious poem with its contrasts of scene and pace, interspersed with flashes of wit, horror and philosophy, is widely regarded as Burns's greatest work, and its popularity has remained undiminished over the centuries since it was first published in the *Edinburgh Magazine* and *Edinburgh Herald* in March 1791.

William Creech had been quite successful with the 1787 edition of poetry and he planned to issue a new one to include poems written subsequently. He wrote to the poet seeking new material in 1791 but received no reply. He tried again in April 1792 more successfully and an understanding was reached. Robert agreed to supply about fifty extra pages but made it clear that he was too busy to give time to the publishing details. He nominated Professor Dugald Stewart, Henry Mackenzie and Alexander F. Tytler as literary advisers and proof readers, but this work was practically all left to Tytler, as it transpired. As to payment, Robert asked only for some copies of the book to give away plus a few other books. He expressed no further interest in copyright. That attitude appears to have been short-sighted, as the copyright of *Tam o' Shanter* alone would have been quite valuable. Tytler took exception to these four lines in *Tam*:

> Three Lawyers' tongues, turn'd inside out,
> Wi' lies seam'd like a beggar's clout;
> Three Priests' hearts, rotten, black as muck,
> Lay stinking, vile, in every neuk.

Those repulsive items were left off 'the haly table' of the Alloway kirk in the 1793 and later editions. Tytler, a senior barrister, clearly found them offensive to his profession and presumably to the kirk.

Burns's friendship with Robert Riddell, apart from leading to the creation of *Tam o' Shanter*, was significant in other ways. Riddell had founded the Monkland Friendly Society with its library to encourage more reading in the district, and Burns gave active support. Before long he was *de facto* librarian. He also supplied Riddell with two hand-written books of poems, letters and commentary, happily preserved today in the National Library of Scotland and known as the Glenriddell Manuscript. Another valuable record given to Robert Riddell was a four-volume interleaved set of the *Scots Musical Museum* with its hand-written notes on Scottish songs.

Farming at Ellisland came to its premature but predictable end in the autumn of 1791. Patrick Miller, the landlord, made no bones about winding up the lease as he had a buyer waiting to take over the property. Burns sold the standing crop – a good one – together with livestock and chattels, and moved into cramped upstairs quarters in Dumfries. The location was Cawart's Vennel, aptly nicknamed the Stinking Vennel. More than a year was to pass before accommodation more suited to a couple with a growing family was available. This was in Mill Vennel, and the building is preserved today as a Burns museum.

DUMFRIES AND PERILOUS POLITICS

Burns's move to Dumfries late in 1791 meant a good deal more than simply turning his back on farming and settling into the routine of a full-time Excise job. With the French Revolution entering its third stormy year, the prospect of reforming the entrenched socio-political system of Britain was engaging the attention of many liberal thinkers, Burns and some of his friends included. The Forty-five aftermath had brought little mitigation of the harshness of feudalism, apart from two enactments – the abolition, in 1746, of *ward-holding*, removing the right of the feudal lord to command the men of his domain to armed service, and the abolition, in 1747, of *heritable jurisdictions*. The latter move ended the lord's right to inflict the severer punishments such as scourging, imprisonment or even execution on his recalcitrant subjects. These two reforms merely transferred the powers concerned to the Crown, being measures directed to the prevention of further rebellious risings. Any alleviation of 'man's inhumanity to man' was only a secondary consideration. Parliamentary democracy, based on absurdly unequal electorate populations, was little more than a pretence.

Prominent among British reform activists whom Burns greatly

admired was Thomas Paine (1737–1809). Paine, like Burns, had been an Excise officer. After he was dismissed for his part in an agitation for better pay in 1772 he crossed to America to support the revolutionary cause there. He wrote his pamphlet *Common Sense*, a work which reviewed the arguments for American independence and which achieved significant circulation in Britain. After some years of meritorious service with the established American republic, Paine returned home to England, to become a prominent votary of the revolution looming in France. Up to this time, the American revolution appears to have made only minor impact on Burns. His 1787 song *When Guilford Good* (Guilford: Lord North, then chief minister of George III) (K.38) is little more than a historical narrative. Basically, the revolution had been a successful revolt against colonial domination, and although personal liberty was a component feature it did precisely nothing for three million black slaves. And of course Burns was only seventeen years old in 1776. The French Revolution was another matter.

By 1791 Burns had become thoroughly familiar with the issues of the French situation. He had read books by the Enlightenment writers – persuasive treatises which had long been paving the way for the explosive climax of 1789. He was well aware of the plight of commoners subject to domination by the aristocracy and a monopolistic merchant class enforcing unjustifiable privileges, and he would have been scornful of the power long exercised by high-ranking clergy. He was personally familiar with the climate-related crop failures of the 1780s – failures which had fuelled the rebellious discontent of people threatened with starvation and concurrently subject to a taxation burden imposed selectively and unfairly.

As the Revolution continued on its course of merciless savagery, with refugee aristocrats arriving in substantial numbers, the British government stood in dread of the movement taking hold of their own land, particularly in Scotland with its relatively recent history of rebellion. There was no dearth of conservative individuals ready to inform on sympathizers. Edmund Burke released his anti-revolutionary book *Reflections on the Revolution in France* late in 1790, and it brought a vehement response from the extremely radical Thomas Paine in the form of a two-instalment book *The Rights of Man*.[8] Part I exposed the bias in Burke's commentary without mercy, while Part II, published with difficulty in 1792 after Paine's return from a visit to France, was a trenchant attack on the state of

British society and politics. It poured scorn on titles and inherited power and privilege, on a church established by law, on the term of parliament being subject to government whim, on commercial monopolies and even on the monarchy itself. Paine's arrest on the capital charge of treason was ordered. However, on being warned in time by the poet William Blake he was able to escape to France and safety.

Receiving encouragement from the Revolution and the radical *The Rights of Man*, the cause of electoral reform and individual freedom was embraced by growing numbers of progressive thinkers in British society. Many Societies of Friends of the People were formed, and their limited aim was the introduction of universal suffrage, annual parliaments and the right to petition both Houses of Parliament. Membership of one of those societies would have placed the job of a civil servant in jeopardy, and although Burns wisely refrained from making any formal link, he left no one in doubt about his sympathies through his words and actions. The first General Convention of the Societies was held in Edinburgh in December 1792, the leading speaker being the Vice-President, Thomas Muir of Huntershill. On 2 January 1793 Muir was arrested, charged with sedition, and released on bail. He crossed to France.

One can readily envisage Burns's shock and fear when he was informed at this very time that his political views and his indiscreet words were to be the subject of a departmental inquiry. Had he been able to foresee the political and legal developments in the following August and beyond, the effect on him would have been quite terrifying.

Muir's return from France to face trial had been delayed because of the state of war that had arisen between Britain and France. The only available ship route home was *via* America and Ireland, and on arrival at Portpatrick he was seized and taken to Edinburgh in chains. He was tried on the sedition charge in August 1793 under conditions of scandalous bias, found guilty, and sentenced to fourteen years transportation to New South Wales. In the following September the Reverend Thomas Palmer, an unassuming Unitarian minister of Dundee, was similarly tried and sentenced to seven years transportation. In January 1794 William Skirving and Maurice Margarot, and in March Joseph Gerrald, were in turn arrested and tried on the same charge and sentenced to fourteen years transportation. Of Scotland's five Reform Martyrs only Margarot survived to see his native land again. The whole shameful interlude had been an over-reaction to activities which today would be regarded as commonplace and innocent – issuing a few handbills making a case for parliamentary reform and addressing meetings to that end with no incitement to any violence. In Muir's trial, much was made of his passing copies of Paine's book to a few friends. But defence witnesses attested that Muir had emphasized that he considered *The Rights of Man* a book 'foreign to their purpose' and 'one which might be dangerous to people of weak minds'. It is no wonder that Burns quickly passed his copies of *Common Sense* and *The Rights of Man* to his friend George Haugh, a Dumfries blacksmith, for safe keeping as soon as he was told of the pending inquiry.

Politically, Burns had been under a cloud since 1787 when he had recklessly advertised his anti-Hanoverian and pro-Jacobite views on the window of the Stirling inn, leaving the lines to be read by scores of the travelling gentry. A Mrs Stewart had already blasted him face to face for the disloyal expressions while in Edinburgh (L.189), and his thwarted attempt to send four carronades to the French Convention (even though it was before the declaration of war and therefore not illegal) would probably not have been kept a secret.

The departmental inquiry to which Burns was subjected around the time of Muir's arrest turned out to be not at all draconian, merely taking the form of a more or less informal visit from William Corbet, General Supervisor of Excise, who gave him a dressing-down and a stern warning. One may well assume that at no time was Burns in any real danger of dismissal or of incurring more severe punishment. The exercise seemed to be directed towards giving him a timely warning, and initiated by somebody who held him in high regard – even by Mrs Dunlop herself and not 'some envious, malicious devil' in Dumfries (L.529). (Mrs Dunlop was a close friend of Mrs Corbet – a possible channel of communication?) Burns, despite the protests of Mrs Dunlop, had repeatedly expressed pro-revolutionary views in his letters to her. In December 1792 he had told her of shouts of 'Ça ira' and 'groans and hisses' drowning out 'God save the King' in the Dumfries theatre. ('Ca ira' became the title of one of the most famous songs of the French Revolution. It is said to have originated in the response by Benjamin Franklin when asked whether America would win the war against Great Britain (1785). Literally meaning 'It will go', it could be translated as 'We will win' or 'It will work out OK'.) Burns added:

> For me, I am a *Placeman*, you know, a very humble one indeed, Heaven knows, but still so much as to gag me from joining in the cry. What my private sentiments are, you will find out without an Interpreter.
>
> (L.524)

Burns's immediate response on being told of the pending inquiry was to write a panicky letter to Commissioner Graham, pleading the cause of his dependent wife and children. In a second letter, written a week or so later, he did his best to refute the charges set out in Graham's reply to his first. He told lies and struck an attitude of injured innocence. It was all a bit overdone, as no record of the charges was ever filed in the Excise minutes. Nevertheless, Burns the disparager of the Hanoverian line and admirer of the Stuarts, the votary of the French Revolution and reform at home, had been gagged. Like Colonel Fairfax, he was 'Free, yet in fetters held'.

Perhaps because of memories of the Forty-five, the government reaction against reformers in 1793–5 was far more savage in Scotland than in England. (Thomas Hardy, founder of the London Corresponding Society, Horne Tooke, and eleven other arrested radicals were acquitted by London juries.) Both Fox and Sheridan spoke up for Muir after his trial and sentencing, and even the maligned Henry Dundas told an Oppositon speaker in reply that Joseph Gerrald would not be sent to New South Wales were the decision his. But as the trial transcripts reveal, in Scotland the attitude to the reformers, even that of middle-class citizens, was the reverse of merciful. In the list of the ten jurors at Gerrald's trial are recorded two names of significance to students of the Burns saga – those of 'William Creech, bookseller' and 'Peter Hill, bookseller' – none other than Burns's Edinburgh publisher and one of his closest Edinburgh friends. In the trial preliminaries, Gerrald challenged the eligibility of Creech to serve on the jury, his actual words in the transcript being:

> My lord, I object to William Creech; I understand that he has

repeatedly declared, in private conversations, that he would condemn any member of the British Convention', if he should be called to pass upon their assize; and I wish to refer it to his own conscience, and his oath, whether he has not pre-judged the principles upon which I am to be tried.[9]

Gerrald's valid objection was unanimously disallowed by the trial judges (Robert M'Queen of Braxfield as Lord Justice Clerk, Lords Henderland, Eskgrove, Swinton, Dunsinnan and Abercrombie) and the trial reached its close with all ten jurors finding Gerrald guilty of sedition. So much for the standard of justice prevailing in Scotland in 1793–4. It is obvious that Burns never learned of the part his two friends played in the Gerrald case; otherwise he would hardly have written that cordial letter to Creech a year later, enclosing sixteen epigrams and the song lyric *My Chloris, Mark How Green the Groves* (K.470, L.671), and a sequence of very friendly letters to Peter Hill. He also continued to send Hill a kippered salmon each year, and at times a hare.

The warning that had been served on Burns did not deter him from seeking the company of radical friends like Dr William Maxwell, back from France after having taken an active part in the Revolution, and John Syme of the Dumfries Stamps Office. It would appear that such communing reinforced his radical beliefs and tempted him to lower his political guard as time went by. His inscription in a book (De Lolme's *The Constitution of England*) that he gave to the Dumfries Library – 'Mr Burns presents this book to the Library & begs they will take it as a creed of British Liberty – untill they find a better' – was clearly suspect, and the donor, having reflected overnight on the loaded nature of the passage, hurried back and obliterated the inscription.

One may wonder whether Burns's failure to maintain a discreet silence on his support of revolutionary politics was based on simple courage, ostrich-style refusal to comprehend reality, or alcoholic lubrication. The temptation to raise double-meaning, or openly suspect, toasts at gatherings became almost chronic. Lockhart relates the traditional account of Burns seeking to amend a proposed toast from 'The health of William Pitt' to 'The health of a greater and better man, George Washington.'[10] Dr Moore in his diary records a Burns toast more transparently disloyal, reported by one Mr Allen who was present:'Here's the last verse of the last

for the
a very
ircum-
regret,
istance
ate the
nfortu-
th the
ounsel,
trans-
uld be
a gen-
s, qua-
useful
lord, I
uld be
ild be
nighly.
   unin-
pology
a man,
laws of
; would
ing the
consis-
ny lord,
pannel
per and
ny lord,

THURSDAY, MARCH 13, 1794.

When the Court met, the interlocutor on the relevancy was read over, and the following gentlemen were chosen as jurors :—

David Deuchar, Seal-engraver, Edinburgh.
Peter Hill, Bookseller, there.
John Bell, Bookseller, there.
James Hunter, Merchant, there.
Andrew Miligen, Watch-case-maker, there.
Sir William Forbes, Bart. Banker, there.
Peter Mathie, Jeweller, there.
Alexander Gardner, Jeweller, there.
William Creech, Bookseller, there.
Thomas Hutchison, Merchant, there.

Mr. GERRALD.—My lord, I object to Mr. William Creech ; I understand he has repeatedly declared, in private conversations, that he would condemn any member of the British Convention, if he should be called to pass upon their assize ; and I wish to refer it to his own conscience, and his oath, whether he has not prejudged the principles upon which I am to be tried.

Lord HENDERLAND.—My lord, the objection is, that he has prejudged the principles upon which Mr. Gerrald is to be tried ; that he said he would condemn every member of the British Convention : it is stated in a loose way ; it is not stated

From the transcript of the trial of Joseph Gerrald, Scottish political martyr, 1794. *The Trial of Joseph Gerrald*, Muir, Gowans & Co., Glasgow 1835.

chapter of the last book of *Kings*.'[11] We are not informed of any immediate reaction to the latter, but we are to one proposed by Burns in Dumfries when a regiment was stationed there: 'May our success in the present war be equal to the justice of our cause.' Burns himself made clear the perilous outcome to Samuel Clarke Jnr in a letter, in which the recipient was begged to try to mollify one Captain Dods who evidently was all out to settle the matter with 'a brace of pistols' (L.631).

Burns overstepped the mark in a letter to Mrs Dunlop dated 12 January 1795 (L.649). Their mutual friend Dr Moore had written a journal about the French situation, and after reading it Burns wrote 'I cannot approve of the honest Doctor's whining over the deserved fate of a certain pair of Personages. What is there in delivering a perjured Blockhead & an unprincipled Prostitute to the hands of the hangman.' Offended, Mrs Dunlop stopped writing letters to Burns, and pleas for a resumption of correspondence were ignored – except for a final plea in July 1796 that brought him a reply when he was close to death. The term 'whining' aimed at her friend, and the callous reference to the execution of Louis XVI and his queen, would have been resented by the lady. Such a reaction becomes even more credible on recalling that she had recently become the mother-in-law of two French refugees who had managed to escape from the Terror.

Looking back at the politically critical years of 1792 to 1795 in Britain, one is drawn to conclude that lucky timing had been on Burns's side in his avoidance of really serious trouble. The fear of the revolutionary infection spreading to Britain reached a peak with the execution of Louis on 21 January 1793 and with France's declaration of war a few days later. In Paris in September 1792, a bloody massacre had taken 1,200 lives, and that had been a curtain-raiser to events affecting British action. In that 1792 to 1975 period was passed a series of very harsh Acts for the strict maintenance of the established order, and identifiable reformers became marked men. Had the decision to inquire into his alleged disaffection come a year or so later than December 1792, Burns might well have found his name added to those of the five martyrs. The complaint lodged against him could well have reached a level higher than the Excise Board, and instead of a visit from William Corbet and a reprimand there might well have been an un-heralded swoop by the Lord Advocate's sleuth-hounds for a search of his house. What might they have found? For a start, there was his copy of Tom Paine's *Rights of Man*. A search of his papers could have revealed his epigram on Edmund Burke. Burke, himself an ardent reformer in earlier years, had broken with Fox and crossed the floor of the house in May 1791 to take his place as an even more ardent champion of the existing Constitution than Prime Minister Pitt himself. Burns had written:

> Oft have I wondered that on Irish ground
> No poisonous reptile ever had been found.
> Revealed the secret stands of Nature's work:
> She preserved her poison to create a Burke!
>
> (K.478)

For obvious reasons this epigram was not published in Burns's lifetime: it survived for our eyes only as a transcript made by John Syme. Read out in court to Braxfield and his fellow law lords it would surely have qualified as a seditious libel. And there was plenty more in the Second Common Place Book and the Glenriddell Manuscript. In the former Burns had written *The Bonnie Lass of Albanie*. Primarily, that poem was one more manifestation of the Jacobite obsession that Burns never cast off. The Jacobite cause had become permanently lost by the 1790s, offering only memories for sentimental song and story. But aiming gross insults at the reigning Hanoverians was quite another matter. The bonnie lass referred to was Charlotte, the daughter of Bonnie Prince Charlie and his Scottish mistress Clementina Walkinshaw. Charlotte, just a few years older than Burns, had been retrospectively legitimized (!) by the French parliament in 1784 under the seal of Louis XVI and given the title of 'Duchess of Albany'. (Albany was an ancient name for the Scottish Highlands.) The poem was probably written soon after the death of Prince Charles Edward in 1788, but prior to Charlotte's own untimely death less than two years later. In the poem Burns championed a case for the establishment of Charlotte as the heir apparent, incidentally ousting the Prince of Wales from that exalted status. This was regardless of the lady's Roman Catholic faith – totally unacceptable under the Constitution – and the unavoidable acceptance into the Court of the three bastard children she had borne to the 'celibate' Archbishop of Bordeaux. Stanzas 4 and 5 run:

But there is a youth, a witless youth
    That fills the place where she should be,
We'll send him o'er to his native shore
    And bring our ain sweet Albanie.

Alas the day, and woe the day,
    A false Usurper wan the gree,
That now commands the towers and lands,
    The royal right of Albanie.   (K.188)

The 'witless youth' was George Augustus Frederick, the eldest son of George III, and the 'false Usurper' was the first Hanoverian king of Britain, George I. In reality, the Jacobite fervour for the Stuart surname was quite wrong-headed, as George I carried the same share of Stuart blood as did James Edward, the Old Pretender. (Well, almost the same. One chromosome out of 46 was not remotely Stuart, as the Y chromosome is inherited only by male progeny. The Old Pretender inherited Darnley's Y chromosome – but who would boast about that?) Both were great-grandsons of James I, George differing only in having received his Stuart aliquot through two female generations. In Braxfield's court, Burns's poetic insult to the current royal family would have weighed heavily against him. It would have taken its place alongside another damning court exhibit, the *Lines on a Stirling Window*, awaiting rediscovery in the Glenriddell Manuscript. To describe the reigning monarch as one of the 'idiot race, to honour lost' at that particular time would have aroused a very sharp judicial reaction. The King had made a good recovery from the mental disorder that had struck a few years earlier; a recovery that had aroused public rejoicing with processions and fireworks displays. King George's personal write-off of revolutionary France (in a letter to Grenville dated 9 February 1793) as 'that unprincipled country, whose aim at present is to destroy the foundations of every civilized state', clearly summarized and echoed the views of his government, and certainly the views of the even more reactionary Scottish law lords.

Anti-revolutionary fervour brought out spies from all ranks of society. The evidence of Anne Fisher played a major part in the conviction of Thomas Muir. A servant in the home of Muir's father, she told the court of several incidents involving Muir using those premises for passing Paine's book to selected friends. In reply

Muir told the court 'This domestic and well-tutored spy is brought to prove words which may irritate your minds against me.' We may rest assured that had Burns been brought to court there would have been spies ready to report the disloyal toasts, the carronades incident, incautious remarks and letters clandestinely pried into. Fortunately for Burns, his chief confessor Mrs Dunlop remained loyal and careful, actually cutting out and destroying two loaded passages from one of his letters (L.529). No Botany Bay for Robert Burns, but he was a bit lucky.

Burns's active involvement in politics in his Dumfries years was not confined to the sensitive international scene. He gave electioneering support in verse to Patrick Miller Jnr in the latter's successful bid for the Dumfriesshire seat in 1790, and to Patrick Heron when he stood, also successfully, for the Stewartry of Kirkcudbright in 1795.

Some idea of the unbridled belligerency which could intrude into electioneering in the eighteenth century is given by Burns's racy narration, in a letter to Mrs Dunlop (L.403), of events leading up to Miller's election. More than 200 armed colliers and lead miners had been assembled by the Duke of Queensberry in support of Miller, but on sighting near Lochmaben a much larger armed contingent backing the rival candidate (Sir James Johnston) they turned and fled in disarray. Burns had been summoned, in the feudalist tradition, to attend with his servants bearing arms, by Queensberry, but the letter suggests that he only went along as an observer. More to his taste was his contribution to the campaign in verse. In *The Five Carlins* (K.269) he praised the personal qualities of Miller Jnr:

> He wad na hecht them courtly gifts,
>   Nor meikle speech pretend;
> But he wad hecht an honest heart
>   Wad ne'er desert a friend.

In support of Patrick Heron's campaign in 1795, Burns wrote no less than four election ballads (K.491–4), but these topical and dated compositions attract only passing interest today.

Burns's hopes for favoured advancement in the Excise by the patronage of the members of Parliament he had supported were but thinly disguised. (See, for instance, his letter to Heron of March 1795: L.660.) If such hopes were not fulfilled he at least

saved postage on the numerous letters franked for him by both
Miller and Heron when they were in Dumfries. Burns concluded a
letter to Miller in London, dated 8 March 1795, with a highly
significant comment: 'When you return to the country, you will
find us all *Sogers.*'

Early in 1795, with the bulk of the armed forces deployed
abroad, a decision was made to create two militia companies in
Dumfries for home defence. They were given the title, the Dumfries
Volunteers, and Arent Schuyler de Peyster, veteran of the war in
America, was elected to the post of Colonel. There was a ready
response to the call for recruits, many of whom saw the move as an
opportunity to prove – or appear to prove – their loyalty to the
King and his government. Dr William Maxwell, steadfastly pro-
French, remained aloof, but Burns and his friends John Syme and
John M'Murdo joined up. One may presume that enlistment
carried with it some prospect of social reinstatement for Burns in
Dumfries. In Dr W.J. Murray's words, 'Burns took out further
insurance against political persecution.'[12] To the same end he
wrote the song *The Dumfries Volunteers*, a rallying-cry against
'haughty Gaul'. But the closing lines reveal that, although occulted
for some observers by a uniform, the reformer spots on the poetic
leopard were still there unchanged:

> But while we sing, *God Save the King*,
> We'll ne'er forget *the people*!

> (K.484)

Approval of the French Revolution was less disguised in *Is there for
honest poverty*, often given the alternative title *A man's a man for a' that*
(K.482), written during the same period. With its eloquent plea for
the underdog, this song ranks among Burns's best and it is
deservedly popular. Obviously unaware of the fame for which it
was destined, Burns sent it off to his Edinburgh song editor George
Thomson in January 1795, nonchalantly describing it as 'two or
three pretty good prose thoughts inverted into rhyme' (L.651).
Along with it he sent the bawdy *Ode to Spring* (K.481). An ill-
matched poetic pair, indeed, but then Robert Burns was a many-
sided man.

From this time onwards Burns maintained a cautious profile on
radical politics; in fact, by the time another year had passed, those
who 'dare be poor for a' that' had become the *Swinish Multitude* (an

expression he had obviously borrowed from Edmund Burke – if only for Mrs Dunlop's information: L.688), threatening riot in Dumfries through food shortages.

IMPORTANT DUMFRIES FRIENDSHIPS

It did not take long for Burns to form new friendships after the family moved to Dumfries, and the first, strongest, and most lasting was with John Syme. Syme had been sent to Dumfries, as Collector of Stamps, just a few months before Burns arrived, and by an odd coincidence his office had been set up on the ground floor of the very building in which Burns was later to establish his domicile on the floor above. The two men had much in common from the outset. Both would have had few local friends; both were civil servants; both were intelligent and both leaned to the radical side in political views. Unfortunately for probing biographers, their day-to-day proximity meant that letter-writing was almost completely unnecessary. (Only one letter from Burns to Syme – an inconsequential one at that – was available to J. de L. Ferguson for his published collection in 1931.) Burns became a frequent guest of Syme at his villa, Ryedale, on the west bank of the Nith, for convivial soirées.

Syme accompanied Burns on a horseback tour of Galloway in July 1793. Events in that short interlude were later recounted by Syme in a letter sent to Dr Currie for inclusion in the famous biography of 1800.[13] It gives us some graphic and interesting details. After staying with the Gordons of Kenmure, where the poet reluctantly complied with Mrs Gordon's request for an epitaph on her deceased lap-dog Echo (K.416), the pair became drenched in a rainstorm on the way to Gatehouse. At Gatehouse they found consolation in 'getting thoroughly drunk'. Next morning, Burns ripped his new boots while trying to pull them on and flew into a rage – a rage which partly abated at Wigtown but only fully subsided at Kirkcudbright where the travellers spent a happy evening with Lord Selkirk. The inspiration to write the famous *Scots Wha Hae Wi' Wallace Bled* may have stemmed from the rugged scenery and wild weather of Galloway, but the record of this is confused. (See Kinsley's *Commentary*, Item 425, for a full analysis.)

Syme proved his constancy and loyalty to the end. He had accepted his friend's sporadic outbursts of temper calmly during five years of close acquaintance, and he performed his executor's duty assiduously and wisely in the interests of Jean and the children for some years after the testator died.

Robert Riddell's attractive young sister-in-law, Maria Riddell, also came into Burn's life early in his Dumfries period, and a warm friendship developed. Maria's literary and political views had much in common with those of Burns, but one may suspect that the association was not wholly of the intellect. The poem *The Last Time I Came O'er the Moor* (K.405) brings in the expressions 'bosom swelling' and 'the guilty lover', plainly addressed to Maria. She was intellectual, well educated and beautiful, although somewhat flirtatious and capricious, and the susceptible poet succumbed to her charms. A letter to Maria, undated but presumed to be of November 1793 (L.596), points to frustration with Maria's continuing fidelity to a husband (Walter Riddell) whom Burns disliked intensely: 'Impossibility presents an impervious barrier to the proudest daring of Presumption, & poor I, dare much sooner peep into the focus of Hell, than to meet the eye of the goddess of my soul!' Burns was certainly smitten. Another letter to Maria (L.594) reveals a jealous reaction on finding that an officer in uniform had entered her theatre box ahead of him, so he did not attempt to stay. His metaphors are colourful: 'the first object which greeted my eye was one of those lobster-coated Puppies, sitting, like another Dragon, guarding the Hesperian fruit'. A climax was looming, and it came, cataclysmically.

When a person subject to bi-polar depression, as Burns certainly was, drinks to excess with jovial company the sweep of mood change can be excessive and socially adverse. Just such an incident was exemplified at the home of Robert Riddell around Christmas 1793 or early January 1794. Documentation of detail is sparse, being limited to one letter of abject apology (the 'letter from Hell': L.608), written by the culprit on the day following, and one much later letter from Rachel Kennedy to Dr James Currie when he was assembling material for the 1800 biography. (That second letter was published for the first time in 1963 by professor R.D. Thornton.)[14] From the two letters it would appear that Burns, affected by alcohol, made such an offensive advance to Maria during a carousal by some of the men present at a party, that he became forthwith *persona non grata* to the whole Riddell family and many of their friends. It was a bitter blow to the poetic offender, both from the loss of Robert Riddell's valued friendship and hospitality, and, more acutely, from the sudden break with the captivating Maria. His reaction to the lady's rejection was long-sustained and caddish. He soon wrote this epigram:

> *Pinned to Mrs R . . . 's Carriage*
> If you rattle along like your Mistress's tongue,
>   Your speed will outrival the dart:
> But, a fly for your load, you'll break down on the road,
>   If your stuff be as rotten 's her heart.

(K.448)

These mean lines about a lady who had not initiated the row cannot be written off as a drunken, angry reaction of the moment, as Burns sent a copy to Patrick Miller Jnr for him to pass to the *Morning Chronicle* in London for publication, and later he sent a copy to William Creech. In April 1794 Robert Riddell died, and Burn asked Riddell's sister Elinor to return the Glenriddell manuscripts. He then wrote the savage epigram into that collection. One likes to believe that Maria never saw a copy. The verse was not to be the final purging of the splenetic reaction, as around mid-year 1794 Burns wrote his *Monody on Maria* —— (K.443) and posted it off to Mrs Dunlop – of all people – and he later sent a copy to Clarinda. The *Monody* is an epitaph for Maria, in imagination deceased. One of its six verses is about the choosing of flowers to place on her bier, ending with the lines:

> But chiefly the nettle, so typical, shower,
> For none e'er approached her but rued the rash deed.

That Burns was still resentful of rejection in the closing months of 1794 is evident from his writing *Epistle from Esopus to Maria* at that time. It reveals not only year-long nursing of wrath over Maria, but also the social ostracism he was suffering in Dumfries. These are six of its eighty-four lines:

> The shrinking Bard adown an alley skulks,
> And dreads a meeting worse than Woolwich hulks –
> Tho' there his heresies in Church and State
> Might well award him Muir and Palmer's fate:
> Still she, undaunted, reels and rattles on,
> And dares the public like a noontide sun!

(K.486)

To her credit, Maria Riddell reached reconciliation with Burns late in 1794, and this became some consolation for his loss of Mrs Dunlop's friendship soon afterwards. Soon after his death in July 1796, Maria wrote a scholarly tribute to Burns for publication in the *Dumfries Journal* (August 1796) using the *nom de plume* 'Candidior', and that valuable character analysis has been widely reprinted. It was described by Henley and Henderson in their centenary biography of Burns (1896) as being 'so admirable in tone, and withal so discerning and impartial in understanding, that it remains the best thing written of him by a contemporary critic'.

Demanding inclusion in this shortlisting of important friends of Burns's Dumfries period – one whom Burns never actually met – is George Thomson of Edinburgh. Thomson must, without question, be accorded the status of significant benefactor to the living Burns, even though that status has suffered unfair impairment from pejorative assessments made by some twentieth-century writers. Thomson was Clerk to the Board of Trustees for the Encouragement of Manufactures. With the help of some fellow-amateurs he had set himself the task of compiling and publishing *A Select Collection of Original Scottish Airs*. From Edinburgh he wrote to Burns in 1792, asking him to 'improve' the lyrics of some of the old songs to make them acceptable in polite circles, proposing that he deal with 'twenty or twenty-five' of them.[15] This number was eventually to exceed one hundred, as Burns's enthusiastic response was not to abate as long as he lived. We need only peruse the very extensive preserved correspondence to realize that Burns found his collaboration with Thomson a source of continuing interest and pleasure, filling what could otherwise have been gaps of boredom in the exciseman's last four years. Each of the pair argued his case for particular airs, stanza form and word choice frankly, sometimes stubbornly, and at other times conceding a point. Thomson has been found guilty of making gratuitous changes in some Burns lyrics before sending them to the press, particularly in the volumes published after the Bard's death, but overall the collaboration has to be seen as adding to the fame of Scottish song. Thomson has been labelled 'prudish' from such injunctions to Burns as 'Let her [the Muse] not write what beauty would blush to speak, nor wound that charming delicacy which forms the most precious dowry of our daughters.'[16] But Burns knew well that Thomson simply had in mind his Presbyterian market for his *Collection*, and never hesitated to send Thomson the latest bawdy item for his personal amusement. On a copy of the extremely bawdy and witty *When Princes and Prelates* (K.395) sent to Thomson (L.632) is appended the footnote 'What a pity this is not publishable. G.T.' We will get back to Thomson in Chapter Three and in Appendix F.

THE SANDS RUN OUT

The last two years of Burns's life were blighted by financial problems and physical suffering, and his tenacity throughout that sad period is to be admired. He allowed nothing to dissuade him from his song-writing for both Johnson and Thomson, and he took time off from Excise work only when quite incapacitated. To seek relief from his painful illness (discussed in detail in Chapter Seven) he went, on 3 July 1796, to the Brow resort on the Solway coast in the hope that sea-bathing would relieve his distressing symptoms, and the evidence as to whether that move was supported or opposed by Dr Maxwell remains controversial. Although Burns wrote of some easing of his pains it was not the answer to his problem; indeed it may have speeded up the onset of his final collapse. During the Brow stay, Maria Riddell proved herself a true friend – sending her personal carriage to bring the Bard to her home on a visit. Weak and emaciated, his first words on seeing Maria were 'Well Madam? And have you any commands for the next world?' This question appears more poignant on reflecting that Maria herself was to die aged only thirty-six, at an even younger age than did Burns who lived to complete thirty-seven and a half years. As July advanced, a change in the tidal cycle ruled out sea bathing, and on 16 July Burns asked John Clark of Locherwoods for the loan of a gig to drive back to Dumfries, fearing the exposure of a horseback ride home. On his arrival, already feverish, he immediately wrote to James Armour; pleading with him to send his wife to look after Jean in her imminent confinement, and that letter was to be his last. His feverish and anxious state progressed to delirium, and to death on 21 July. One additional week of life would have accorded him dual solace – the pleasure of seeing his last-born child and Jean in caring hands, and the arrival of funds from Montrose and Edinburgh to avert the money crisis which had thrown him into a panic at Brow. But that extra week was denied him.

Details of the cash crisis which beset Burns in his last days have not been elucidated. He had been on quite a good salary for more than four years since quitting the Ellisland farm, but he never acquired the wisdom of putting aside some savings for emergency use. In his last letter to Gilbert (10 July 1796) he admitted this failing: 'I have contracted one or two serious debts, partly from my illness these many months & partly from too much thoughtlessness as to expense when I came to town.'

Burns's chronic shortage of cash was evident long before his final illness. The account for the erection of the memorial stone over Fergusson's grave remained unpaid for two years after it was submitted (L.495). He repaid John M'Murdo six guineas in December 1793, adding the remark 'I have owed you money longer than ever I owed it to any man' (L.604). He even got behind with his house rent in 1794 (about £10 or £12 per annum). He explained this embarrassment to his landlord, Captain John Hamilton, in July of that year (L.633) but six months later he was still in arrears. On 29 January 1795 he sent Hamilton three guineas in part payment with a promise of the balance 'soon' (L.653) but he avoided mentioning that he had borrowed that sum from Stewart of Closeburn (L.652). The later cash shortages were due in part to the salary reduction from £70 to £35 when he was off duty sick, but we may find a more convincing cause in the natural generosity in his make-up. He had lent James Clarke money in 1792 and it was not all repaid in June 1796 (L.698). For Jean and the children he bought good clothes and furniture. The most-discussed of his money problems, however, was the one which was to cast him into frantic despair during the last two weeks of his life.

While at Brow Burns received a payment demand, described in two letters he wrote on 12 July 1796. One was to James Burness, his cousin at Montrose:

A rascal of a Haberdasher to whom I owe a considerable bill taking it into his head that I am dying, has commenced a process against me, & will infallibly put my emaciated body into jail. Will you be so good as to accomodate me, & that by return of post, with ten pound.

(L.705)

40

The other letter was to George Thomson, in similar pleading terms, asking for five pounds and describing the creditor as 'a cruel scoundrel of a Haberdasher' (L.706). Allan Cunningham, with no real justification, identified the creditor as Mr Williamson, the Dumfries draper who was owed £7 4 shillings by Burns for his Volunteers uniform, but Robert Burns Junior was to declare in later years that Williamson's account, received routinely through his solicitor Matthew Penn, contained no threatening expressions.[17] But the assertion by Cunningham (who had been roundly condemned as a fabricator) has been widely accepted by writers on Burns, seemingly because the Volunteers uniform interpretation puts the poet in a good light – suffering because of his patriotism in joining up. There are good reasons to doubt the case against Williamson. He was a clothier, not a haberdasher. He was owed £7 4 shillings but Burns desperately needed £15. The popular explanation of Burns's panic is that he was in a state of mental disturbance at the time and unable to grasp the correct significance of Williamson's account, but this is dubious as his other letters at the time are models of realism and balance. The 'cruel scoundrel of a Haberdasher' just has to be some other individual with whom Burns had dealings, and dealings that he kept to himself. One possible candidate for the role would be the *haberdasher* who had supplied contraband French gloves for Maria Riddell in 1793 (L.560), no doubt at an exorbitant black market price, and there could well have been other items for other people. In his official position Burns would have dreaded exposure of involvement in contraband commerce – hence the 'cruel scoundrel' description of a blackmailing creditor, and his decision to seek help only from distant Montrose and Edinburgh, in letters which were not overly explicit.

The money sought from both his cousin and from his editor had been posted promptly, but it arrived too late. The task of banishing the spectre of the debtors' prison from the troubled mind of the poet became one not for generous Burness and Thomson, but for the Reaper.

Despite Burns having wryly said in his last hours to John Gibson, a brother Volunteer, 'John, don't let the awkward squad fire over me',[18] his funeral on 26 July 1796 was on the grand scale with full military honours. John Syme gave Dr James Currie a detailed description of the proceedings for inclusion in the 1800

41

biography, and copied versions have appeared in numerous subsequently written biographies. The Dumfries Volunteers led the funeral procession and took post in the churchyard, and the Fencible Infantry of Angusshire and a regiment of cavalry of the Cinque Ports, then stationed in Dumfries, lined the street from the town hall to the churchyard, a distance of more than half a mile. Some thousands of the inhabitants of Dumfries and surrounding districts swelled the procession crowd in the wake of the Volunteers. It was all a generous gesture of respect for the late Bard and his famed achievements. Rather less than generous were the anonymous obituaries published in Edinburgh and London, the former probably written by Alexander F. Tytler and drawn upon by an unidentified journalist for much of the detail of the latter. (See Appendix F for a probe into that authorship.)

Jean and the children were not left to suffer the stresses of poverty. Money raised by a public appeal was invested, supporting the family until the profits from Dr Currie's four-volume biography – which sold very well – provided a fairly good income.

Chapter Two

PROFANE RHYMER
(L.125)

EARLY DAYS

Contrary to impressions conveyed by Robert Burns's tangles with the kirk, the eighteenth century had seen the end of the worst evils in the course of religion throughout Scotland. The century had witnessed the last witchcraft execution, the retirement of sword and gibbet from religious politics, and the end of magisterial backing in the enforcement of kirk edicts. But religious harmony was not to reign thereafter, as the new freedoms also brought freedom to pursue internal strife and to execute secession coups. It is against that disordered backdrop that the religious life of Burns is to be viewed, and what has been written of that life abounds in inconsistency. For instance, R.J. Macintyre[1] has Burns a 'regular worshipper' at St Michael's in Dumfries, while James Barke[2] wrote that Burns disliked St Michael's and attended there only twice. And no writer seems to have paid any attention to the strong influence of John Locke in the religious path taken by the Bard.

Nowhere in Scotland had the dogma and discipline of Calvinism been more firmly implanted than in the south-west. It was at Sanquhar that the last-ditch Covenanters Richard Cameron and James Renwick issued their Declarations and founded their own strict Calvinist church – the Cameronians – which even ignored the Revolution Settlement of 1690 and survived intact until the end of the nineteenth century. Stone memorials to Covenant martyrs stand as reminders of cruelty in all too many of the towns of Ayrshire, Dumfriesshire, Wigtown and Kirkcudbright. Mauchline, famed for ever in the Burns story, has its martyrs' monument for five men hanged there for refusing to accede to episcopal control of the kirk.

William Burnes, father of the poet, was not a native of the south-west and he arrived there with his Calvinism already a little blunted by the Arminian influence slowly radiating from Edinburgh. But this moderation remained more or less covert in his adopted countryside and his children were born in a prevailing strict Calvinist *milieu*, as had been his wife. It never occurred to young

43

Robert to question the dogma and discipline of the kirk in his boyhood years; later writing of the 'idiot piety' which governed his beliefs and behaviour at that phase (L.125). Religion was a prominent theme in his early poetry, framed within a conformity which indoctrination had rendered automatic. But all that was to change as he approached maturity, and from his Edinburgh period onward one may note the conspicuous absence of religion from his verse – apart from one angry satire and occasional deistic phrases. Less than two years before his death he confessed 'heresies in Church and State' in the *Epistle from Esopus to Maria* (K.486). In analysing Burns's religious stance from about 1786 on the researcher becomes dependant almost entirely on his letters.

Every respectable Scottish home in the days of Burns gave pride of place to a family Bible, and not just as an ornament, with a nightly reading and prayer by the gudeman as habitual and regular as the consumption of oatmeal. The simple dignified language of the James I Authorized Version had a profound effect on Scottish speech and literature, playing an important (albeit regrettable) part in the displacement of the old Lowlands language by English. The description of a devout father reading scripture to an attentive household in *The Cotter's Saturday Night* (K.72) would equate with the scene of the Burns family during the Mount Oliphant and Lochlea years, and to that limited extent the revered poem is biographical.

The religious instruction that the youthful Robert Burns received from his devout father was supplemented by the teaching of the equally devout youthful schoolmaster John Murdoch. And it would seem that the latter was a rather better teacher on the secular side than the general run of parish dominies of the day. At the promptings of the kirk, Parliament had passed Acts in 1646 and 1696 that compelled the heritors of every parish to pay a modest salary to a teacher and provide or improve school premises. One consequence was that Scots in general, particularly in the Lowlands, were better educated in the eighteenth century than were the socially equivalent classes in England. The motivation that led to these excellent Acts was a worthy one, but like all blanketing schemes incorporating an element of compulsion they had weaknesses. The heritors of the parish tended to be tardy in meeting their obligations, and the replacement of departed schoolmasters was at times long delayed by the smallness of the pittance offered. Mackinnon[3] relates how one perquisite was allowed the teacher – on Fastern's E'en the children were allowed to arrange a cock-fighting contest, paying a small fee to the teacher who also received all dead birds afterwards. By this yearly windfall many schoolmasters living in a state of near-starvation were well nourished for a few days, little concerned by the Fast of Lent. (The celebration of Easter had been long since denounced by Knox: 'All worshipping, honouring, or service invented by the brain of man in the religion of God, without his own express commandment, is idolatry.' *Works*, 111. 34. David Laing's edition in 6 volumes. Fastern's E'en is Shrove Tuesday.)

It is not hard to understand William Burnes's motivation to independent action when the Alloway school lost its teacher by transfer soon after Robert and Gilbert first attended, for had he not acted the vacancy could have persisted for many months, finally to be filled by some inefficient individual whose main qualification was the basic one of having embraced Knox's Confession of Faith. William Burnes roped in four collaborating parents to finance the teacher's quarterly salary payments and young John Murdoch was appointed after his qualifications had been well scrutinized. The five parents took turns at providing his board and lodging. Murdoch was fortunate in getting the job and the Alloway boys were fortunate in getting Murdoch. We have good information about Murdoch's teaching methods from his letter written in 1799 from London.[4] He concentrated on the spelling and meaning of words; on parsing and grammar, presenting a limited number of books of poetry and prose, among which the Bible was prominent. He has been sneered at for an addiction to pretentious phraseology, but no criticism can take from him the credit of having been the cicerone of Burns's youthful journey to the foot-hills of Parnassus.

Murdoch was a pious young man and religious instruction was given due priority. When William Burnes wrote his *Manual of Religious Belief* for his children it is likely that Murdoch assisted him: a copy in his handwriting may be seen today in the Birthplace Museum at Alloway.[5] Murdoch left Alloway in 1768, when Robert was aged nine, but there was a renewal of contact five years later when Murdoch took a post at Ayr. It was during this phase that he taught Robert some French, and, more importantly, lent him Pope's works. The influence of Pope in Burns's poetry was to be substantial – introducing him to the weapon of satire with which he was to assault religious dogma in later years. To the kirk-persecuted Rev. John M'Math he wrote in 1785:

> O Pope, had I thy satire's darts
> To gie the rascals their deserts,
> I'd rip their rotten, hollow hearts,
>   An' tell aloud
> Their jugglin' hocus pocus arts
>   To cheat the crowd.

(K.68)

From the age of nine, with Murdoch departed, Robert's general education – and that of the other Burns children – was taken over by the father. Books were borrowed to this end – predominantly on religious topics – and they included such works as Derham's *Physico-Theology* and *Astro-Theology*, Ray's *Wisdom of God in the Creation* and Stackhouse's *History of the Bible*. In the long Moore letter (L.125) Burns set down some details of books he had read in the Mount Oliphant and the Lochlea years. A scientist is liable to be expectantly surprised on noting 'Boyle's lectures' included. Robert Boyle (1627–91) holds a place of veneration in the history of science for formulating his law of gas properties and for pioneering discoveries in chemistry. But the Boyle-and-Burns admirer can relax. Boyle was deeply religious, and he bequeathed funds for the delivery and publication of 'Lecture Sermons'. The Boyle's lectures referred to by Burns turn out to be the two Derham works referred to above – not lectures *by* Boyle. Dr Currie misread the Burns holograph for his biography of 1800, passing the item to the printer as 'Bayle's lectures'. The error was perpetuated by Robert Chambers in his 1850 biography; a footnote explaining that he had been unable to identify 'Bayle'. Currie and Chambers may have been tempted to link the name with that of the French philosopher Pierre Bayle (1647–1706) – one of Voltaire's often-quoted idols – but if so they both correctly refrained. The spelling of the name was corrected by William Wallace in his valuable revision of Chambers's four-volume work in 1896, but it remained for the German biographer of Burns, Hans Hecht, to identify the 'Bayle's lectures' as the Derham sermons in 1936.

Gilbert Burns, in the long letter written to Mrs Dunlop after his brother's death, wrote that the Lochlea period (Robert aged eighteen to twenty-four years) was 'not marked by much literary improvement'. This statement must not be taken too seriously as Gilbert seemed to be confused on dates. He placed his brother's reading of Richardson's *Pamela* and Smollett's *Ferdinand Count Fathom* and *Peregrine Pickle* well back in the Mount Oliphant period (around 1773), whereas Robert wrote of reading *Pamela* and *Ferdinand Count Fathom* in Irvine (1781–2). With easy access to Tarbolton, it was during the Lochlea years that Burns must have greatly extended his reading, to include Fergusson's poems and the works of many of the writers who became his favourites. One such was Henry Mackenzie, whose *Man of Feeling* was later described by Burns as 'a book I prize next to the Bible'. Just how that sanctimonious and sentimental work appealed to Burns is a puzzle to all who have looked into the poet's cultural flowering, but he could have gained from it some solace during his bout of depression in Irvine. It was probably in the Lochlea, or at least the early Mossgiel, period that he began his sustained admiration of John Milton, a life-long fighter for freedom and rebel against Calvinist dogmatism. From as early as April 1786 (L.29) to his last days (L.697) he was moved to quote lines from *Paradise Lost* in his letters, and more than once expressed admiration for Milton's Satan ('a very respectable Personage'; 'my favourite hero'). As noted by Professor Kinsley, Burns drew freely on *Lycidas* and *Comus* for images and phrases for his poems. He even acquired a pocket edition of Milton in 1787, to have it on hand during his travels. Although we lack supportive evidence, it is tempting to suppose that Burns also sought out some of Milton's important prose works; works that would have been available to him in Edinburgh if not in Tarbolton. *Areopagitica*, Milton's famous plea for freedom of speech and publication, with its keynote sentence – 'Give me liberty to know, to utter, and to argue freely, according to conscience, above all liberties' – would have shone effulgently to the eye of Burns. That claimed liberty obviously lay behind Milton's adherence to unitarianism.

JOHN LOCKE

If we are left guessing about some details of Burns's early reading of heterodox tests, there is no doubt about the two he specifically mentioned in his famous Moore letter – John Taylor's *Scripture*

Doctrine of Original Sin, and, of far greater significance, John Locke's *Essay Concerning Human Understanding*. The former called for doubt on the reality of original sin: the latter called for doubt about almost anything.

To the end of the Mount Oliphant period or perhaps for some years later, young Robert Burns had been a conforming Presbyterian, Calvinist or Arminian – the doctrinal difference is insignificant. The devout father's lifestyle example and his fervently-sustained teaching influence would have ensured this, and there would have been a ban on the reading of heretical books in the house. Taylor on original sin was in that obvious category and Robert evidently read it clandestinely. The message of Locke's voluminous *Essay* would have been not at all obvious from its title, and had William Burnes spotted it and flipped through its pages he would have regarded it as an acceptable work of philosophy, enriched with religious references. (Locke's *Essay* is rather heavy going: the reader must really keep at it to grasp its messages.) Had William settled down to read the whole work – all of its 300,000-odd words – he might have discovered its potential for undermining the established Presbyterian faith. Evidently Robert kept his discovery to himself, even refraining from commenting on it to Gilbert. This could well explain Gilbert's silence on Locke's *Essay*, and on Taylor's book, in the detailed biographical letter he wrote to Mrs Dunlop in later years; a letter supplying a great deal of detail on his brother's early reading.

As for many other pleasures, to John Knox dancing was taboo. Young Robert Burns, in the Mount Oliphant period, attended country dancing classes. He later wrote of the parental reaction in his Moore letter: 'My father had an unaccountable antipathy against these meetings; and my going was, what to this hour I repent, in absolute defiance of his commands!' (We have Gilbert's later reassurance that their father's attitude to the dancing relaxed later, with younger members of the family also attending to share the enjoyment. William was not blindly stubborn – just a bit set in his Presbyterian stance when first confronted.) That first and rather trivial defiance was a foretaste of the religious rebellion in Burns which was soon to be felt by the kirk itself in Ayrshire. Locke's *Essay Concerning Human Understanding* could well have provided an early stirring of the posset, but its likely significance has been anomalously ignored by writers on Burns. Mrs Carswell,

John Locke. Freeman, after Sir Godfrey Kneller. From *An Essay Concerning Human Understanding*, by John Locke, William Tegg & Co., London 1853.

in her very comprehensive biography, did not mention Locke at all, and the meticulous and encyclopedic William Wallace, in listing and analysing the religious writings read by Burns, in two Appendices to his revision of Chamber's *Life and Works*, made no mention of the important *Essay*.[6] The continuing oversight is a serious one. The influence of Locke is evident not only in the life of Burns but in the trend of philosophy throughout the world in subsequent centuries.

The place of Locke among the intellectual greats of the seventeenth century is a prominent one. That important century had seen ancient authority dismantled in many fields of human knowledge: in medicine by Harvey; in astronomy by Galileo and Kepler; in physics and chemistry by Newton and Boyle. But what those geniuses tackled in their special fields now seems to have been basically empirical when set alongside the task of revising the age-entrenched mix of abstractions that had congealed variously as different sectarian doctrines of belief, each stubbornly regarded by its adherents as the only rigidly true doctrine. The task demanded not only wisdom: it demanded a special sort of courage. Spinoza, born the same year as Locke (1632), set about the task sooner than his English contemporary, but he had barely started before his Amsterdam synagogue excommunicated him. Undeterred, he devoted his whole short life to his new look at religion and philosophy. Locke was well aware of the hazards and sanctions in the path of his objectives and was fairly successful in avoiding them. As we know that his major work was read by Burns and probably influenced his religion and poetry, a closer look at the great philosopher would seem to be in order.

John Locke (1632–1704) was born in Somerset in a period of rising puritan power. As a seventeen-year-old scholar at Westminster school he would have been in the thick of the politico-religious turmoil which culminated in the beheading of Charles I. He went on to Oxford in 1652 and graduated MA in 1658, and in 1660 – the Restoration year – he was awarded a tutorship, but soon became dissatisfied with the traditional Oxford curriculum and the intolerance of puritans. As an advocate of unfettered inquiry he abandoned his original plan for a career in divinity, turning instead to philosophy, science and medicine. If any additional encouragement was needed to consolidate his devotion to the cause of civil and religious liberty, it was undoubtedly provided by a new-found and close friendship with Baron Ashley (soon after to become the first Earl of Shaftesbury) who had benefited from Locke's medical skill. Shaftesbury's brilliance had earned him influential offices, but his independence and his opposition to the naming of Catholic James as successor to Charles II were to bring him arrest and trial on a charge of high treason. After a London grand jury acquitted him, he crossed to Amsterdam in 1682. Realizing that no confidant of Shaftesbury was safe in England, Locke also went over to Amsterdam in the following year. Charles II responded by cancelling his senior studentship at Oxford.

Locke found happiness in Holland and leisure well suited to philosophical reflection and writing. Holland at that time was Europe's haven of liberty and religious toleration, and provided the appropriate atmosphere for Locke to press on with the *magnum opus* he had commenced in 1670. *An Essay Concerning Human Understanding* was completed in Rotterdam and published in 1690. The Glorious Revolution of 1688–9 meant that Locke could return to England without risk to his personal freedom and publish his *Essay* unrestricted by sectarian politics. He was actually aboard the vessel which brought Princess Mary Stuart to London to be crowned, jointly with her husband William, as Queen Mary. For the rest of his life Locke lived in tranquillity at Oates, enjoying visits from many friends, including the great Isaac Newton. He continued to write. His two *Treatises of Government* in which the divine right of monarchs is rejected would have brought him bad trouble had they appeared prior to the Revolution. Treatises on education (1693) and finance (1691 and 1695) were followed by his more famous essay *The Reasonableness of Christianity* (1695) which claimed that mere inability to explain mystery does not in itself stand as the disproof of faith.

A comprehensive summary of the *Essay Concerning Human Understanding* would be out of place here, but attention may be drawn to some of the passages which had powerful potential for influencing the religious outlook of Robert Burns. Refuting some ideas formulated by Descartes, Locke claimed that there were no *innate* ideas in humans, and that all appeals to universality for proving the reality of such must fail. He held that the mind begins its existence like a blank sheet on which all the individual will eventually know has to be written by the imprints of observation and experience, or by reflecting on the interactions of these in a manner analogous to mathematical calculation. He even went as far as to claim, in direct oppositon to Calvin's assertions, that our awareness of the existence of God is not innate, and therefore it has to be acquired by penetrating observation, experience and reasoning. To illustrate this point he quoted the reports of world travellers who had found communities in Asia and Brazil where atheism normally prevailed. Such communities were atheistic simply because in their isolation they had neither received divine revelation nor applied their reasoning and observations to arrive at the concept of God. But he hastened to add that the mere absence of an innate notion of God in no way argued against the existence of God. An important consequence of these views was that there was no place at all for any assertion of abstract dogma which had no basis of revelation, no matter how elevated the rank of the asserter, be he Pope, priest or presbyter.

One can readily envisage the surprise with which Robert Burns encountered such iconoclastic claims. At long last could come a challenge to the rigid kirk dogma which hitherto was never to be questioned. Dissatisfaction with the rigidity of puritanism had moved Locke, recalling his reaction as a young man at Oxford, to write satirically: 'I found that a general freedom is but a general bondage, and that the popular asserters of liberty are the greatest engrossers of it too, and not unjustly called its keepers.' The young man Burns was in his turn realizing that acclaimed certainties could be at the same time illusory as concepts and despotic in their application.

Locke still left room for the concept of *probability*, when decision must fall short of *certainty* because of the limits of the senses and the restraints which operate against the boundless accumulation of relevant experience. He insisted on the need for assiduous examination of pros and cons whenever a decision must be made on the basis of probability, and emphasized the importance of 'mutual charity and forbearance' before a decision is reached on such grounds. He pleaded for this attitude in matters political, social and religious. Such a plea leads us to see him as a sensitive, compassionate man; one of the sort not always found in high places. The concluding paragraph of his 'probability' chapter deals with *divine revelation*, which he held to be the most reliable of all testimonies which can reach the human senses. At the same time, he strongly emphasized that one must be sure that what is stated to be divine revelation is in absolute fact divine revelation. Only then does one's assent to such a matter become 'faith'. He then proceeded to a critical discussion of the value of the historical record in deciding on what assertions are acceptable and what should be rejected or remain tentative.

Join Taylor's tilt at 'original sin' with Locke's reservations on 'faith', and you have a rather formidable duo confronting the 'idiot piety' long since and confidently implanted in young Robert by his father and Murdoch.

Clearly, Locke had both politics and the church in his sights when he attacked accepted doctrine built on venerable antiquity only:

> How many men have no other ground for their tenets than the supposed honesty, or learning, or number of those of the same profession? As if honest or bookish men could not err; or truth were to be established by the vote of the multitude! Yet this, with most men, serves the turn. 'The tenet has the attestation of reverend antiquity; it comes to me with the passport of former ages, and therefore I am secure in the reception I give it; other men have been and are of the same opinion,' (for that is all is said) 'and therefore it is reasonable for me to embrace it'. A man may more justifiably throw up cross and pile for his opinions, than take them by such measures. All men are liable to error; and most men are, in many points, by passion or interest, under temptation to it. If we could but see the secret motives that influenced the men of name and learning in the world, and the leaders of parties, we should not always find that it was the embracing of truth for its own sake that made them espouse the doctrines they owned and maintained. This at least is certain, there is not an opinion so absurd which a man may not receive upon this ground. There is no error to be named which has not had its professors; and a man shall never want crooked paths to walk in, if he thinks that he is in the right way, whenever he has the footsteps of others to follow.
>
> (Book IV, Ch. 20, 17)

There is ample evidence in the later letters of Burns that passages such as the above had made a deep and lasting impression. The message is prominent in his letter to Mrs Dunlop written on New Year's Day 1789 from Ellisland. After a dissertation on souls and beautiful things in nature, he went on:

> I own myself partial to such proofs of those awful & important realities, a God that made all things, man's immaterial & immortal nature, & a world of weal or woe beyond death & the grave, these proofs that we deduct by dint of our own powers of observation. However respectable, Individuals in all ages have been, I have ever looked on Mankind in the lump to be nothing better than a foolish, headstrong, credulous, unthinking Mob; and their universal belief has ever had extremely little weight with me.
>
> Still I am a very sincere believer in the Bible; but I am drawn by the conviction of a Man, not the halter of an Ass.
>
> (L.293)

Again, when writing to Mrs Dunlop in July 1790 to console her on the death of her son-in-law, the same questioning of traditional belief is revealed:

> Though I have no objection to what the Christian system tells us of Another world; yet I own I am partial to those proofs & ideas of it which we have wrought out of our own hearts and heads.
>
> (L.403)

Locke's influence on philosophy and religion has been vast, particularly in the development of eighteenth-century religious rethinking and in the progress of enlightenment throughout Europe. Voltaire admired and repeatedly quoted him. In Locke's own lifetime the main body of adverse reaction gained little momentum. (George Berkeley, who became the most prominent opponent of Locke's ideas, was only five years old when the *Essay Concerning Human Understanding* was first published.) There was, however, an immediate response on his chapter on identity and diversity by the Bishop of Worcester. Locke had asserted that 'identity of self' exists only in the constant identity of the mind or the soul. He held that the material body had no constancy, with 'the same continued life communicated to different particles of matter'. In that view he had anticipated today's precise bio-chemical knowledge about the never-ending turnover of component elements in the body by nutrition, respiration and excretion. The assertion upset the committed prelate who in the notion foresaw serious problems on the Last Day, when everybody's physical elements had to be reassembled for resurrection. Locke answered in the form of a note added to subsequent editions of his *Essay*. (Some *note*. About thirteen thousand words!) He had conceded that in the case of the resurrection of Jesus there was no problem – the body was raised as it was at the time of death, wounds and all, and uncorrupted. But for the long dead the bodily elements became widely dispersed after decomposition, and some could be taken up by plants and become the substance of other individuals using such plants for food. (One can envisage disputes on the Last Day over whose molecules were whose.) But the bishop produced his ace of trumps – divine revelation. The Bible clearly foresaw 'this corruptible' putting on 'incorruption' (I. Cor. 15, 52–5). Locke was trapped. He was not prepared to reject, *overtly*, the words of Paul as having been divinely inspired so he admitted error in his note, without attempting any further explanation. We are surely entitled to assume, in retrospect, that this one recantation made by Locke had much in common with an earlier one by Galileo on a motionless earth. Locke worshipped as an Anglican, but after his death his Common Place Book revealed that he had been a unitarian in belief and was therefore prepared to doubt Paul's infallibility.

In proclaiming distrust of intuitive reasoning and of inductive and syllogistic argument, Locke stands out as the first great post-Galileo empiricist. He was fortified in his faith in the deductive procedure by the findings of his friend Isaac Newton (writing of the latter's 'never-enough-to-be-admired book' in the *Essay*) although he held fast to the ultimate significance of God as the bestower of reasoning-power on mankind. His influence on a new generation of philosophers was to be quite overwhelming, in particular on Edinburgh's courageous David Hume, the most celebrated of all empiricists to this day. Hume extended the argument for scepticism of inductive reasoning to its limit, going beyond Locke all the way to religious agnosticism – maintaining that mere historical evidence was utterly inadequate as a basis of belief in the miraculous. Hume set the scene for a new and widely accepted philosophy of logic and science, but paid the penalty by being rejected for both the chair of Moral Philosophy in Edinburgh and the chair of Logic in Glasgow. His insistence on the essentiality of experience and experiment in the advancement of unimpeachable knowledge, and his rejection of conjectural conclusions from anything unobservable, held fast into the twentieth century. An element of change came with the formulation of relativistic limitations to the long-standing and seemingly immutable Newtonian system of physics by Einstein, and opened a gap for a new philosophy founded by Sir Karl Popper. Popper's startling insistence on the essentiality of falsification in the progress (or lack of progress) in science has had both supporters and energetic detractors,[7] but Hume's reservations on the inductive process stay firm as a corner-stone in Popper's philosophy.

There is no direct evidence of Burns ever having read Hume's works, but one negative remark by Gilbert Burns suggests that he did so. In his long letter to Mrs Dunlop, Gilbert stated that in his Mount Oliphant years his brother 'remained unacquainted . . . with Hume, with Robertson, and almost all our authors of eminence of the latter times'. This implies a presumption that he read Hume's works later. In any event, he would hardly have missed out on relevant discussion in the learned circles in Edinburgh, where Hume's tilting at bigotry and superstition had been exercising many liberal minds.

Suffice it to be said that Burns's scepticism of irrational dogma, so evident in his pre-Edinburgh satires, was probably gleaned from Locke, and it may well have been later reinforced by Locke's successor Hume and others of like persuasion. But unlike Hume, Burns stopped short of any admission of outright agnosticism in anything he wrote or is reported to have said.

If direct evidence of Hume having influenced Burns is lacking, some highly persuasive evidence of the influence of Locke is to be found in at least two of Burns's poems, one written at Mossgiel and the other in his Dumfries period. The early poem is *A Dedication to Gavin Hamilton Esq.* (K.103). Hamilton was both the poet's landlord and the admired friend who had emerged victorious from a disciplinary dispute with the Mauchline kirk minister and his elders – one of the latter being the Burns-immortalized 'Holy Willie' Fisher. In stanza seven are these heretical lines:

> Ye'll get the best o' moral works,
> 'Mang black *Gentoos*, and Pagan *Turks*,
> or Hunters wild on *Ponotaxi*,
> Wha never heard of Orthodoxy.

As mentioned above, in his *Essay* (Book I, Ch. 4) Locke had discussed the atheist communities of Brazil, the Caribbeans, China etc., some of which had displayed notable skills in art and the sciences, and made pointed comparison (in their favour) between their lifestyles and 'the lives and discourses of people not so far off'. Burns's four quoted lines are almost a précis of those observations by Locke, with names varied for metrical and rhyming convenience. He needed a community to equate with Locke's wild natives of Brazil and came up with the pre-Columbian-sounding name *Ponotaxi* to rhyme with *Orthodoxy*. (There seems to be no mountain called Ponotaxi: Kinsley suggests he was thinking of the Andean volcano Cotopaxi.)

The second example to be noted is in the first verse of the famous radical song *Is There for Honest Poverty* (K.482):

> The rank is but the guinea's stamp,
> The Man's the gowd for a' that.

In the Epistle Dedicatory introducing the *Essay*, Locke had used the stamped-and-unstamped gold metaphor:

> But truth, like gold, is not the less so for being newly brought out of the mine. It is trial and examination must give it price, and not any antique fashion; and though it be not yet current by the public stamp, yet it may, for all that, be as old as nature, and is certainly not the less genuine.

The same gold metaphor had been used by Wycherley in his play *The Plain Dealer*, and Locke may have taken it from that source. But Burns almost certainly got it from Locke – it is most unlikely that he had read the Wycherley play.[8] There is direct evidence that Burns continued to study and admire the philosopher long after his early reading of the *Essay Concerning Human Understanding*. In 1788 in a letter to Clarinda he asked:

> Have you ever met with a saying of the Great and likewise Good Mr Locke, Author of the famous essay on the human understanding. He wrote a letter to a friend [The friend was Anthony Collins, Locke's executor, and a deist.] directing it 'not to be delivered till after my decease'; it ended thus – 'I know you loved me when living, and will preserve my memory now I am dead. All the use to be made of it is this; that this life affords no

solid satisfaction, but in the consciousness of having done well, and in the hopes of another life. Adieu! I leave my best wishes with you.

J. Locke
(L.182)

It is clear from the quoting of the above letter that Burns would not have forgotten his introduction to Locke's persuasive religious philosophy. That philosophy, with its questioning formula, had steered Locke along a Socinian path, but his residual respect for the Bible as a source of revealed truth had stopped him at a point short of deism. It is not hard to detect a similar progression in Burns from the time he read the *Essay Concerning Human Understanding*. Overt expression of change was suppressed while his Calvinist father was alive, but we get a hint of it dawning from his reminiscent account of how: 'I, ambitious of shining in conversation parties on Sundays between sermons, funerals, &c. used in a few years more to puzzle Calvinism with so much heat and indiscretion that I raised a hue and cry of heresy against me which has not ceased to this hour' (1787, L.125). But we may feel assured that those arguments were not persuaded within the hearing of his pious father.

A VULNERABLE KIRK

The death of his father early in 1784 was to Robert Burns at once a bereavement and a liberation of intellect and body. His unchained mind became poised to rise to one of the most phenomenal peaks of power in the world's history of poetical creativity; his body to the indulgence of well-endowed sexuality. Within a few months the servant girl Lizzie Paton was pregnant, and she and the confessed father-to-be were commanded to appear on a specified Sunday for public rebuke from the Calvinist pulpit of the Rev. William Auld, minister of Mauchline. A simple acceptance of such disciplinary power by the people of a parish seems unreal by today's standards. To comprehend its cogency in 1784 we need to take a look at the train of events which gave Scotland her kirk, and at some of that kirk's tenets.

With its long history of disputation with the Roman church, no country was more ready to embrace Reformation changes than

Scotland. Under the fervid sponsorship of John Knox and Andrew Melville, Calvinism was welcomed by nobles and lairds, and its austerity suited the dour nature of the humbler folk. In the framing of his doctrinal system, Calvin (1509–64) had intruded little that was new – his *Institutio* in four books following the Apostles' Creed sequence was in effect a revival of Augustine's scheme set down in the fifth century on the basis of Holy Scripture. Two basic postulates of Calvinism are the inheritance of original sin by all mankind, and the absolute sovereignty and omniscience of God. But God, not being without mercy, elected his chosen to salvation from eternal punishment and, axiomatically, the non-elect were reprobate and damned. The mercy of God was in time offered to the world by the incarnation of the Son and the atonement for inherited sin. To complete the doctrinal scheme, Calvin taught that the benefits of the atonement were received automatically by the elect, who thereby entered into a state of grace which was irreversible, while the non-elect could attain grace through an external agency – the church. Through that agency, Christ could regenerate the non-elect through baptism, exhortation to member-ship, guiding individuals on a pilgrimage of discipline, self-denial, prayer and repentance, to perfect faith. But Calvin emphasized that this pilgrimage could only be initiated in those first called to it by God, and this component of the holy plan made Calvinism a strongly evangelical type of religion. Whether any individual was of the elect or the non-elect was unknowable, and therefore it was vital for the church to maintain its evangelical pressure on all to the end of life if souls were to be saved. Many ministers over-played the power of fear in carrying this out, concentrating much of their preaching on terrifying descriptions of the torments of hell. The sin of fornication, usually provable in females by simple observation, demanded their special attention.

The history of punishment for fornication in Britain has chapters of the utmost savagery. In puritan England under Cromwell it brought a sentence of death for both parties, and 'without benefit of clergy'. Things were a bit milder in Scotland. An Act of 1567 provided for the punishment of fornicators with a fine of £40 and having to stand bare-headed in the market-place for two hours, and the punishment was heavier for subsequent offences. The fine for a third offence was as much as £100 (a huge sum then) plus public ducking three times in a filthy pond. Deprived of the collaboration of the Scottish civil authorities by the Act of 1690 which put an end to the severe social consequences of excommunication, the kirk lost its ultimate disciplinary measure. Prior to that enactment an excommunicated person became a miserable outcast, debarred from holding lands or receiving rents, excluded from appointment to any public office or even appearing as a court witness, and the Calvinist theocrats applied the provisions unrelentingly. The Toleration Act of 1712 saw the virtual end of state collaboration in the enforcement of holy discipline by removing the power of magistrates to enforce kirk summonses and penalties. From then on the kirk was left with one principal weapon – the threat of humiliation and shame in the eyes of the local community. It was applied energetically for the prevalent sin of fornication, particularly against the female participant. Many a girl committed suicide when her pregnancy became apparent or killed her baby if she had succeeded in reaching term without being found out, rather than having to face the wrath of the kirk. (The original emphasis of the term fornication was on organized whoring, the term being derived from the Latin *fornix*: a vault. The Roman brothels were usually below ground level. Fornication was not an offence under Roman or Mosaic law, but adultery committed by a married woman was a serious crime as it could impose the care of spurious offspring on her husband.)

Presbyterianism in Scotland met a critical challenge towards the end of the seventeenth century when the restored monarch Charles II, who hated the Presbyterian system, made moves to restore prelacy and patronage in minister appointments in defiance of the two Covenants it suited him to sign in 1649. Opposing Covenant adherents continued to conduct services in barns and fields where they were savagely harried by royalist troops, but they fought back with single-mindedness, convinced of their divine election and the rightness of their cause, the struggle ending only when forces they rallied were routed by a powerful contingent under Monmouth at Bothwell Brig in 1679. Many hundreds of lives had been lost in the campaign and the period has been called the 'killing time'. It required the Revolution of 1688–9 to restore a wholly Presbyterian system to the kirk, with Calvinism, and freedom from prelacy and patronage, assured by law under the Act of 1690.

Not only had Holland given Scotland a new monarch in the

person of William III, but it also had offered a variant on Calvinism, one which in time was to achieve substantial acceptance. This was Arminianism, formulated by the Dutch professor James Hermensen – better known by the Latinized name Jacob Arminius (1560–1609). Although the points of divergence in Arminianism were little more than matters of interpretation of scriptural semantics, the Calvinists of the Continent and Britain bitterly opposed any of the clergy adopting the new doctrine in the seventeenth century. Arminius's followers had codified his dogma system in a *Remonstrance* in 1610. It did not exclude the certainties of original sin, predestination and the efficacy of the atonement to ensure salvation by faith, and as in Calvinism, calling was a prerequisite to regeneration as free will alone was insufficient in human beings, all descendants of Adam and accordingly all loaded down with inherited sin. The main point of difference in Arminianism is its insistence on the conditional nature of predestination, and that salvation is only assured to those persevering to the end in belief in Christ, and that it is possible to lapse from the state of grace. But we are brought back very close to the Calvinist view by the *Remonstrance* stating that God foresaw from all eternity just which individuals would persevere in faith, and those others who would not and so merit eternal torment after death. The difference between the two systems of dogma seems to be slight enough to astonish us today when we read of the sacking and exiling of Arminian clerics ordered at the Synod of Dort in 1618–19. The two systems even divided early Methodists, Wesley adopting Arminianism and Whitefield holding fast to Calvinism.

Many Scottish clerics were drawn to the Arminian doctrine and formed a separate party which came to be known as the Moderates, or New Lights, rivalling the Calvinist residue which acquired the name Evangelicals, or Old Lights. Both parties persisted within the official Church of Scotland with no resultant secession occurring. The doctrinal differences dividing the Evangelicals and Moderates were less significant than their differences in academic background, personality and preaching style. Moderate ministers' sermons tended to reflect the broadening influence of intellectual teachers of the stamp of Francis Hutcheson, Adam Smith, Adam Fergusson and Thomas Reid, with their preaching characterized by tolerance and charity rather than undue emphasis on hell-fire and the extremes of discipline. One good consequence was the cessation of the execution of alleged witches. (The last of these vile incidents occurred in 1727 when an old woman accused of turning the daughter of a sheriff of Dornoch into a pony was duly strangled.)[9] Another consequence was wryly commented on by the Scottish historian James Mackinnon: 'Certain it is that, if the services became more decorous and refined, the churches were far less crowded than formerly.'[10]

One may suspect that at least part of the strategy of Evangelical ministers in their energetic thunderings from the pulpit was to keep the congregation awake, many old folk having walked five or more miles to church and arriving very tired. The Rev. K. Hewat relates that in some churches a kirk official was provided with a rod with which he advanced on slumberers and prodded them awake.[11] Sleeping in church, however, was never exclusively a failing of the Calvinist or other Scottish congregations, if note is to be taken of the popularity of the topic among eighteenth-century cartoonists. (Particularly satirical is Hogarth's *The Sleeping Congregation* of 1736, with the preacher reading the text 'Come unto me all ye that labour and are heavy laden, and I shall give you rest'. B&C 164, Plate 8.)

Doctrinal differences were quite secondary to the issue of patronage and other politically based disputes in spawning a series of secessions from the Church of Scotland, from the first in 1733 to the last, and biggest, in 1843. But something in the make-up of seceders seemed to make them prone to secede from seceders, and the history of all the resulting collateral churches in Scotland makes a bewildering story. Space cannot be given to details in this text, but they are set out in flow-chart form in Appendix A. In the legislation for the Union of Parliaments in 1707 the disallowance of patronage had been explicitly re-stated, but this provision was flagrantly reversed by the Westminster Parliament of Queen Anne by the passing of the Patronage Act of 1712, and it was not without the support of many Scots. View this cynical about-face as you will, it must be conceded that it had its virtues. Nobles and lairds tended to be well-educated and discerning, and their choice of new ministers to fill vacancies was reflected in a general raising of the erudition levels of the clergy of their day. Not unexpectedly, Moderates frequently won out over Evangelicals. But the thoroughly bad side of patronage in an old Covenanting countryside was its divisiveness.

It would appear that up to the age of about seventeen or

The Sleeping Congregation. William Hogarth. *Courtesy of the Trustees of the British Museum.*

eighteen Burns had accepted the prevailing kirk dogma and discipline without question, although he probably found 'three-mile prayers and hauf-mile graces' thoroughly irksome. His religious indoctrination had given him something he could cling to amid the stresses of family poverty, his father's illness and his own bouts of pathological depression. Those of his very early poems that have survived, roughly the first twenty of Kinsley's chronological sequence, are dominated by submissive religious introspection, at times revealing the end point of depression, the death wish. All that was to change – drastically.

TARGETS FOR A PROFANE RHYMER

Before surveying in some detail Burns's famed assaults on eighteenth-century Presbyterian orthodoxy, let us briefly review the component tenets of that orthodoxy which were to become his targets. The starting point, naturally enough, has to be *peccatum originatum* – the inheritance of Original Sin by the whole human family, the descendants of Adam, and consequential eternal damnation for the unredeemed when life on earth is terminated. The belief is given prominence today mainly in revivalist movements. In most churches of Christendom it tends to be rather muted – but not discarded, as without it redemption would be relevant for sin committed by the individual only, and the emergency baptism of newborn infants likely to die would have greatly diminished significance. The Biblical authority for belief in the inheritance of original sin and its consequences tends to be indirect; the passages that are cited for its support requiring an element of imaginative extrapolation. Typical is I Cor. 15.22: 'For as in Adam all die, even so in Christ shall all be made alive.'

The indirectness of the scriptural basis for belief in original sin inheritance moved John Taylor to write *The Scripture Doctrine of Original Sin Proposed to Free and Candid Examination*, a work first published in 1740. As already noted, Burns had read that treatise at Lochlea, presumably without his father knowing. As it confronted beliefs expressed unequivocally in his *Manual of Religious Belief*, the book would have been anathema to William Burnes. (A précis is available in the Wallace-Chambers *Life and Works of Robert Burns* I, p. 461.)

While the words of Paul are found to be somewhat recondite for the inquirer seeking divine backing for belief in the inheritance of original sin, they are relatively explicit on predestination, election and calling:

> And we know that all things work together for good to them that
> love God, to them who are called according to his purpose. For

whom did he foreknow, he also did predestinate to be conformed
to the image of his Son, that he might be the first-born among
many brethren. Moreover whom he called, them he also
justified, and whom he justified, them he also glorified.

(Rom. 8. 28–30)

The meaning of this and some other scriptural passages seemed
clear enough to the influential bishop Augustine (354–430), and his
conclusions on predestination, election and reprobation became embodied in formal Catholic doctrine. They survived the Reformation,
passing into the Anglican Thirty-nine Articles; also into the
Westminster Confession adopted by the Scottish kirk. On reprobation, both of the above formulations are silent, but its
implication had to persist as the logical consequence of non-
election to grace or of lapse from grace. Never let it be said that
those ancient points of dogma were Calvinist inventions.

The agony and argument engendered by the old concepts no
longer occur because they have long been swept under various
ecclesiastical carpets. Roman Catholic theologians see them as
insolubly metaphysical but of historical interest. The typical lay
Anglican will probably look blank if quizzed about them,
presumably because the Thirty-nine Articles are printed on the
remoter back pages of his Book of Common Prayer and are
unlikely to be studied analytically. Christian churches in general
tend to settle for the Arminian compromise of believing grace
available to all by accepting the pathway to faith that each teaches,
and a consequential lapse from grace facing the backslider.

During the early years of the Reformation, the novel but execrable
notion of Antinomianism – from the Greek 'against law' – was
formulated by the German theologian Johannes Agricola (1495–
1566). He asserted that the Gospel only should be preached,
ignoring the requirements of civil law and popular concepts of
morality, so avoiding the wrong path of 'salvation by works'
instead of 'justification only by faith'. This doctrine was opposed
by Luther and his successors as its implications had been
condemned by Paul (Rom. 6.15). The Antinomian idea provided
blanketing indulgence even in respect of the Mosaic decalogue,
claiming that killing, stealing, adultery and other moral transgressions involved no penalty for the elect in the after-life. Being
unalterably elect, such offenders would proceed to heaven

regardless of their earthly record, but of course they took their chances with the civil law in the mortal world. Any invoking of Antinomianism was sharply condemned by both Evangelicals and Moderates in the Scottish eighteenth-century kirk, although the privileges were liable to be claimed by off-beat schismatic groups.

ATTACK

Let us now return to the scene of our twenty-five-year-old Robert Burns and Lizzie Paton ordered to appear before the Old Light minister and congregation of the Mauchline kirk to be dealt with for the sin of fornication. Such a routine would have been no novelty for the congregation, Burns included, but it was the first time he had been in the hot spot. How that sensitive and proud young genius must have hated standing there, unable to hide from the sea of solemn, accusing peasant faces! His mother, brothers and sisters probably were there too, sharing his embarrassment and wondering which way to look. The volley of reproving words was duly fired, hitting that part of his persona where it would have hurt the most – his pride. At last, filing out of the church silently and setting out for home with his equally silent family he would have been acutely embarrassed and inwardly fuming, turning his thoughts towards the counter-attack weapon he knew he could wield adroitly – satirical verse. He was soon to open fire with a clever Epistle, the addressee of which was well chosen in the person of 'Rough, rude, ready-witted Rankine' – a tenant farmer friend whose conscience was not burdened by kirk standards. The *Epistle to John Rankine* (K.47) leads off with four stanzas in which Rankine is satirically asked to spare the Evangelical ministers, the third being:

> Hypocrisy, in mercy spare it!
> That *holy robe*, O dinna tear it!
> Spare't for their sakes wha aften wear it,
>   The lads in *black*;
> But your curst wit, when it comes near it,
>   Rives't aff their back.

In the fourth stanza the poet couples Rankine's and his own backsliding in the expression 'ony unregenerate Heathen, like you or I'. In another six stanzas he turns to his lapse with Lizzie Paton with bravado, using the apt metaphor of hunting a hen partridge with his gun and bringing her 'to the grun', without hurting her much. Sustaining the symbolism he relates how his 'poaching' was reported, resulting in a fine. But his easy conscience is underlined by a resolve to repeat the procedure: 'Lord, I'se hae sportin by an' by, for my gowd guinea'. Copies of the *Epistle to John Rankine* were made and passed to like-minded friends. It was a small masterpiece of the rhyming art, and Burns, confident that the symbolism was recondite, was to include it in his published editions of 1786, 1787, 1793 and 1794. With an air of picaresque fun, Burns had performed his first chastisement of the kirk with his poetical whip. Chastisement with scorpions was to follow soon afterwards – with the writing of *Holy Willie's Prayer*.

Holy Willie's Prayer (K.53) was written after the citation of Gavin Hamilton, Burns's new landlord and friend, for some minor breaches of holy discipline. He denied the charges and was cleared, despite kirk appeals to the Ayr Presbytery and Synod. It would appear that the kirk elder William Fisher had been Dr Auld's ardent prompter, both in raising the charges and in the hearings. Burns, still piqued from the humiliation of his own recent public rebuke, must have been elated by Hamilton's victory, and saw in the whole business a perfect scenario for revenge in verse. Fisher was his *nominal* target, and the personal attack would have been warranted if the man had in fact been the loose-living hypocrite he was made out to be. But Burns's real target was the kirk itself and all that it stood for in his eyes. The poem is indirectly a savage attack on the evangelical faith, and it has misled uncritical admirers of Burns who have accepted it as the definitive description of Old Light Presbyterianism. Ridicule is heaped on the doctrine of election to grace in a manner never directed to its Biblical origin. Even such a respectable cleric as the Reverend R.J. Macintyre wrote as recently as 1912:

> An ultra-Calvinism was preached to the people, the chief recommendation of which was the Divine election of the preacher and a few others and eternal damnation of all the rest.[12]

The expression 'ultra-Calvinism' makes no more sense than other modified absolutes. Both Calvinist and Arminian doctrine had long been codified in strict formulations, allowing no additions nor diminutions. When Burns clashed with the kirk his targets were individuals, and those individuals tended to be Calvinists in his own, and nearby, parishes. Had they been Arminians he would have been up against the same entrenched dogma of predestination and damnation – indeed the possibility of lapse from grace made persuasive preaching more urgent for them. The New Lights may have demanded conformity and sinless behaviour less blatantly, but for the unrepentant sinner the threat of hell would have been no less positive in their sermons.

In the disdainful assertion quoted above, Macintyre reveals his agreement with Burns's one-to-ten guess as to the ratio of elect to non-elect in *Holy Willie's Prayer*:

> O thou that in the heavens does dwell!
> Wha, as it pleases best thysel,
> Sends ane to heaven and ten to hell,
>   A' for thy glory!

Macintyre went on to emphasize that this word-picture drawn by Burns was 'no caricature of the doctrines which Burns regularly heard in the Ayrshire kirks'. But Calvin and Calvinist ministers, and of course the Arminians too, had no predilection towards making such ratio quantifications as they believed the elect state to be one of God's secrets not revealed to living man. Each minister would have liked to feel that his own chances were good, but entitled to feel quite certain, on the basis of accepted doctrine, that a few or most of his flock were not of the elect and therefore in dire need of regeneration by the processes of the kirk. There is no evidence external to *Holy Willie's Prayer* that Fisher believed himself to be of the elect. Burns put words into his mouth that assert that he did:

> When from my mother's womb I fell,
> Thou might hae plunged me deep in hell,
> To gnash my gooms, and weep, and wail,
>   In burning lakes,
> Where damned devils roar and yell
>   Chained to their stakes.
>
> Yet here I am, a chosen sample,
> To shew thy grace is great and ample:
> I'm here, a pillar o' thy temple

Strong as a rock,
A guide, a ruler and example
To a' thy flock.

Inevitably, *Holy Willie's Prayer* 'alarmed the kirk-Session so much that they held three several meetings to look over their holy artillery, if any of it was pointed at profane Rhymers' (L.125). Burns was to find out in the following year that he was 'point-blank within the reach of their heaviest metal'. He was of course alluding to the consequences of getting Jean Armour pregnant within four months of the birth of little Elizabeth, his 'love-begotten Daughter' by Lizzie Paton. Whether William Fisher played any active part in the hounding of Burns over the second fornication offence is not recorded, but *Holy Willie's Prayer* was to be only the first of quite a cavalcade of satires on the kirk and its officials.

Because there had been a subsequent rumour that William Fisher had stolen money from the Mauchline kirk poor-box, as picked up much later by Burns in his poem *The Kirk of Scotland's Garland* (K.264):

Holy Will, Holy Will, there was wit i' your skull,
When ye pilfer'd the alms of the poor;

and because Dr Auld in later years had to rebuke Fisher for excessive tippling, commentators on *Holy Willie's Prayer* have been disposed to pin an Antinomian label on Fisher. (Dr J.D. Ross, in his *Burns Handbook*, pointed out that there is no official record of William Fisher having helped himself to kirk funds.) But Burns, in three poems involving Fisher, made no accusation which may be so interpreted. Had he believed Fisher to be the claimant of such immunity, he would have had no reason to present the hated elder confessing to God his sexual lapses 'wi' Meg' and 'wi' Leezie's lass', nor his asking God to bear in mind that all men are 'Defiled wi' sin' – so off-loading blame for his vulnerability. If Antinomianism had at times intruded into Scottish Calvinism we may rest assured that it was always dealt with sharply. Burns would have known that if William Auld had any suspicion that his elder had invoked the perverted notion to justify breaches of moral standards he would have acted against Fisher vehemently. It was not that Burns was ignorant of the strange doctrine – he had previously told his

Montrose cousin how the Reverend Hugh Whyte had been dismissed from his Irvine Relief Church charge for linking up with the Buchanites, a small group that embraced the belief (L.17). (In his letter to James Burness, dated 3 August 1784, Burns related how the spiritual mother of the group, 'old Buchan', administered to her flock: 'She pretends to give them the Holy Ghost by breathing on them, which she does by postures & practices that are scandalously indecent; they have likewise disposed of all their effects & hold a community of goods, & live nearly an idle life, carrying on a great farce of pretended devotion in barns, & woods, where they lodge & lye all together, & hold likewise a community of women, as it is another of their tenets that they can commit no moral sin.')

If satirizing of Antinomianism was absent from *Holy Willie's Prayer*, pungent treatment of Original Sin was there in full measure, and not only in that poem. He has Holy Willie saying:

> I, wha deserv'd most just damnation,
> For broken laws
> Sax thousand years ere my creation,
> Thro' Adam's cause!

In *A Poet's Welcome to his Love-begotten Daughter* Burns implies the same assumption:

> As a' the Priests had seen me get thee
> That's out o' hell.
>
> (K.60)

Quite obviously the Bard had agreed with John Taylor, whose book questioning Original Sin had been part of his early reading. When John Goldie, a capable industrialist and amateur theologian, published his six-volume treatise *The Gospel Recovered from its Captive State* (1784), highly critical of Calvinism, Burns wrote him a witty *Epistle*. Stanza five runs:

> It's you and Taylor are the chief
> To blame for a' this black mischief;
> But could the Lord's ain Folk get leave,
> A toom tar-barrel

> And twa red peats wad bring relief
> And end the quarrel.

> (K.63)

It was a grimly satirical reminder of the fate in store for heretics in earlier centuries when death by burning was a legal punishment. (It has been said (but not proved) that Calvin himself was a party to the burning of the heretic Servetus in 1553. The statute *De haeretico comburendo* of 1401, which brought the stake to Britain, not only survived the Reformation – it came to be more zealously applied thereafter. It was repealed in the reign of Charles II.)

Burns's satirical humour aimed at Original Sin was never better than in his hilarious *Address to the Deil*:

> Ye came to Paradise incog,
> An play'd on man a cursed brogue,
> (Black be your fa'!)
> An' gied the infant warld a shog,
> 'Maist ruined a'.

> (K.76)

The old Pauline assertions on predestination and election are so far-fetched that they even tend to be passed over by high-pressure revivalists today. Modern writers have frankly passed them off as 'absurd' in applauding the campaign mounted by Burns.[13,14] For some inconsistent reason, that applause is not extended to his satirizing of the inheritance of Original Sin, the very basis of the fanciful extrapolations.

All the hard-hitting religious satires of Burns, bar one, were written in his Mossgiel period. In *The Holy Tulzie* (K.52), also named *The Twa Herds* in some editions, he was enjoying the amusing spectacle of two Old Light ministers, Moodie and Russel, brawling over the delineation of their parish boundaries before the Irvine presbytery. The topic is localized and dated. The same two ministers are introduced in taunting terms in the *Epistle to John Goldie*, already mentioned. An even more merciless satire, *To the Rev. John M'Math* (K.68), was only to come to light in 1808, in Cromek's *Reliques*. M'Math, an unhappy Moderate, had got wind of *Holy Willie's Prayer* at Tarbolton and asked Burns for a copy. He got his copy plus a wonderful bonus, the Epistle. M'Math must have thoroughly enjoyed every stanza of both compositions, the

Epistle reading as an obvious follow-up of the satire on Fisher:

> I own 'twas rash, an' rather hardy,
> That I, a simple countra bardie,
> Shou'd meddle wi' a pack sae sturdy,
>   Wha, if they ken me,
> Can easy, wi' a single wordie,
>   Louse hell upon me.

Contempt for the Old Lights clergy is revealed in stronger terms as the poem continues:

> But I gae mad at their grimaces,
> Their sighan, cantan, grace-prood faces,
> Their three-mile prayers, an' hauf-mile graces,
>   Their raxan conscience,   (stretching)
> Whase greed, revenge, an' pride disgraces
>   Waur nor their nonsense.

There is a lot more besides. Taking Burns's word for it, there must have been some contemptible individuals within the ranks of the Scottish clergy of 1785, but it is hard to believe that they were other than a minority. Burns had little to say about the others. Surely there were many neither greedy nor revengeful.

The Holy Fair (K.70) is another kirk satire, but of a rather different kind. It stands as a significant contribution to kirk history, but one must keep in mind a possible slant in Burns's value judgements when reading it. It describes in detail the annual Communion meeting at Mauchline, depicting satirically not only the relays of high-powered preaching but all that was happening on the side as well – eating, drinking to excess, and in particular, amatory assignations. As neighbouring parishes joined in to swell the crowd to over a thousand, tents were provided to accommodate the communicants. But the poem is unbalanced in its failure to make any reference to Communion. Burns was poetically thrashed for this misrepresentation by James Maxwell of Paisley in his *Animadversions* (1788):

> The most solemn ordinance Christ hath ordain'd,
> Which hath in his church, since his passion, remain'd,
> This infidel scoffer calls that but a Fair
> To which rakes and harlots together repair,

To make lewd appointments of carnal delight;
Thus is it described by this hellish wight.&c.

Burns took delight in satirizing the devil. He dealt with him in
Address of Beelzebub, Tam o' Shanter, and in a few epigrams, but his
Address to the Deil (K.76) is the masterpiece. Offered as cheeky *lèse-
majesté* for His Satanic Majesty, one senses an ingredient of
admiration – even affection – for his arch-villain. The personal vein
in which he rounds off an account of mischievous activity is
unique:

> An' now auld Cloots, I ken ye're thinkan,
> A certain Bardie's rantin, drinkin,
> Some luckless hour will send him linkan,
> To your black pit;
> But faith! he'll turn a corner jinkan,
> An' cheat you yet.

The Ordination (K.85) is a satire on kirk politics. To take in its
message it is necessary to know some facts about happenings in
Kilmarnock in 1785. The congregation of the Laigh Kirk,
predominantly Moderate, was to have imposed on it by patronage
the Evangelical Calvinist James Mackinlay as second in charge to
Mr Lindsay, a Moderate. Anticipating trouble, Burns wrote the
smart fourteen-stanza satire. But time was soon to prove it rather
pointless as Mackinlay became a very popular minister.

A Dedication to Gavin Hamilton (K.103) was almost certainly
written to head the forty-four poems of the Kilmarnock book. But
our poet dropped it back to twenty-fifth place when the copy went
to press. Why? Probably because he thought better of giving it such
prominence with its stinging attacks on orthodox Calvinism. There
was no point in antagonizing a large fraction of potential readers
before they came to *The Twa Dogs, The Cotter's Saturday Night, To a
Mouse* and other poems, devoid of religious controversy. Another
kirk satire, *The Calf* (K.125), first appeared in the 1787 Edinburgh
edition. Burns described it as 'a bagatelle'. It *is* a bagatelle.

In the autumn of 1785 Burns wrote his brilliant cantata *The Jolly
Beggars* (K.84), based on a carousing company he saw in Poosie
Nansie's tavern. The concluding chorus, below, has for its last line
what could be considered Burns's most savage jibe at the kirk, even
though it is represented as being voiced by semi-fictional

characters. Pure poetic creativity, or a poet's credo? Probably both:

> A fig for those by law protected
> Liberty's a glorious feast!
> Courts for cowards were erected,
> Churches built to please the Priest.

The foregoing religious satires were all written before Burns went from Ayrshire to Edinburgh to discover new lifestyles. With a wider world opening up, he found new interests and new priorities. Next the heady involvements of Edinburgh were to yield place to the calm of Nithsdale, and the kirk squabbles in Ayrshire no longer seemed to concern him. But his fierce satirical Muse was to be aroused once more with some news filtering through from his old presbytery in 1789. Dr William M'Gill of Ayr had been denounced from the pulpit for what seemed to be heretical views on original sin and the Trinity in a published essay, and he was charged with heresy before the Synod of Glasgow and Ayr. Burns rose to the heights of savage satire, writing *The Kirk of Scotland's Garland – a New Song* (K.264). (The alternative title *The Kirk's Alarm* appears in some editions.) Burns called it a song: it could be better described as a catalogue aria, dealing with a score of individuals in sequence. He led off with John Knox, and then with mock horror complimented first M'Gill himself and next his supporters Ballantine, Dalrymple and Aiken – the last-named being the lawyer 'Orator Bob' who defended M'Gill. The main theme is extended in stanza five:

> Calvin's Sons, Calvin's Sons, seize your spiritual guns –
> Ammunition ye never can need;
> Your *hearts* are the stuff will be *powder* enough
> And your *sculls* are a storehouse o' *lead*.

Then follows a sequence of flailing stanzas on the Evangelical ministers of Ayrshire, with the hated elder William Fisher included for a share of the Burns venom. The stanza on the Rev. William Peebles, clerk of the Ayr presbytery, is scatologically coarse. Burns was evidently very pleased with his viperish effort and couldn't wait to finish it for Mrs Dunlop, sending her a first draft in July 1789 with instructions not to reveal the authorship (L.352). Before long, copies of the completed version had been posted to John Logan (L.356), Graham of Fintry (L.373) and, of all people, Lady

Cunningham – a sister of the sick Earl of Glencairn (L.379). The Earl had exercised his patronage in presenting the Evangelical Mackinlay several years earlier to second charge of the Kilmarnock kirk, and that same Mackinlay was now being insulted and ridiculed:

> Simper James, Simper James, leave the fair Killie dames,
>> There's a holier chase in your view:
> I'll lay on your head that the *pack* ye'll soon lead,
>> For *puppies* like you there's but few.

Not very tactful, to say the least. Burns told Mrs Dunlop that he planned to have two or three dozen copies printed and sent to Ayrshire folk on both sides of the dispute, but he must have felt very flattened on learning that after a drawn-out hearing, M'Gill had expressed his regrets to the presbytery and promised, in what could have been another recantation in the Galileo and Locke vein, to adhere to orthodox kirk doctrine in the future.

By now we are left in little doubt about Burns's doctrinal maverick stance. Rejection of all orthodoxy seems to have corresponded in time with his reading of Locke's *Essay*; become overt after his first rebuke for fornication with the writing of *Holy Willie's Prayer* and other kirk satires of the period; and well confirmed four years later in *The Kirk of Scotland's Garland*. When Burns raised the New Light cause as a taunting threat to the Old Lights it must not be read as his adherence to the New Light doctrines. For the last seven years of his life, Burns gave scant attention to religion in his poetry.

Many Burns admirers like to hark back to the scene depicted in *The Cotter's Saturday Night* as good evidence for the poet's religious conforming, but that much-admired poem can be misleading on the issue. It is factually biographical in only a partial way, with Burns's emphasis on the central father figure providing a parallel with his own devout father whose memory he was honouring. But he could not help revealing a little of his own protesting self in stanza seventeen:

> Compar'd with this, how poor Religion's pride,
>> In all the pomp of *method*, and of *art*,
> When men display to congregations wide,
>> Devotion's ev'ry grace, except the *Heart*!

Through the Mossgiel period, as head of the household, Burns had *outwardly* submitted to the discipline of the kirk. He needed Dr Auld's help to get clear of his perplexing marriage tangle in mid-1786. From that negotiation the often-criticized Dr Auld emerges as no tough, pound-of-flesh bigot, particularly when taking into account the second fornication offence which had led to yet another rebuke from the pulpit for Burns, that time with Jean Armour. Wayward Robert told his equally wayward friend Richmond in a letter dated 9 July 1786:

> However, the Priest, I am inform'd will give me a Certificate as a single man, if I comply with the rules of the Church, which *for that very reason* I intend to do.
>
> (L.33)

(Italics mine.) He related the outcome to David Brice of Glasgow soon afterwards:

> I have already appeared publickly in Church, and was indulged in the liberty of standing in my own seat. I do this to get a certificate as a bachelor, which Mr Auld has promised me.
>
> (L.34)

If there were indeed ministers then who displayed 'Devotion's ev'ry grace, except the Heart', lenient Dr Auld was not one of them, despite his energetic style of sermon delivery. (He was to be described by Burns later as 'that Boanerges of Gospel power' in a letter to Gavin Hamilton (L.157): Boanerges was the surname given to James and John, sons of Zebedee, by Jesus on account of their thundering voices and religious fervour (Mark 3.17 and Luke 9.53–54). We should remember Dr Edgar's characterization of Dr Auld in *Old Church Life in Scotland*:

> There was, however, a stately courtesy, with much kindness of heart, underneath his austere and rigid manners. While a terror to evil-doers, he was the praise of those who did well.[15]

Despite his merciless attacks on the kirk, Burns never lost an underlying respect for Dr Auld, the man. One may even detect a note of affection from his occasional reference to the minister as 'Daddy Auld'.

Reading Burns's satires against the kirk and thoroughly enjoying the wit he wove into them so deftly, one may well wonder whether the overall picture presented by the Bard is factual, or unfair. In 1931 the Reverend A. Burns Jamieson, in his informative book *Burns and Religion*, made a reasoned plea for a balanced appreciation of eighteenth-century Calvinism and for a realization of the incompleteness of the view of it that Burns had engendered.[16] His case appears to have been largely ignored, and there remains a popular tendency to ridicule the Evangelicals for their over-zealous preaching and their retention of the doctrines of predestination, election and reprobation. As Jamieson pointed out, this is quite unfair to those earnest preachers of past years, whose long fiery sermons were directed towards the furtherance of regeneration in those of the flock who might have been of the non-elect. Otherwise, those ministers would appear to us today as a misguided pack of ranting blockheads, wasting their own time and energy, and the time of their congregations, on needless exhortations for the elect, and useless exhortations for the non-elect. Why ever bother to harangue and terrify simple folk with lurid accounts of hell and eternal torment if nothing could be done to avert such a destiny? No, they simply preached on those lines because Calvin had pointed the way to regeneration in Book IV of his *Institutio*. If the Calvinist line on piety is to be found lacking it must be for giving no special prominence to secular virtues: kindness, generosity, self-denial and good works. But there again, Calvin had simply followed Paul's directive to ignore 'works' (Rom. 9.11). Calvin emphasized that salvation of the souls of the non-elect was achieved by a means external to the man – the Church, which was the Body of Christ, offering redemption through baptism, exhortation to membership and faith, and the Eucharist. Such processes still operate in Christian churches today; only the style has changed. If Paul's assertions on election and its implications are to be taken as 'revealed truth', Calvin was wholly consistent when he embodied them in his dogmatic canon.

SUMMATION

It would be biographically tidy to set down a single succinct label for Burns's religious persuasion, but he left to posterity no recorded attestation of such. The discernible alignment however, is *unitarianism* verging on *deism*. If he was in fact a unitarian he was following

77

in the wake of distinguished intellectual predecessors such as Milton, Locke and Newton.

Since the third century various formulations of unitarianism, all claimed to be within the pale of Christianity, had made an appearance. (In a literal sense, Jews and Moslems are also unitarians.) The most influential of these was probably Socinianism, so named after its much-persecuted founders, Siena-born Lelio Sozzini (1525–62) and his nephew Fausto Sozzini (1539–1604). Socinian belief embraces the concept of a merciful and omniscient God who appointed Jesus Christ, a mere man, to teach His will to other men. The resurrection implied no redemptive purpose, serving only to teach the reality of immortality by a special and spectacular example. Socinianism achieved some penetration of eighteenth-century Scotland, mainly in Moderate flocks. Principal Shairp wrote that even some of the kirk's ministers embraced the heresy, adding, with a note of cynicism, 'most of them shone less in the pulpit than at the festive board'.[17]

Deism is more a *church-emptying* theological philosophy than one destined to give rise to big congregations. It has been called 'natural religion' – involving complete rejection of the Scriptures as a certificate of divine revelation. The concept of God is retained, but only as the creator of the universe and the power behind its continuance. Deism became prominent in the second half of the seventeenth century and in the first half of the eighteenth from the writings of a few liberal and courageous intellectuals, prominent among them being Thomas Woolston (1670–1733) whose subversive *Discourse on the Miracles of Christ* cost him his Cambridge fellowship and brought him arrest and trial for blasphemy. Unable to pay a heavy fine and surety, Woolston languished and died in King's Bench prison. Deism was opposed by Locke but supported by his close friends Anthony Collins and the Earl of Shaftesbury. Without even being aware of the meaning of the word deism, a good proportion of the people deserting the churches today would be deists.

One must hesitate to regard Burns as having been an out-and-out deist. He held the Bible in very high regard, although at times making fun of selected Biblical characters. In a reflective letter written to Alexander Cunningham in 1790 he stated: 'I hate a man that wishes to be a Deist, but I fear, every fair, unprejudiced Enquirer must in some degree be a Sceptic.' (L.392). Such a confession suggests that, deep down, he entertained deistic thoughts, but these were not compelling enough to drive him past all the red lights of indoctrination, dim though some had become. Burns invariably maintained reverence and humility when he brought the Almighty into his verse or prose, but from the kirk's formula for salvation he made no secret of his dissent – a dissent which left for him a troublesome gap in his religious philosophy. The kirk would have been affronted by such a passage as 'I firmly believe, that every honest, upright man, of whatever sect, will be accepted by the Deity' (L.176, to Clarinda), and by his quoting 'O that some courteous ghost would blab it out' (L.105, to Mrs Dunlop from Robert Blair's *The Grave*, a blank verse poem of some 800 lines, later illustrated by William Blake). The kirk needed no blabbing ghosts; it had all the answers already.

Support for the supposition that Burns had long been a unitarian (in effect from his reading of Locke) lies in negative evidence. We have no record of his admitting trinitarian belief. His nearest approach to the recognition of the divine status of the Son was in non-committal statements, as to Clarinda – 'Jesus Christ, a great Personage, whose relation to Him we cannot comprehend' (L.174). In the one extant record of his even mentioning the Trinity, a letter written to Gavin Hamilton as early as 1787, there is a note of cynicism: 'I beseech the Holy Trinity, or holy somebody that directs the world' (L.157). The most telling scrap of evidence of Burns having found his religious compromise in unitarianism, or of even drifting further, lies in a single adjective aimed at him by a friend. The friend was the ever-frank William Nicol: the adjective was in the starting greeting of a witty effervescent letter written early in 1793, strongly advising the politically-victimized poet to emulate the song-celebrated Vicar of Bray in coping with his trials. He began: 'Dear Christless Bobbie . . . '

Why? Let us remember that Burns and Nicol had shared a coach for sixteen days in their rambling tour of the Highlands in 1787. Nicol was a remarkably well-read fellow, his studies having embraced in sequence theology, medicine and the classics, and he shone in letter-writing and conversation. We can be certain that he and Burns delved into many philosophical topics and exchanged intimate confidences in the course of their long journey. The discerning Nicol would not have used the jibe 'Christless' unless he knew it was appropriate. A true word had been written in jest.

Burns's reply is one of the gems of his witty prose (L.537 of 20 February 1793). It was published by Currie in 1800, and it has been widely reprinted. It contains no direct mention of the adjective under discussion – only a volley of facetious sarcasm aimed at Nicol's wisdom:

> May one feeble ray of light of wisdom which darts from thy sensorium, straight as the arrow of Heaven against the head of the Unrighteous, & bright as the meteor of inspiration descending on the holy & undefiled Priesthood – may it be my portion; so that I may be less unworthy of the face & favour of that father of Proverbs & master of Maxims, that antipode of Folly & magnet among the Sages, the wise & witty Willie Nicol! Amen! Amen!

Burns wisely refrained from spreading abroad his personal brand of faith. Unitarians were often politically radical, and both attributes probably played a part in the sacking of the home of Joseph Priestley in 1791, and in the conviction and transportation of the political martyr Thomas F. Palmer in 1793. Burns was already suffering plenty of ostracism in his later Dumfries years without attracting additional snide animadversions of kirk bigots. In writing to friends that he trusted he even revealed a deistic aproach when he alluded to God in his later letters: as to Mrs Dunlop, 'The Great Disposer of Events' (L.491), 'the Religion of God & Nature, the Religion that exalts, that ennobles, Man' (L.605); to Maria Riddell, 'the Author and Director of Nature' (L.516); to Alexander Cunningham, 'nature's God' (L.619). When he was confident that a friend would appreciate a touch of satire on kirk matters he was not inhibited. When giving Cunningham the latest news about his twenty-two-month-old son in 1788 he interposed: 'By the bye, I intend breeding him up for the Church; and from an innate dexterity in secret Mischief which he possesses, & a certain hypocritical gravity as he looks on the consequences, I have no small hopes of him in the sacerdotal line.' (L.257). For his erring comrade Ainslie, at last a legitimate father, he could not resist some Scripture-linked banter:

> Call your boy what you think proper, only interject Burns.
> What do you say at a scripture name; for instance –
> Zimri Burns Ainslie

or

Achitophel, &c., &c. –

look in your bible for these two heroes. If you do this,
I will repay the Compliment.

(L.130)

(Zimri was a chief of the tribe of Simeon who brought a Midianite
woman back to his camp. For this both were slain. Achitophel
(spelt Ahitophel in the Authorized Version) joined Absolom's
revolt against David and later hanged himself in fear and remorse.)
In a later letter to Ainslie he related how 'a Taylor' who was a
regular commuter to and from his rural Nithsdale library took his
advice about learning theology by strapping an old Concordance,
given to the library by a neighbourhood priest, between his
shoulders 'as doctors do a blistering plaister' and how 'Stitch, in a
dozen pilgrimages, acquired as much *rational* Theology as the said
Priest had done by forty years perusal of the pages' (L.561). It was
a hilarious made-up yarn, but Burns, by italicizing the word
rational, would have left Ainslie in no doubt about his contempt for
fundamentalism.

Writers doing their best to enhance his religious image have
emphasized that Burns, while at Ellisland, conducted regular
religious services for his household and later attended regularly at
St Michael's in Dumfries. Just how regular these observances were
is not known. We may take a hint from his letter to M'Auley in
which he interposes 'in my family devotion, which, like a good
presbyterian, I *occasionally* give to my household folks' (L.346,
italics mine). But the Reverend R.G. Macintyre has Burns
conducting family worship *every* evening at Ellisland. The same
writer refers to the Burns family pew at St Michael's 'where he was
a regular worshipper'.[1] As mentioned in the opening paragraph of
this chapter, James Barke stated that Burns disliked St Michael's
and attended there only twice. That is not to say that Jean and the
children were not regular attenders in their time at Dumfries.

There is no evidence that Burns was a staunch adherent of any
New Light kirk. It is true that he often put forward the Arminian
cause in his satires, but primarily as a taunt aimed at particular
Calvinist ministers who had earned his detestation. His antipathy
was directed to bigotry-based injustice associated with any variant
of religious faith – not to the metaphysical basis of that faith nor its

organized structure as such, whether hierarchic or egalitarian. This is evident from his warm admiration of Dr John Geddes, Roman Catholic Bishop of Dunkeld (see L.148). A succinct statement of his indifference to sectarian formality occurs in a poem supporting and complimenting Gavin Hamilton, who had been in trouble with the kirk:

> Some quarrel the presbyter gown,
>   Some quarrel Episcopal graithing,
> But every good fellow will own
>   Their quarrel is all about – naething.

(K.99)

Despite his rejection of holy discipline, Burns admired the single-mindedness and bravery of the Covenanters in their life-and-death defence of Calvinism against royalist episcopal domination. Late in life, probably in his last year, he wrote:

> The Solemn League and Covenant
>   Now brings a smile, now brings a tear.
> But sacred Freedom, too, was theirs;
>   If thou'rt a slave, indulge thy sneer.

(K.512)

To this point, the chapter has been concentrated on the kirk's influence on Burns. What of the reactive consequences – his influence on the kirk? There have been over-blown statements on this. Christina Keith was undoubtedly right in observing that *Holy Willie's Prayer* was 'Burns at his supreme best', but a bit off the mark in adding 'it was the last and final nail in the eighteenth-century Scots kirk. It was driven triumphantly home.'[18] She obviously meant the Evangelical kirk – Burns's habitual target for satire – but the fact is that the Moderates had been increasing their dominance in kirk leadership for more than fifty years before the Burns satires were written. Their influence reached a peak in the 1770s under the inspiring leadership of Principal William Robertson. However, contrary to Miss Keith's enthusiastic claim, from the *Holy Willie's Prayer* period onwards the Evangelicals achieved a steadily *rising* influence, and this was maintained well into the nineteenth century by great writers of the calibre of Dr Thomas Erskine (1788–1870) and by brilliant preachers of the stamp of Thomas Chalmers. True, the kirk was plagued by a sequence of squabbles, but it was not religious doctrine that caused the rifts – it was the festering sore of lay patronage.

Lay patronage flouts the very principle that gives Presbyterianism its name – kirk administration by locally elected elders. It was the issue behind the secession splits of 1733, 1761 and 1843. The Burgher Oath and the Old and New Light disagreements were trivial in comparison with the patronage issue. In the early decades of the nineteenth century, lay patronage progressively lost the refining effect it tended to bring in the eighteenth century as the educational levels of both laity and clergy continued to rise, and it came to be more and more resented by the democratically-minded Scots. After a bewildering series of legal wrangles it was thrown out for good in 1874 by Act of Parliament.

One might have expected that a thoroughly consistent Robert Burns, widely hailed as a Scottish champion of democracy, should have been fighting patronage in kirk appointments, but his antipathy towards many Evangelical ministers and elders stayed his hand. His influence in any kirk changes was negligible, perhaps because he refrained from publishing his stronger kirk satires. The doctrinal row that split the burgher section of seceders into separate Old and New Light churches (not involving the established church) was over by 1799 – two years before Stewart was to give *Holy Willie's Prayer*, *The Holy Tulzie* and *The Kirk of Scotland's Garland* any wide readership in his published Burns collection. The Disruption of 1843, which split asunder the established church, was centred not on religious doctrine but on the right of civil courts to deal with ecclesiastical dispute, and on the lay patronage issue. *Nec tamen consumebatur.* In the end, intelligence was to prevail over stubborn prejudice, and the abolition of lay patronage by civil law in 1874 cleared a path for the reunions of 1900 and 1929, and the last of the secessionists came back to the fold in 1957. (See Appendix A.)

Chapter Three

DISTANT SHONE, ART'S LOFTY BOAST

(K.62)

MUSICAL ART

We need no reminding that the fame of Burns rests on his mastery of the art of using words. On the other hand, the appraisal of his appreciation of other great arts – musical and visual – can be elusive. Music first. We get off to a puzzling start if we go right back to the schoolmaster John Murdoch's often-quoted comments on young Robert and his brother Gilbert:

> I attempted to teach them a little church-music. Here they were
> left behind by all the rest of the school. Robert's ear, in
> particular, was remarkably dull, and his voice untunable. It was
> a long time before I could get them to distinguish one tune from
> another.[1]

If we reject the notion that Murdoch was a liar – and we should, surely – we are left looking for the facts behind his cold and un-compromising statement. Dr Currie's observations on the teaching of church music, published in 1800, give us a good clue:

> This branch of education had, in the last reign, fallen into some
> neglect, but it was revived about thirty or forty years ago, when
> the music itself was reformed and improved. The Scottish system
> of psalmody is however radically bad. Destitute of taste or
> harmony, it forms a striking contrast with the delicacy and
> pathos of the prophane airs.[2]

This passage raises two tempting alternative or additive prop-ositions. The first is that Murdoch's music-teaching prowess was rather less than adequate, stemming from a dubious induction into the required techniques in his day. The second propositon is that the mentally agile Robert and Gilbert became thoroughly bored as the class droned on with Murdoch's selections from Knox's Psalter; the two responding to the young dominie's exhortations with convincingly-feigned ineptitude. Had young Robert been in fact a tin-ear he would have grown up to join the ranks of those unendowed individuals who inflict a tuneless mosaic of sound on the ears of singers when they attempt to join in (and they seem impelled to join in, with gusto). But Burns's later intimate involvement with more than three hundred songs makes nonsense of the dull ear and untunable voice story. Furthermore, heeding Dr Currie's observations on bad psalmody and 'the delicacy and pathos of the prophane airs' we can quickly set the record straight for Burns. Back home from school it was no dull ear that responded whenever his mother burst forth with one of Scotland's folk songs; not a few of which were decidedly 'prophane' in a suggestive or ribald sense. Burns was later moved to quote the words of one such song as the wind-up to a letter to Dalrymple of Orangefield in 1787:

> Kissin is the key o' love,
>   An' clappin is the lock,
> An makin o's the best thing
>   That ere a young man got
>
> An auld Sang o' my Mither's.

(L.84)

Perhaps young Burns was taught more than a sang by his Mither's rendition of the above, but that is another story.

The first documented instance of Burns attempting to blend his words with an old air was related by him in his long letter to Dr Moore. He wrote that when aged fifteen he succumbed to the charms of 'a bewitching creature who just counted an autumn less':

> Among her other love-inspiring qualifications, she sang sweetly; and t'was her favourite reel to which I attempted giving an embodied vehicle in rhyme.

Two Edinburgh-based writers stand as a sort of time fence between the two main phases of Burns's creative life – the Ayrshire phase marked by phenomenal poetic creativity against a backdrop of religious disputation, and the Dumfriesshire phase of song-writing with political embroilment at times intruding. If that assertion be accorded the status of a rule, a few overlap exceptions either way are there to prove it. With its Ayrshire-located theme, *Tam o' Shanter* was both a Dumfriesshire creation and the last of

Burns's truly great poems. In the reverse direction, the first of the truly great song lyrics – *Corn Rigs, The Rantin Dog the Daddie o't*, and some songs woven into *The Jolly Beggars* cantata sequence – are sample foretastes of the bounteous Dumfriesshire harvest to follow. (Some, but by no means all, Burnsians would include *Mary Morison* and *The Lass o' Ballochmyle* in that small group.) Burns would have included *The Jolly Beggars* in the first Edinburgh edition of his works but he omitted it on the promptings of his small group of advisers, of which the Reverend Hugh Blair was a prominent member. Blair condemned the cantata as coarse, degrading and unfit for publication with its very vivid description of the licentious behaviour of an assembly of vagrants in a low tavern. However much we may now disagree, for the anticipated readership of his day Blair may have had a point. Blair is not to be written off as just a narrow-minded cleric: he was an intellectual kirk Moderate and had been one of the few champions of David Hume in kirk circles. Burns kept no copy of the cantata after its discouraging reception, but happily it was preserved by some Mauchline friends, eventually to come into the hands of the Glasgow publisher Thomas Stewart for printing in 1799.

Burns must have been set back by the reception met by one of his most imaginative and substantial lyrical works, perhaps by then even feeling that song-writing was not his forte. But any such doubt was to evaporate a few months later when he met James Johnson in Edinburgh, to be told about an ambitious venture. In that venture Robert Burns was to be offered an almost limitless outlet for new poetic creativity – a creativity with a different emphasis – the writing or amending of song lyrics for the existing airs of Scotland. Johnson, noting the scattered distribution of the extensive corpus of published Scottish airs, had set about applying his skill as an engraver to consolidate them in a single publication. Burns needed no convincing of the merits of the venture, and joined forces. In his own words:

> An engraver, James Johnson, in Edinr. has, not from mercenary views but from an honest Scotch enthusiasm, set about collecting all our native songs and setting them to music; particularly those that have never been set before. Clarke, the well-known Musician, presides over the musical arrangement; and Drs Beattie & Blacklock, Mr Tytler, Woodhouselee, and your

humble servt. to the utmost of his small power, assist in collecting the old poetry, or sometimes to a fine air to make a stanza, when it has no words.

(L.145, to James Hoy, Oct. 1787)

In another letter:

Songs in the English language, if by Scotchmen, are admitted, but the music must be all Scotch. Drs Beattie and Blacklock are lending a hand, and the first musician in town presides over that department. I have been absolutely crazed about it, collecting old stanzas, and every information respecting their origin, authors, &c. &c.

(L.147, to John Skinner, Oct. 1787)

The first volume of Johnson's collection, which its editor named *The Scots Musical Museum*, was well under way when Burns came into the picture, with a hundred songs ready for the press. Burns added three more. Volume II, released in March 1788, was followed by Volume III in 1790, and that volume was intended by Johnson to complete the set. But from Burns's enthusiastic efforts three more volumes followed, the last being issued in 1803, long after Burns had died.

Johnson had a five-year start on a song-publication series by George Thomson, who chose for it the name *A Select Collection of Original Scottish Airs*. In September 1792 Thomson wrote to Burns seeking his aid in providing new or amended lyrics for 'twenty to twenty-five airs'. Unlike Johnson's, Thomson's clearly-stated aim was to offer old Scots songs in a form that would suit decorous mixed company in the middle- and upper-class drawing-rooms of Britain, requiring the replacement of 'loose and indelicate' words and of rhymes which were 'mere nonsense and doggerel'. Unlike Stephen Clarke's *Museum* settings – the melody line plus the deceptively simple figured bass – Thomson offered, in large format, full 'piano forte' accompaniments, aware of the growing popularity of the new Broadwood instruments. Each volume cost one guinea, and for an additional six shillings there were separate violin and cello parts available. Like *The Museum*, *A Select Collection* progressed well beyond the target issue, running to six volumes, the second last of which, issued in 1818, included the grat *The Jolly Beggars* cantata, to a setting by England's Henry Bishop.

George Thomson's song publications, which were extended to cover the old airs of Ireland and Wales as well as those of Scotland, earned wide acceptance and praise to the end of the nineteenth century. Neither Wallace nor Henley and Henderson, both publishing major definitive works on Burns in 1896, were critical of Thomson and his achievements. But the general acceptance was suddenly and emphatically reversed by the assertions of James C. Dick, whose detailed studies of the songs of Burns were published in 1903 and 1908.[3] As an ardent worshipper of Burns, he assailed Thomson trenchantly for amending many words and lines, and poured scorn on him for at times preferring an air other than the one nominated by Burns. However, he conceded that Thomson was right in rejecting Burns's air for *Auld Lang Syne* in favour of the one now universally sung. Dick could hardly have done otherwise.

Burns's industrious study of traditional Scottish bagpipe, fiddle and flute airs, and his insight into the potential of these for fusion with his words, were outstanding. Equally so was his ability to write better words for existing songs; such modifications ranging from minor word changes to the creation of entirely new lyrics to replace old ones calling for rejection on the grounds of triviality or coarseness. That said, his, and Johnson's, monumental work was not 'folk song collecting' in the strict sense – typified by the relatively recent searches made by enthusiasts like S. Baring-Gould, John and Lucy Broadwood, Mary Neal, Marjorie Kennedy-Fraser, Cecil Sharp and Percy Grainger. Those researchers travelled far and wide to set down the unpublished folk-songs directly from the voices of local singers, usually elderly, preserving all the rawness and irregularity implanted by oral tradition. On the other hand, the airs used by Burns and his two publishers were virtually all available in some written form. True, Burns did write about some songs 'taken down' from the singing of Jean and others, but while he could readily record the words in that way his command of musical skill was hardly adequate for putting the air to paper as it was sung – a view quite at variance with claims made by J.C. Dick. Burns's letters, however, reveal that Clarke at times filled that role during visits to Dumfries (definite instances in Letters 568, 636, 637, and probable instances in 557 and 644). Dick also made overstated claims about Burns's ability to hear a song, remember the air, and write it down later. Such a claim is hardly supported by Burns's remark to Thomson about an attractive alternative air for the song *Hughie*

Graham: 'I neglected to take down the notes, when I first met with it; & now, it is out of my power' (L.586).

Burns was always self-effacing when referring to his musical competence. He wound up a discussion on the tune *The Grey Cock* in a letter to Thomson with the admission: 'Of the poetry, I speak with confidence; but the Music is a business where I hint my ideas with the utmost diffidence' (L.587). Dick's assertion that Burns could capture the nuance of an air almost instantly must be seen as an exaggeration. The claim is hardly given support in a letter to Thomson:

> Laddie, lie near me – must lie by me, for some time. I do not know the air; & untill I am compleat master of a tune, in my own singing, (such as it is) I can never compose for it.

> (L.586)

It is a pity that Burns was unable to set down the unwritten folk music of his country in notation. Had he been able to do so he would surely have revelled in the task. But plenty remained to be done in bringing together and 'mending' the already printed lyrics and airs from their disparate locations. The early eighteenth century had witnessed the printing of a series of music publications in Scotland. (In this context we can ignore the few earlier manuscripts in lute tablature, and Playford's *English Dancing Master* of 1657, which would have been almost certainly unavailable to Burns and Clarke.) In 1720 appeared Tom D'Urfey's *Pills to Purge Melancholy*, soon to be followed by Thomson's *Orpheus Caledonius* (1725–33) with fifty Scots airs with flute accompaniment. Alexander Stuart issued his *Musick for Allan Ramsay's Collection of Scots Songs* (i.e. for the *Tea-Table Miscellany*) in 1726. It contains seventy-one songs. Adam Craig issued his collection of Scots tunes set for the harpsichord or spinet in 1730, and at about the same time appeared *Watt's Musical Miscellany* – six volumes of Scots airs and songs. But it was the prolific publishing by James Oswald, a Dunfermline violinist and dancing-master, from 1740 to 1742, that seems to have been highly significant in the Burns story. His best-known set is *The Caledonian Pocket Companion*, in twelve parts. Burns's own copy has been preserved, and his numerous marginal notes reveal that he exploited its resources freely. A succession of additional collections – including those of J. Walsh, F. Barsanti, W. M'Gibbon, R. Bremner, Burke Thumoth, J. Reid, J. Clark, the

Earl of Kelly, N. Stewart, D. Dow, F. Peacock, C. M'Lean, A. M'Glashan, A. Cumming, P. Macdonald, J. Ritson, Niel Gow (Gow did spell his name Niel: not Neil as often printed), Pinkerton, Witherspoon, Aird and others – brought song publishing activity right up into the years of Burns, Clark and Johnson.

Once Burns had grasped the merits of a Scottish air, his own words were sure to be in place before long, but when a fine match already existed, as in *Loch Lomond* and *Lochaber No More*, he made no attempt at intrusion. Burns as a songwriter is to be seen as something of a rarity, in that he worked in the reverse direction – creating or improving the lyric for a pre-existing air as the need became evident. For this reason he is not to be grouped with great songwriters who were primarily composers of music: celebrities like Schubert, who set the expressive words of Schiller and Goethe (and even Ossian!); with Grieg who looked to Ibsen, Björnson and Andersen; with England's Roger Quilter who found his inspiration in Shakespeare, Herrick, Tennyson and others.

In many ways Burns outreached his musical collaborators in the conception and making of songs. Take, for instance, his apt approach to the old song about a drunken binge, *Hey Tutti Taiti*:

> Landlady count the lawin,
> The day is near the dawin,
> Ye're a' blind drunk, boys
> And I'm jolly fou.

(K.206)

The tune (which was available to Johnson from Oswald) greatly appealed to Burns, who saw in it the perfect musical frame for his *Scots Wha Hae Wi' Wallace Bled* (K.425). In pressing the case to George Thomson he revealed much about his musical sensitivity and knowledge:

> You know that my pretensions to musical taste, are merely a few of Nature's instincts, untaught & untutored by Art. For this reason, many musical compositions, particularly where much of the merit lies in Counterpoint, however they may transport & ravish the ears of you, Connoisseurs, affect my simple lug no otherwise than merely a melodious Din. On the other hand, by way of amends, I am delighted with many little melodies, which the learned Musician despises as silly & insipid. I do not know

whether the old air, 'Hey tuttie taiti', may rank among this number; but well I know that, with Fraser's Hautboy, it has often filled my eyes with tears.

(L.582)

The first point to note is the poet's minimal contact with a greater world of music. One may wonder how he would have responded had the entrepreneur Salomon taken Haydn on tour to Scottish cities, to electrify audiences with his new symphonies as he had done in London in 1791 and 1794. That we will never know, but Burns's response to Fraser's hautboy (oboe) tells us how a fine melody could stir his sentience. In the same letter he went on to relate the tradition of the air *Hey Tutti Taiti* being Bruce's march tune at Bannockburn. That (doubtful) tradition may have indeed suggested to Burns that the tune would suit *Scots Wha Hae*, but the important point is that he could readily dissociate it from the established drunken binge context. Thomson, and a group of his friends in Edinburgh, could not. Their verdict was that the tune was too devoid of grandeur to be the right setting for 'the noblest composition of the kind in the Scottish language', and Thomson put the case for using the air *Lewie Gordon*, even though it involved minor line changes in the verses. He published *Scots Wha Hae* with the latter tune in his 1799 volume, but, to his credit, he was to admit to being in error and republished to to *Hey Tutti Taiti* in 1803. The innate charm of the air was later to be underlined by Baroness Nairne choosing it, greatly slowed in tempo, for her poignant *The Land of the Leal*. Many years later, the German composer Max Bruch (1838–1920) used it to provide a stirring finale for his beautiful *Scottish Fantasy*. Inability to appreciate an air for its innate qualities, isolated from a familiar context, is by no means uncommon. Grainger provoked a not-unexpected reaction by pointing out that the hallowed 'An Die Freude' climax to Beethoven's Ninth Symphony was close, in line, rhythm, type and form to the air of *Yankee Doodle*.[4] (The main reaction was stunned silence.)

How does one define a good song? The short answer is a flawless blending of an excellent lyric with an excellent air. Within the air specification, the technicalities of tempo, rhythm, slurs, scale, cadence, pitch range, ornament and volume control all have a part to play. The lyric may have its mood setting at any point between the extremes of tragedy and merriment. Thereafter, the performer's sensitivity takes over as the critical factor. (Ignorantly bad performance of lyric or air is abominable. Too often we hear 'For *the sake* of auld lang syne', and the poignant *Loch Lomond*, perhaps the saddest song ever written, roared out in foxtrot tempo.)

Burns was sensitive to the subtle appeal of a fine air and went to endless trouble in the matching of an appropriate lyric; not only aesthetically but technically – in the avoidance of any clumsy stress that would interfere with the flow:

> My way is: I consider the poetic Sentiment, correspondent to my idea of the musical expression; then chuse my theme; begin with one stanza; when that is composed, which is generally the most difficult part of the business, I walk out, sit down now and then, look out for objects in Nature around me that are in unison or harmony with the cogitations of my fancy & workings of my bosom, humming every now & then the air with the verses I have framed: when I feel my Muse beginning to jade, I retire to the solitary fireside of my study, & there commit my effusions to paper; swinging, at intervals, on the hind-legs of my elbow-chair, by way of calling forth my own critical strictures, as my pen goes on.

(L.586)

On the entirely separate question of Burns's *technical* expertise in music (which J.C. Dick overstated, and which does not matter very much) we are left with uncertainties. Early in his poetical career he wrote in his Common Place Book: 'I am not musical scholar enough to prick down my tune properly', but we may presume that this deficiency was remedied to some degree as he progressed to deep involvement in note-values and phrasing, poring over many printed collections and exchanging views with his two editors. As a young man he acquired a fiddle and played a little, but whether he played only by ear or learned to sight-read a printed line is not known. The Bard's occasional resort to technicalities in his correspondence with Thomson, e.g. the 'crochet (sic) stops' in *O When She Cam Ben She Bobbit* (L.644), and his admission of a problem 'with the verses to fit these dotted crotchets' in the *Caledonain Hunt* air (L.647), suggests some familiarity with elementary music technique. He even went as far as jotting down two bars of notation to make his point of a better flow of syllables in *O Saw Ye Bonie Lesley* (L.514). Mrs Carswell included in her biography a reproduction of two lines of *The Wee German Lairdie* set down on music manuscripts paper by hand, with words in Burns's handwriting.[5] There is no proof, however, that Burns wrote in the music notation. One must not fall into the trap of regarding Burns as a *composer* from his many references to his 'composing' a song, when he obviously meant no more than writing the lyric. Burns was no composer of music. His eminence in the field of Scottish song stemmed from his ability to write or amend lyrics to suit airs which his numerous predecessors, usually of unknown identity, had composed.

James Johnson was poorly educated. Burns at times had to correct his errors of quite elementary spelling (see L.690), and as might be expected he uncritically published anything handed to him by Burns and Clarke. The main limitations of his *Museum* are easily traceable to Clarke's laziness and 'near enough' attitude. He often failed to transpose flute or fiddle settings to an acceptable pitch range, confronting singers with high notes that would tax the powers of Cleo Laine. He also left in bowing slurs when adapting fiddle settings, serving only to mislead the singer, for whom they have a different significance.[6] Characteristically, Johnson took no liberties with Burns's text. He can only be criticized today for his tendency to make an incorrect guess at a lyric signature when Burns, sadly, was no longer available to check proof sheets. (Henley (1896) was confident that the B signature to *A Red, Red, Rose* would have been changed to Z (derived work) had Burns lived to see the proof.)

George Thomson, on the other hand, could not resist making changes in the works sent to him by Burns. Most changes were minor and unimportant, as may be noted from Kinsley's footnotes, but some were major and have been deprecated. Although in their exchanged letters Burns and Thomson debated many points of disagreement, often with spirit and to good effect, it is well to note that Burns insisted on both his editors retaining an option to accept or reject. To Johnson:

> I have sent you a list that I approve of, but I beg & insist that
> you will never allow my opinion to overrule yours.

(L.331)

And to Thomson in October 1792:

Now, don't let it enter your head that you are under any necessity of taking my verses. I have long ago made up my mind as to my own reputation in the business of Authorship; & have nothing to be pleased, or offended at, in your adoption or rejection of my verses.

(L.511)

He gave further assurance of freedom to switch lyrics and airs in November 1794 (L.646). In those letters Burns probably meant acceptance or non-acceptance of lyrics *in toto*, but Thomson could have read more into that offered licence, making minor phrase 'improvements' – as when he had Duncan Gray's company fu' on new-year's night rather than on Burns's 'blythe Yule night'. It would appear that Thomson thought that being drunk on new-year's night would be acceptable to his customers while being drunk on a religious feast night could offend. But he also manipulated stanzas and changed airs. Later publishers have set Burns lyrics to inferior tunes without drawing the fire that has injured Thomson's reputation; a reputation that lies in disarray, particularly in the eyes of those who can discern nothing but perfection in every phrase and stanza the bard wrote.

J. C. Dick's criticisms, in effect, declared an open season on George Thomson, with his character and doings becoming the subject of vicious attacks in other directions: his copyright attitude, the editing of his letters prior to publication, his falsely alleged stinginess, his prudishness, and the completely unfounded charge of having written two tasteless obituaries on the recently-deceased poet who had helped him so magnificently during the previous four years. (The case for reinstating the personal character of George Thomson is set down in Appendix F. Please read it.)

Returning to the much-criticized musical settings published by Thomson, let us pause and try to see the situation from that editor's point of view. For a start, it should be emphasized that folksong – and many Burns songs are revived folksongs – loses its primary quality when *any* accompaniment infests it. It is a joy to hear Burns's songs rendered unaccompanied, liberated from Stephen Clarke's desceptively simple figured basses, Thomson's 'piano forte' with or without his added 'symphonies', or indeed from any other more modern setting. There would be few Burns enthusiasts living beyond Australian shores who have shared with

A SELECT COLLECTION

Original Scottish Airs

OF

FOR THE VOICE

With Introductory & Concluding Symphonies
And Accompaniments for the

PIANO FORTE VIOLIN OR FLUTE & VIOLONCELLO

By

Pleyel Haydn Weber Beethoven &c

WITH

Select & Characteristic Verses both Scottish & English
Adapted to the Airs
Including upwards of One hundred Songs by

Burns

The whole collected by G. Thomson F.A.S. Edinburgh. in Five Volumes.

Now see where Caledonia's Genius mourns
And plants the holly round the tomb of Burns

Price of each Vol. One Guinea   Vol. I Ent.d at Stationers Hall.   The Vio. or Flute & Vio.llo 6/Sh

London Printed & Sold by Preston 71. Dean St Soho. And by G. Thomson the Editor & Proprietor Edinburgh.

Title page of Thomson's *Select Collection of Original Scottish Airs*, Preston, London, and Thomson, Edinburgh. 1826.

the writer the pleasure of hearing Dr Jeff Brownrigg's talks on the songs of Scotland's Bard, generously interspersed with the lecturer's unaccompanied lyric tenor renditions. Those so deprived can turn to the recordings of Ewan MacColl, particularly his unaccompanied *Ay Waukin O* in all its perfection (Folkways Records FW 8758). Another example is Jean Redpath's singing of Burns's *Lament of Mary Queen of Scots* (Philo Records PH 1093), in which the accompanists lapse into silence for the final stanza. The effect is dramatic and moving.

Stephen Clarke seemed to have at least some glimmerings about the importance of an unobtrusive backing for the old songs. Thomson headed off in the opposite direction, determined to gild the vocal lilies with showy accompaniments. For him, bass chords were not enough, and in any event the complexities of figured bass, demanding an advanced knowledge of harmony for their full exploitation, were beyond the capabilities of the general run of amateur keyboard players. Furthermore, he would have been aware that the system was already falling into disuse in the late 1790s. He just had to have the newer style of setting for the drawing-room pianist and the new Broadwood pianos, and if other instruments could be combined, so much the better. From that standpoint, and having the limited skills of an amateur violinist and vocalist, presumably having heard no rustic folk-singers far away from the metropolis, he believed that his song-books should present only elegant settings for performers and audiences a cut above the very people who had created the song heritage. He was wrong of course, but that is what he believed, evidently quite sincerely, and so did a few million other people of Britain.

Thomson was no composer and he needed expert professional help for his song settings. To whom could he have turned for top-bracket compositional expertise? Britain had entered her sad century of composing sterility by 1792. The great Thomas Arne had been dead for fourteen years and Henry Bishop was an obscure little boy of six. The creative renascence given to Britain by Parry, Stanford and Sullivan was not even to begin in Thomson's lifetime, but there were luminaries across the water. So he commissioned Ignaz Pleyel, an Austrian composer then living in Paris. When war with France hampered the mails he switched, lamentably, to Leopold Kozeluch – Mozart's forgettable successor as Court Composer at Prague. Volumes I and II of the *Collection* contained only Pleyel and Kozeluch settings, but the name of Joseph Haydn, already famous through his visits to England, was soon to eclipse the first two, and the settings in Volumes III and IV were all Haydn's. Haydn became very proud of his contribution to the *Collection*, later writing of it to Thomson, in Italian, 'I boast of this work, and by it I flatter myself my name will live in Scotland many years after my death.' Coming from the revered composer of 104 symphonies, 85 string quartets and a lot more, this was pretty heady stuff to lay on a venturesome Scottish civil servant – a veritable air-drop of publicity manna. Haydn's contributions ceased some years before his death in 1809 and his place was taken by Beethoven, Weber and others. The *Select Collection* is largely ignored today, its settings of Burns songs, at times mutilated, serving mainly as historical and biographical references. The Burns-Thomson *correspondence* is of far greater value and interest. The European composers were in no positon to capture the special qualities of Scottish song, in particular the subtleties of the Scottish humour that so often pervades them. What would Pleyel's Germanic sense of humour have made of:

> Duncan sigh'd baith out and in,
> Grat his een baith bleer't an' blin',
> Spak o' lowpin o'er a linn;
> Ha, ha, the wooing o't.?

The *Select Collection* served a purpose in its day, effectively unfolding its version of at least part of the Scottish song heritage, alongside that of Ireland and Wales, for the British public at large. Johnson's *Scots Musical Museum*, the more comprehensive and less unblemished collection, lacking Thomson's glamorous style of promotion, achieved less prominence in the nineteenth century throughout Britain. Both Johnson and Thomson were showered with praise from Burns himself for their achievements. The Bard's praise of Johnson's volumes was based on an intimate knowledge of their contents, even though Volume VI was assembled and printed after his death. Burns had been the main supplier of its contents. In his Preface to Volume V, Johnson wrote of the contributions of Burns: 'Prior to his decease, he furnished the Editor with a number, in addition to those already published, greater than can be included in one Volume.' Burns's praise of George Thomson's *Select Collection* must, on the other hand, be viewed with qualifications as he lived to see only the first volume of the series, impressive in its glamour. Whether he would have sustained his praise had he lived on to examine the rest is another matter. The 'lofty boast' of Art in Thomson's work began and ended for Burns at a distance, both in space and time, and nothing can make that boast shine more distant than death.

The foregoing half-chapter is no more than a brief account of Burns's enthusiastic contribution to Scottish song and his sustained collaboration with his two editors. For more detailed analyses of the topic the reader is referred to scholarly studies by James C. Dick,[7] Thomas Crawford,[8] James Kinsley,[9] David Daiches[10] and Cedric Thorpe Davie.[11] The important recension by Dick has been already discussed. Kinsley's three-volume set *The Poems and Songs of Robert Burns* has become a standard reference with the melody line of the Bard's favoured air printed with every lyric. His separate essay *The Music of the Heart* covers historical aspects of Burns's contribution. In his masterly book *Burns: A Study of the Poems and Songs*, Crawford includes a long chapter on Burns the songwriter. A specialized essay on Burns's cautious links with Jacobite song has been presented by Daiches, that other prolific writer on Burns. Cedric Thorpe Davie's penetrating essay *Robert Burns, Writer of Songs* should not be missed by Burnsians seeking a balanced survey, not only of the music and lyrics but also of their first publishers and the work of later commentators.

VISUAL ARTS

Turning from the great art of music to the visual arts in the life of Burns, we can discover points of interest that have received little attention in standard Burns commentary. There is no evidence that the Bard ever tried his hand at drawing or painting, but, to fall back on the hackneyed but hard-to-replace expression, he knew what he liked. In particular, we know that he greatly admired the work of Hogarth, and almost certainly drew upon that work for some verbal imagery.

The puritans had done a very thorough job in suppressing the painting art in Britain, but the Restoration cleared a path for a lively revival in the century to follow. The favoured model for the new generation of painters of eighteenth-century Britain was the portraiture of Van Dyck, court painter to Charles I, its stereotyped style becoming staple fare for a busy new art world, but, as we might expect to discover in that century of Enlightenment, there were some talented artists finding satisfaction and fulfilment in more imaginative departures. William Hogarth (1697–1764) was the most important of those art liberators, exploiting the rich field of historical, moral and satirical genre painting and engraving. Joseph Wright (1734–97), and David Allan (1744–96) depicted aspects of the Industrial Revolution with penetrating skill.

On a population basis, eighteenth-century Scotland could claim a good share of outstanding portrait painters. One of the first was Allan Ramsay (1713–84), son of the Edinburgh poet. As a young man he studied painting in Italy, and on his return he soon became established as a portrait painter. Quickly, his endowments brought him the patronage of Lord Bute, and a move to richer fields in London soon followed. In 1767 he was appointed Painter-in-Ordinary to George III. Burns never met him, and probably never saw any of his work, but he remains significant in the Burns story as having been the early art teacher of Alexander Nasmyth (1758–1840), the artist approached by Creech to paint a portrait of Burns for the first Edinburgh edition of poems. He not only carried out this important task without charging a fee – he made two duplicates. The three portraits are preserved today – in the Scottish National Gallery, the Kelvingrove Art Gallery in Glasgow, and the National Portrait Gallery in London. Burns and Nasmyth became good friends and took many walks together in Edinburgh's environs, but there is no evidence of Nasmyth ever inducing Burns to try his hand with brush or pencil. Scotland was never to have in Burns her own doubly-gifted Blake.

A Scottish artist whom Burns greatly admired, but never met, was David Allan (1744–96). Allan received early training in Scotland's pioneering Academy of Arts, established on the lower floor of Glasgow University's library as a salon on the Italian model by Robert and Andrew Foulis in 1753. Allan is famed for his genre works, which included scenes in the Earl of Hopetoun's lead smelting works at Leadhills in Lanarkshire,[12] and, more symbolically, *The Origins of Painting*. He illustrated Ramsay's pastoral *The Gentle Shepherd*, an achievement that Burns admired warmly. (Burns wrote regretfully of his inability to buy a copy of that work in a letter to Alexander Cunningham, L.620, of March 1794.) Rather more interesting in the present context are Allan's illustrations for

Robert Burns. H. Robinson, after Nasmyth. *The Poets and Poetry of Scotland*, ed James Grant Wilson, Blackie & Son, London, n.d.

The Cotter's Saturday Night, Tam o' Shanter, and a further twenty for George Thomson's *Select Collection*. The original of *The Cotter* picture was given to Burns by Thomson; a gift that delighted the poet from its inclusion of himself as the cotter's son: 'My phiz is *sae kenspeckle*, that the very joiner's apprentice whom Mrs Burns employed to break up the parcel (I was out of town that day) knew it at once.' He went on to assert 'Several people think that Allan's likeness of me is more striking than Nasemith's, for which I sat to him half a dozen times'. He also expressed delight at the resemblance (obviously fortuitous) between a depicted youngster, assaulting a cat's tail, and his own 'wee rumble-gairie hurchin' – four-year-old William Nicol Burns.[13] (L.670, to Thomson, May 1795).

No general comment on eighteenth-century Scotland's portrait painters should exclude the greatest of them, Sir Henry Raeburn. Why did Burns not sit for him? (In this context we may well forget the Raeburn touch-up of the Nasmyth portrait sent to Currie's publishers in 1803.) Raeburn did in fact return to Edinburgh in 1787 after a two-year stay in Rome, but Creech was probably committed to Nasmyth when he arrived. Another possible reason could have been that Raeburn's services were not to be had free of charge, as were Nasmyth's. Not being able to view a Raeburn portrait of Burns alongside those of, say, Sir Walter Scott or the very forgettable Henry Mackenzie, not only leaves a gap in the Raeburn hall of fame; it denies us any chance of seeing what the poet looked like in the eyes of a top-ranking portraitist. (Echoes of the Mozart dilemma: half a dozen undistinguished portraits, all different.) There are differences and limitations in the portrayals by Reid – praised by Burns himself (L.658), – Nasmyth, Skirving, Beugo, Freeman and Taylor. In paint and crayon we seek in vain that *vivida vis animi* and 'the fiery glances of insulted and indignant superiority' that inspired the capable pen of Maria Riddell, and no less distant is 'the coarse physiognomy' of Currie's Burns. If they were ever there, the pock-marks attested to by Gilbert Baird and Marion Hunter have all been levelled. Only that one tiny portrait on ivory by Alexander Reid offers us some reality in the form of a left-side full profile, with a faint smile caught on the face of the wag who wrote *Address to the Deil* and *Tam o' Shanter*.

Apart from the occasional commissioning of paintings to honour prominent people on, or approaching, retirement, the art of formal portraiture today has largely moved across to the photographer's studio. But in pre-photographic times, formal portraiture (preferably flattering) was the mainstay of the artist, and the more *kenspeckle* the features appearing on the canvas the higher soared his reputation for follow-up patrons. But one eighteenth-century artist, William Hogarth, stands out prominently as a rebel against the art establishment. Although his personal portraiture is magnificent in its projection of character (*vide* his Captain Coram and Lord Lovat), his fame both in his own time and today rests mainly on his vivid commentaries on social conditions and history, on the church, and on his moral exhortations – often in grouped sequences. More than that, he was determined in his aim to penetrate all levels of society, transferring much of his painting to the engraving plate to make copies available to middle and lower ranks at small expense.

In all Burns's poetry we look in vain for any message of adoration of the skill of any visual artist except Hogarth. We rightly disregard the lines covering Burns's gift of a pull of the Beugo engraving, sent to Tytler of Woodhouselee (K.152):

> I send you a trifle, a head of a bard,
> A trifle scarce worthy your care;

We first encounter unmitigated admiration of Hogarth's work in *Extempore Verses on Dining with Lord Daer* (K.127). Feeling unequal to the task of finding words to describe his self-consciousness in august company for the first time in his life, his thoughts turned to the artist:

> But O! for Hogarth's magic pow'r,
> To shew Sir Bardie's willyart glowr,
>   An' how he star'd an' stammer'd!
> When goavan's he'd been led wi' branks,
> An' stumpan on his ploughman shanks,
>   He in the parlour hammer'd.

We note that Burns was not invoking inspiration from any 'magic pow'r' possessed by Ramsay, Reynolds or Gainsborough. It was Hogarth's, and for the best of reasons. In 1786 Burns would have been quite familiar with Hogarth's ability to depict humanity at all social levels and in every mood with consummate skill. The prints, run off in hundreds, were distributed far and wide. Years before the time of Burns the Abbé Le Blanc wrote: 'the whole nation has been infected with them . . . I have not seen a house of note without these moral prints.'[14]

We can feel assured that many of those prints had reached as far as Ayr, Tarbolton and Mauchline. Burns would have had even fuller opportunity of seeing a comprehensive range of Hogarth

William Hogarth. Self-portrait; *Courtesy of the Trustees of the British Museum.*

engravings in Edinburgh, the primary distribution point for Scotland for such things. In writing a Pope-style tribute to Graham of Fintry from Ellisland he again brought in his admiration of the artist by referring to Nature's 'Hogarth-art' having been exercised when she created a poet (K.230).

On many counts, more than simple admiration of the skill of the artist would have drawn Burns to Hogarth. From an early age, Burns had been inspired by the poetry of Allan Ramsay, but a warm association between Ramsay and Hogarth had been cemented before Burns was born. This fact probably first came as a pleasing revelation to Burns with the start of his dealings with Creech in Edinburgh.

Edinburgh's poet Allan Ramsay (1686–1758) had, in his earlier years, combined poetical creativity, publication and book selling with his trade of wig-making – a superior and highly skilled trade which drew to his door many *literati* and members of the nobility. By about 1720 he had assembled enough poetry to warrant its publication in book form, and he had no difficulty in signing up four or five hundred subscribers, his list even including such big names from the south as Alexander Pope and Dr Arbuthnot. In 1726 he moved from his small High Street shop to one more central, overlooking the old Market Cross, and it was there that he established Scotland's first circulating library.

The new shop quickly became the 'howf', not only of the wits of Edinburgh, but of distinguished visitors from England, including the genial John Gay. In the same year Hogarth issued his twelve large plates illustrating Butler's *Hudibras* (a satire on puritanism and hypocrisy) and these were inscribed, in a joint dedication, to Allan Ramsay. Ramsay ordered thirty copies of the set, and his shop thus began its long history as an outlet for the artist's work. One can well envisage Allan Ramsay junior, the teenage artist-in-embryo, intently examining those prints as they arrived at his father's shop in successive batches, and they could well have constituted the first canalizing influence for an art career which was to take him all the way to the court of George III. Ramsay senior continued to superintend his bookshop until 1755, despite a serious financial setback arising from his building of the first drama theatre in Edinburgh. Just as the latter was ready for opening, the 'unco guid' successfully brought pressure on the magistracy to close it down under the terms of the Licensing Act of 1737. There-

Allan Ramsay (Snr). W. Howison, after William Aikman. *The Poets and Poetry of Scotland*, ed James Grant Wilson, Blackie & Son, London, n.d. (c.1876).

after, Ramsay concentrated on his bookselling and publishing and retrieved his fortunes. After his death in 1758 the premises were bought by James Sibbald, the founder of the *Edinburgh Magazine* (in which a review of Burns's Kilmarnock volume was to be printed five weeks before Henry Mackenzie's appeared in *The Lounger*).

Burns first entered Ramsay's old shop late in 1786 in the company of Lord Glencairn to be introduced to the current tenant William Creech, now carrying on the business of publishing and bookselling in the Ramsay tradition and welcoming all-comers interested in cultural matters. From January 1787 Burns was often on Creech's premises to negotiate details of his publication agreement (finalized in April 1787) and later 'racking' accounts, and he certainly had ample opportunity to browse around the stock – a stock which undoubtedly included a good range of Hogarth prints.

Despite Hogarth's years extending into only five of Burns's, the long distance between their home bases, and the different artistic roads they travelled, the two men had many experiences, drives and sympathies in common. In early years both knew the stresses of poverty with both their fathers having insoluble money problems. (Hogarth senior was briefly imprisoned for debt.) Both became Freemasons in their twenties. Both had a Presbyterian upbringing, as boys having to sit through many a tedious sermon from puritan clergy, and it is hardly surprising that both of them, well endowed with the gift of humour and a penetrating power of satirical treatment, were to make devastating attacks on churchmen in their mature years. Hogarth's depiction of *The Sleeping Congregation* (B&C 164, Plate 8), dominated by the reader squinting lasciviously at the generously-revealed bosom of a sleeping girl, has much in common with *Holy Willie's Prayer* and stanza seven of *The Kirk of Scotland's Garland*. Both poet and artist revelled in finding comical aspects of biblical happenings and characters. Hogarth's *Paul Before Felix Burlesqued* (B&C 228, Plate 13) is a hilarious representation of the presiding procurator of Judea being harangued by the apostle, and, on being told of the punishment awaiting his soul (Acts, 24), Felix has a bowel accident which brings an unsubtle response from those nearby. Tertullus the prosecutor tears up his prepared speech in disgust as he glares at Paul. Felix's hope for a bribe is symbolized by a fat female figure representing Justice – *half* blindfolded and weighed down by her money-bag.

Burns, as may have been noted *supra*, often brought in the doings of biblical characters to colour his verses and letters in a spirit of fun, and he too was not above intruding some faecal humour, as in stanza nine of *The Kirk of Scotland's Garland* and in some of his *Merry Muses* contributions.

We can only *suspect* Jacobite sympathies in Hogarth, bearing in mind that in his day the risings were very sensitive issues, while Burns could feel freer in hinting his dislike of the Hanoverian succession. In one of his earliest prints, *Royalty, Episcopy and Law* (B&C 52), released in 1724, Hogarth represented the monarch with a guinea for a head. One of his finest paintings, *The March to Finchley* (B&C 223), depicts the foot guards departing from a brothel district with numerous whores making their farewell gestures as the soldiers march away to combat the forces of the Young Pretender. The painting grossly offended George II, and he rejected the dedication. In 1746 Hogarth seized the opportunity to draw a portrait of that double-dealing Scot, Simon Fraser, Lord Lovat, at St Albans when on his way to London for execution as a consequence of his involvement in the Forty-five Jacobite rising.

Paul before Felix. William Hogarth. *Courtesy of the Trustees of the British Museum.*

This highly expressive portrait, released as an etching (B&C 201), shows Lovat counting on his fingers the clans which came out for the Young Pretender. The atmosphere of the drawing points to affable empathy linking artist and sitter, not at all simply suggesting routine documentation of the *facies* of a condemned rebel on his way to the block.

Hogarth berated the art dealers who pandered to snobbish preoccupation with imported works of art and a down-grading of the British offerings:

> your picture-jobbers from abroad, who are always ready to raise a great cry in the Prints, whenever they think their Craft is in Danger; and indeed it is in their Interest to depreciate every English work, as harmful to their Trade, of continually importing Ship Loads of dead Christs, Holy Families, Madona's, and other dismal Dark Subjects, neither entertaining nor Ornamental, on which they scrawl the terrible cramp Names of some Italian Masters, and fix on us poor Englishmen, the Character of Universal Dupes.
>
> (Letter to The St James's Post, 7–9 June 1737)

In another art context (drama), Burns made a parallel condemnation:

> Why is outlandish stuff sae meikle courted?
> Does Nonsense mend, like Brandy, when imported?
>
> (K.315)

Both Hogarth and Burns presented the undisciplined world of vagrants, not censoriously, but as comment on the human spectrum of which they were part. The *Act Against Strolling Players* of 27 June 1737 made it illegal for roving companies of *actors* to stage performances outside the city limits of London without a licence, but slipshod drafting of the Act meant that females were unaffected. Motley groups of females, old and young, were free to range the countryside and present plays, and in rural areas cut off from city entertainment such groups were well received despite their crudity in stagecraft, 'props' and accommodation. Hogarth's etching *Strolling Actresses Dressing in a Barn* (B&C 181, Plate 14) depicts such a group preparing to perform the farce *The Devil to Pay in Heaven* with females taking the parts of Jupiter, Juno, Diana, Aurora, Cupid, Flora and Night, plus supporting devils, ghosts and pages. Horace Walpole, that discerning art critic of the eighteenth century, considered this product of Hogarth's wit and imagination to be his finest work. In more recent times, V.De S. Pinto analysed its kinship with Burns's *The Jolly Beggars*.[15] Both etching and cantata describe, with splendid balance of busy detail and breadth, gatherings of happy and uninhibited vagrants. The *Strolling Actresses* are depicted in a ramshackle barn attached to a rural inn, and there, sure enough, high in the hayloft a doxy (probably one of the players) is being hugged, undisturbed by all the fuss below. The whole atmosphere of the etching is the atmosphere of *The Jolly Beggars*.

But examples of thematic congruence, however apposite, are one consideration: specific source-and-use links are another. But Hogarth was so eloquent, wide-ranging and prolific in his genre art that it would be surprising *not* to find examples of his limnings carried over into verse by contemporary and later poets. We need not mumble 'plagiarism' about this – if there is any hint of

Strolling Actresses Dressing in a Barn. William Hogarth. *Courtesy of the Trustees of the British Museum.*

plagiarism there it is surely plagiarism in its most innocent and justifiable garb. William Blake almost certainly drew upon Hogarth in the writing of *Auguries of Innocence* (as observed by Pinto[15]):

> A dog starv'd at his master's gate
> Predicts the ruin of the State.
> A horse misus'd upon the road
> Calls to Heaven for human blood.

The first print of *The Four Stages of Cruelty* depicts two tormented hungry dogs, and in the second a horse which has stumbled is being cruelly cudgelled. (B&C 224–5). In the same poem the essayist quoted suggests more Hogarth, without naming specific sources:

> The Harlot's cry from street to street
> Shall weave Old England's winding-sheet.
> The winner's shout, the loser's curse,
> Dance before dead England's hearse.

The sources are not hard to find. The harlot and the evil surrounding her are there in *A Harlot's Progress* (B&C 134–9) and the downfall of gamblers figures in *Scene in a Gaming House* (B&C 159) and in The *Prison Scene* (B&C 161).

As we can readily discover Hogarth in Blake, what then of Burns, known, from his own poetic invocations, to have been a veritable worshipper of Hogarth? We do not have to look far. In *Epistle to Robert Graham Esq., of Fintry* (K.318) are the lines:

> Suppose I take a spurt and mix
> Amang the wilds o' Politics
>   Electors and elected;
> Where dogs at Court (sad sons of bitches!)
> Septennially a madness touches,
>   Till all the land's infected.

Kinsley relegates this stanza, and the three preceding it, to small print, as they are found only in the Alloway MS and not in the version actually sent to Fintry. However, in both the Oxford and Collins Burns they follow on after the first stanza without that separation.

If we now turn to Hogarth's four prints of an Oxfordshire

election, particularly *An Election Entertainment* (B&C 237, Plate 15), *The Polling* (B&C 239) and *Chairing the Members* (B&C 240), we see quite vividly how all the land was infected with a madness. Election goings-on in Dumfries in 1790 would have been not much different to those illustrated by Hogarth for Oxfordshire in 1754, perhaps allowing for some satirical exaggeration in the prints. But Burns's lines in no way preclude bricks hurled through windows, Whig urine-pots being emptied over Tory supporters outside, a Mayor collapsing after eating a gross excess of oysters, and, in particular, excessive drinking of the wealthy candidate's free liquor. (This print is packed with fascinating detail, too involved to cover here. For a fuller description, see the interpretations given by Burke and Caldwell,[16] Lindsay,[17] or, for a more staid but eminently readable version, those of the Rev. Dr Trusler.[18]

When one is moved by interest or curiosity to the winkling out of possible Hogarth influences in the works of Burns, thoughts inevitably turn to the latter's liveliest and most image-rich poem, *Tam o' Shanter*. True it is that the foundation tale of this great work

An Election Entertainment. William Hogarth. *Courtesy of the Trustees of the British Museum.*

111

was one of the three witch stories, associated with Alloway Kirk, which Burns related in the celebrated letter written to Captain Grose in June 1790 (L.401). But the details in the letter describing the scene in the old kirk are meagre. Burns referred to the presence of some recognizable women of the neighbourhood, with one in particular, wearing a revealingly short smock, capturing the rapt attention of a passing farmer who stopped to peep through the window as the group danced merrily to the pipe music of the Deil. But on the reading of *Tam o' Shanter* it immediately becomes evident that Burns had added hugely to the old tale with descriptions of weird and revolting paraphernalia and happenings. One must not be dogmatic on the issue, but it is tempting to refer, once again, to Hogarth's *Strolling Actresses Dressing in a Barn* as possibly having contributed to the framework of Burns's immortal word-picture. In what way? Let us look once again at that Hogarthian masterpiece.

The eye is immediately drawn to the dominating central figure (Diana) who is clothed scantily and revealingly as was 'Cutty-sark'. Just right of centre is a church altar, desecrated by a smouldering tobacco pipe and a tankard of porter, the latter being contentiously shared by two devils. No occupied coffins stand round 'like open presses', but in the far right foreground stands an up-ended chest that had been used in a previous performance as Juliet Capulet's coffin (Trusler). Revolting happenings are depicted – a distressed cat is being bled by a ghost and a page to provide a bowl of blood for the play; a monkey is urinating into a helmet; a babe is being forcibly fed with scalding pap; a Siren is being de-loused by Aurora in the far left of the scene. Finally, note the peeping Tom at a hole in the decrepit roof. Turn now to another famous Hogarth print, *The Reward of Cruelty* (B&C 227, Plate 16). Burns probably never saw a body cut down from a gibbet, and the lines

> A thief, new-cutted frae a rape,
> Wi' his last gasp his gab did gape;

suggest that he had called on more than hearsay in framing them. There is little doubt that the print in question was the source of the graphic details – the body of the thief and murderer Tom Nero being dissected for an anatomy lesson at the Royal College of Physicians. Once seen, this gruesome print is never forgotten. The newly-cut rope remnant is still in positon; the gaping gab practically dominates the picture.

Two fortuitous alliances linked the poetic genius of Burns with one sector of the world's great arena of musical art, to bring him happy fulfilment in his later and sadder years. The light of the visual arts ever shone more distant, but it vouchsafed him some opportune rays.

The Reward of Cruelty. William Hogarth. *Courtesy of the Trustees of the British Museum.*

Chapter Four

RUINOUS BARGAINS

(L.125)

A BACKGROUND

Writers on the life of Robert Burns, particularly those of the twentieth century, seem impelled to say hard things about the farming conditions, particularly the nature of the soils, which the Burns men – William, Robert and Gilbert – had to wrestle with. A picture is painted of capable and conscientious farmers who just seemed fated to draw the short straw. It is no more or less than the picture painted in the letters and poems of Burns himself, and just as the Bard has won for himself a posthumous reputation for vision and integrity, it would seem that his observations on the four farms on which he laboured must, *ipso facto*, be accepted uncritically. A closer examination is warranted.

The first parental farm, Mount Oliphant near the Carrick Border, 'proved a ruinous bargain' (L.125). On the second farm, Lochlea near Tarbolton, William Burnes was to escape the consequences of insolvency by his tragic death. At the third farm, Mossgiel, ends never quite met – first for the brothers together and later for Gilbert alone. The reputation of Ellisland, which Robert leased in his own right, fares no better. Robert described the place to Gilbert as 'a ruinous affair on all hands' (L.381). Such a stigma tends to remain indelible. As recently as 1979 Professor Thornton referred to 'Miller's stubborn soil on the west bank of the Nith'.[1] 'Stubborn' is too strong an adjective: 'unimproved' would be nearer the mark.

Arriving at a balanced assessment of the four Burns farms, and of the Burns men as farmers, is not a simple procedure as many interlocked factors made up the total farming picture in the late eighteenth century. They included the nature, treatment and response of the soils, the painfully slow progress of agrarian enlightenment in its historical setting, climatic problems, and the plutocratic economy that shackled the tenantry. Let us break into this *melange* at a fundamental level – by taking a scientifically critical look at the soils of south-west Scotland; in particular the soil of the Burns farms in Ayrshire.

Soil science, or pedology, is a sort of follow-on component of the major and older subject of geology, and we need not go deeply into the latter. It is sufficient to mention that Ordovician/Silurian sedimentary strata (500 million to 400 million years old) provided the parent material of most of the Nithsdale soils, and the Devonian Old Red Sandstone (350 million or more years old) and some Carboniferous sediments (270 million or more years old) with some volcanic supplementation appearing now and then, supplied the parent material long ago for the soils of the three Burns farms of Ayrshire. While the chemical composition of the original rock largely determines the abundance or lack of plant nutrients in the soil formed from it, other vitally important effects determine the final nature of soil. These are primarily climatic but subsequently human. In the case of the four Burns farms, as for other vast areas of Britain, the initial and overwhelming factor was the last Ice Age, which brought moving ice sheets and glaciers.

The last ice sheet to cover what were to be the four Burns farms of Ayrshire and Nithsdale, identified as the so-called Perth Readvance,[2] lasted for several millenia between 10,000 and 25,000 years ago. Had the ice simply come and melted away without trace we would be little concerned about it in this context, but its effect provides the whole basis of the Burns story. As the ice flowed slowly over the land it smashed the rock below and carried a load of rock pieces in its basal layer. Those pieces, of varying size, were transported for varying distances and finally deposited. But, more importantly for future agriculture, vast amounts of rock were ground as fine as flour in an abrading situation enormously intensified by the weight of the ice above which was typically a mile or more in height. The fine material, mixed with rock pieces ranging between extremes of size, was left smeared over the land surface after the melt as a layer of boulder clay, or till, often of great depth. Till may be regarded as soil-forming material of good potential fertility when its mineral content is favourable. Its state of fine division gives it a 'flying start' in the decomposing process described as weathering, and as it is usually of great depth the easy penetration of tree roots confers an advantage over the shallower skeletal soils, i.e. the soils formed *in situ* on parent rock. But, against that, the usual clayey consistency of till is liable to bring problems of poor natural drainage and consequent waterlogging; problems that were particularly bad in the high rainfall areas on the western lands of Ayrshire.

The soil of all four Burns farms has been classified by the Soil Survey of Scotland as Brown Forest Soil. *Forest* soil? Remembering how Dr Johnson was moved to rib his Scottish friend Boswell about the absence of trees in Scotland, the designation could be puzzling. The enigma disappears if we retrace the post-glacial history of Scotland.

After the melt, the still cold wet land passed to the tundra condition, supporting mainly peat-forming mosses. Over subsequent centuries of slow-warming, small-flowering plants and trees gained a foothold, spreading northerly from the far south which had been spared glaciation. Pollen analysis of a deep Ayrshire peat has revealed that water milfoil was an early arrival, followed in order by birch, pines, hazel, alder and oak.[3] From this and other evidence we now know that Scotland, apart from the coldest elevated areas, acquired a quite luxuriant tree cover from around 4,000 BC: a tree cover that enriched the surface soil by absorbing plant nutrients at depth and depositing them as leaf drop. A different species of organism, *homo sapiens*, came perilously close to converting that surface soil to sterility.

In prehistoric millenia the Mesolithic, Neolithic and Iron Age people arrived and stayed. All those folk, but particularly the last-named with their efficient axes, exploited the forest resources for fuel and other needs, and cleared land was needed for crops and herds.[4] So began the forest destruction that continued inexorably into historic times, with the higher land reverting to moss, heath and peat accumulation. Disturbed at last by the visible consequences in the sixteenth century the authorities passed Acts[5] to restrict tree felling, but forest renewal remained an unobtainable objective with a growing population needing more and more land for crops, and with hungry livestock devouring anything green, including tree seedlings, on the unenclosed land. Soil deterioration was the natural consequence. Prior to the Agrarian Revolution that advanced at slow pace in the eighteenth century, Scotland's rural economy was based on an annual allocation by each laird of a run-rig strip to each of a group of cotters. In effect, the cotters were peasant slaves, subject to call-up for the armed conflicts that plagued the country, and paying for the privilege of subsisting in miserable hovels by handing over a good proportion of their hard-won produce to the laird. The soil of the run-rigs became more and more exhausted and the threat of famine was never far off: all too often it became a tragic reality. The original forest soils were on the acid side, but the acidity became steadily worse as the basic elements – calcium, magnesium, potassium etc. – were taken from the root zone in the form of produce and not replaced. Severe soil acidity reduces the growth of practically every food source plant. The application of lime to correct soil acidity had been adopted on several Ayrshire farms in the sixteenth and seventeenth centuries[6] but the practice seems neither to have spread nor persisted.

Perhaps oddly, it was not a farmer who made the first attempt to disseminate a message of soil improvement to a wide readership. In 1697 James Donaldson, an Edinburgh printer, published his 156-page treatise *Husbandry Anatomized.*[7] The author's emphasis on the application of alkaline material – lime, ashes, marl and 'seaware' – should have received wide attention, but the book could hardly have been issued at a less opportune time. Landowners had gambled every spare shilling on the Darien scheme, and lost every shilling. The Jacobite cause that should have died with Dundee at Killiecrankie in 1689 smouldered on, as did the Covenanting embers which that same Viscount had stirred so savagely a few years earlier. The future of the kirk was seen as the all-important issue, both to a divided nobility and to God-fearing cotters. Donaldson had wasted his time and money.

The first two decades of the eighteenth century were momentous for Scotland in many ways – they witnessed the English Act of Settlement, the Scottish Act of Security, the Treaty and Act of Union and an abortive Jacobite rising – but for agriculture they were sterile decades.

It was not until 1723, with both the Union polemic and the 1715 Jacobite rebellion in the past, that any real farming reform came to Scotland. In that year 'The Honourable Society of Improvers' was founded with a large membership of land-owning members of the nobility, law-lords and academics. Much advanced knowledge was disseminated, and more writers published their individual books to further the reform cause. The Union also meant that influential people were travelling to England and the Continent and learning the benefits of enclosure, rotations, fallowing, sown pasture and new crop plants. The old run-rig system, which meant soil exhaustion and tenant misery, was condemned. Then came the 1745 Jacobite rising to bring another disastrous setback to reform, with the Society of Improvers falling apart. Scotland had to wait until 1757 for the next significant publication on farming – that of Francis Home. This writer expounded on the benefits of enclosure, long leases for tenants, stall-feeding of animals with root crops, and roundly condemned the scourging of the land by over-cropping. Home's book was followed by the notable publications of such men as Sir Archibald Grant of Monymusk and the Rev. Adam Dickson of Duns. And so in the second half of the century the Agrarian Revolution in Scotland started on its spectacular course. Real improvement was further fostered by the concurrent operation of the Turnpike Act of 1751. Under its provisions, Scotland by 1784 had a thousand or more miles of good highways. This excellent development made possible, at long last, the easy cartage of farm produce, lime and coal.

With the ending of the abominable run-rig system and the introduction of individual tenancy with long leases, came some real incentive to achieve long-term improvement of the land. But an adverse factor intruded. The prospect of greater productivity naturally led to the upward creep of rentals. Many tenant farmers stayed near the borderline of insolvency as high rentals always had to be met, but some failed and had to join the miserably paid band of farm labourers. There were enlightened landlords who accepted the responsibility of financing long-term improvement of the land, realizing that as well as helping the tenants they were increasing the value of their own assets. But far too many tenants received little or no assistance in the struggle to make their farms pay, remaining at the mercy of market forces and the weather. A bad season for a penurious tenant could be a devastating set-back. And bad seasons came. Press reports for the year 1767 (William Burnes's second winter at Mount Oliphant) tell a grim story:

> We are informed that the storm has been very severe at Leadhills, and that the roads having been for some time impassable, the inhabitants of that place have been in great distress for want of meal and other provisons . . . in the parish of Crauford-John the people were harrowing the ground, where the snow was least deep, in order to raise the tops of the heath, for

the relief of their cattle, which were all ready to perish with hunger.[8]

And in Ayrshire:

> We hear from Stewarton, that last week a number of horses, loaded with meal, were coming through that place, they were set upon by a mob, who seized the meal, and divided it amongst them, allowing the owners 1s. a peck.[9]

The thaw of that same year caused severe flooding of the lower reaches of the Clyde, submerging much of Glasgow some feet under water.[10] The bad weather story with threatened starvation continued in press reports during 1772 and 1773,[11] but in Selkirkshire one small light of compassion gleamed in the dark picture:

> A correspondent informs us that the Duke of Buccleuch has sent all his tenants receipts for their last half year's rent, as a compliment, on account of their great losses by the uncommon severity of the weather last spring.[12]

One avenue of escape from rural misery in the 1770s and 1780s lay in emigration – for those who could find the passage money or arrange indenture. From Stanraer:

> This morning the ship Gale of Whitehaven, Henderson Jefferson master, for New York, sailed from this port with 230 emigrants on board, including women and children, 72 of whom were shipped at the Water of Fleet, the rest at Stanraer.[13]

Burnsians will recall the reactionary attempt to block the emigration of five hundred Highlanders by Macdonald of Glengary as late as the year 1786 – an attempt that inspired Burns to write *Address of Beelzebub* (K.108), four of its ironical sixty-two lines being:

> They! an' be damned! what right hae they
> To Meat, or Sleep, or light o' day,
> Far less to riches, pow'r, or freedom,
> But what your lordships *please to gie them?*

Better-favoured tenants went on to enjoy relative stability and prosperity by utilizing soil improvement, drainage where required, enclosure and crop rotations which included root crops for winter feed. To an outside observer the overall picture of late-eighteenth-century farming in Scotland would have been a good one, with the benefits of the Agrarian Revolution and rising prices for produce becoming evident. But many hard-working tenants went through exhaustion and ruin as the lead-up to such a picture – a lead-up spanning many decades. That was the frame in which we might now seek the place of William, Robert and Gilbert Burns, and of the all-important landlords with whom their lives were emmeshed.

We do not have to tramp over the old Burns farms today, armed with spade or auger, to get a first-hand picture of the soil problems their famed tenants encountered in trying to survive as farmers. That task has been accomplished for us by the Soil Survey of Scotland, skilfully supported by the scientific staff of the Macaulay Institute for Soil Research, Aberdeen, and the West of Scotland Agricultural College, Dumfries. Pedologists define soil types by pursuing field and laboratory studies, not only of the surface zones accommodating most of the crop roots, but also of the deeper layers down to three or four feet to reveal drainage and other qualities, and finally identifying the parent till or rock at the base of the profiles. Then, just as the biologist arrives at a *species* name within a *genus*, so does the pedologist fix each soil type as belonging to a *series* within an *association*. For each series a physical and chemical description is documented, and its spatial extent within the surveyed area is recorded on colour-coded maps that are made available to the land-using community. More to the point here, they are also available to a writer endeavouring to shed more light on farmers' problems a couple of centuries ago. Let us now pass from the general to the particular – to the daunting problems that faced William, Robert and Gilbert Burns. Their chequered story begins at the Mount Oliphant farm near the Carrick border.

MOUNT OLIPHANT, 1765–77

In late 1765, with his eldest son Robert six years of age, William Burnes signed a lease of the Mount Oliphant farm. It comprised about 85 acres, presumably unenclosed, and was part of a large estate owned by Provost Fergusson of Ayr. Situated about a mile south-east of Alloway and barely half a mile east of the River Doon, it is crossed by the 150 feet contour. It would have received

35 to 40 inches of rainfall annually, and minimal shelter from the prevailing westerlies by the higher country across the Doon. The soils of Mount Oliphant are mapped on sheet 14 of the Soil Survey of Scotland, and are discovered to be of two types. More than half the area has Glenalmond Series soil and the rest, at the north end, has soil of the Glenpark Series.[14]

Glenalmond Series soil developed on red sandy clay loam till derived from the Old Red Sandstone – a parent material of good reputation for fertility and in the earlier prehistoric millenia supporting a luxuriant forest cover. But many centuries of purely exploitative cropping and grazing of the cleared Brown Forest Soil by its feudal occupiers depleted its surface layer of base elements, at the same time exacerbating its original acidity. That was not the only bad development. The deep-rooted trees in their time helped to maintain a balance of water removal against the rainfall, both by leaf transpiration and by leaving deep channels where dead roots rotted, but clearing followed by incessant cropping and grazing grossly disturbed that balance. The result was intermittent waterlogging, with the imperfect natural drainage unable to cope with successive bursts of rainfall. One does not have to await quagmire conditions to recognize a state of imperfect drainage as there is a chemical consequence visible to the naked eye – the condition known as gleying. Gleying is a mottling of the soil with grey and ochreous patches, caused by localized variation of the oxidation-reduction status as the degree of wetness fluctuates between extremes. Glenalmond Series soil exhibits gleying prominently below a spade's depth.

The other Mount Oliphant soil type, the Glenpark Series, has much in common with the Glenalmond. A primary difference lies in the parent rock of the till which is of mixed origin – partly the Old Red Sandstone with the addition of some sediments of the later Carboniferous Sandstone period. The latter component made the till and soil texture a bit heavier and in consequence the natural drainage in the subsoil is even more imperfect than in the Glenalmond soil. Both soils have a sandy loam surface zone making for ease of cultivation, although the abundant glacier-deposited stones had nuisance value. However, the old wooden Scots plough, a heavy cumbersome affair, was well equipped to loosen many stones for progressive removal. One defect of the old plough was its indifferent performance in turning the sod to bury weeds, and weeds infesting a cereal crop would have reduced the yield of grain seriously. Robert Burns in his famous Moore letter made passing reference to the Mount Oliphant weeds, not so much as an agricultural comment but as an aside when describing his youthful romantic attachment to his reaping partner, Nelly Kilpatrick: 'my pulse beat such a furious ratann when I looked and fingered over her hand, to pick out the nettle-stings and thistles.' But it was not just poor cultivation technique that favoured weed competition against crop growth: it was also both the intermittent waterlogging and that ever-worsening surface soil acidity that was characteristic of so much Scottish soil in the eighteenth century. The original Brown Forest soils typically had an acidity around two degrees of pH below the point of neutrality, i.e. around pH 5, and long-cultivated soils had become a good deal worse. (The chemist's pH scale of acidity-alkalinity can be confusing to the non-scientist beause decreasing figures indicate increasing levels of acidity. Neutrality exists at pH 7. Familiar fluids range above and below neutrality, for example, dilute caustic soda at pH 12, sea water around pH 8, blood 7.35 to 7.5, vinegar 3 or less, and human gastric juice is normally 1.7. The actual pH figure is the base-10 logarithm of the reciprocal of the hydrogen ion concentration.)

Although broadleaf forest trees flourish with surface soil at pH 5, such a level of acidity is too severe for nearly all useful pasture and crop plants, in fact any value below pH 6 may be regarded as too acid for the optimal growth of wheat, oats, barley, rye, kail, potatoes, flax, peas and the better pasture grasses and clovers. The effect of acid conditions on such plants is indirect – by rendering soluble toxic elements such as manganese and aluminium to harmful levels.[15] Today, it is common knowledge that soil acidity is readily corrected by applying lime, either in the form of crushed limestone (calcium carbonate) or as burnt lime (calcium oxide). The latter form is more concentrated, and as it breaks up during burning it requires no crushing.

There is an added bonus in liming acid soil. By the calcium becoming chemically bonded with the clay, the stickiness of the latter is greatly reduced, giving the soil a crumb structure and friability that makes for easier cultivation and better drainage qualities. It so happens that the oat plant is to some degree tolerant of soil acidity, although it gives its best yields in soil of pH 6.5, i.e., very slightly acid. This acid tolerance appears to be the factor that made oatmeal dominant in the standard diet in old acid-soiled Scotland. Dr Johnson, in his day, was simply stating the obvious in his Dictionary entry on oats: 'A grain which in England is generally given to horses, but in Scotland supports the people'. Even so, the people would have been better supported with soils less acid, not only in respect of oat yields but in terms of agricultural diversification.

From scraps of information available to us today it would appear that William Burnes's Mount Oliphant landlord, Dr Fergusson, was a kindly fellow and well disposed towards his conscientious tenant. However, as a successful medical man retiring from his London practice to settle in Ayr, his knowledge of farmland improvement was sadly lacking. True, he did advance £100 to William for the purchase of a few cows and horses, but he was mistaken if he believed that unimproved Mount Oliphant would earn him a continuing rental of £40 rising to £45 annually, and comfortably support a tenant with a large and growing family. The land demanded substantial capital for the improvements which liming and drainage could effect; capital which he – not his tenant – should have provided. Enlightenment on such essentials had not come to Dr Fergusson, although it was already paying off for many landlords. When he signed his twelve-year lease, William was probably no better informed. To him, drainage would have meant little more than the ploughing of ditches at the sides of humped rigs, and these could not take away subsoil water, however well they appeared to work for surface run-off. A grid of deep ditches, partially filled with large and small stones covered with an ample layer of brushwood before refilling, was the recognized method of underground drainage at the time.[16] (Tile drainage was to become the standard method some fifty or more years later.) There was ample stone at hand at Mount Oliphant, but the labour needed for thousands of feet of ditch-digging was out of the question, even with labourers' pay no more than three or four pounds a year. As for lime – vitally important for the soil after centuries of acid build-up – it is doubtful if William ever bought an ounce of it, let alone the hundreds of tons which should have been burnt, spread and harrowed in before any seeding was undertaken. It is no wonder that yields were poor; probably no more than three or four grains harvested for each one sown. It is also no wonder that there was no money to spare for such luxuries as bought meat and the family lived on oatmeal, skim milk and whey, with perhaps a little cheese and a few eggs. Raising the cash for successive half-yearly rent payments was a constant battle.

The financial strain and worry increased after Dr Ferguson died in November 1769, with the management of the estate passing into the hands of a factor. In all his reminiscences, both epistolary and poetic, Robert Burns described no other man of his acquaintance with more sustained malignity than he did with that factor. In the Moore letter he wrote of 'the scoundrel tyrant's insolent, threatening epistles, which used to set us all in tears'. He became 'th' Oppressor, Rejoicing in the honest man's destruction' in the Common Place Book poem *A Penitential Thought in the Hour of Remorse* (K.5), and he was to be maligned in *The Twa Dogs* (K.71):

> I've noticed on our Laird's court-day,
> An' mony a time my heart's been wae,
> Poor tenant-bodies, scant o' cash,
> How they maun thole a factor's snash;
> He'll stamp an' threaten, curse an' swear,
> He'll apprehend them, poind their gear,
> While they maun stand, wi' aspect humble,
> An' hear it a', an' fear an' tremble!

As did Jurgen for the Devil[17] – dare I venture a word or two in defence of the unnamed factor? – with no expectation of anything like Jurgen's reward. The new owners of the Fergusson estate would have seen William Burnes as just another ineffectual nobody, usually in arrears for the rent and overdue for eviction. They would have kept prodding the factor for results and he would have needed no telling that his job depended on getting results. Given that his energetic methods call for condemnation, at least we must recognize his difficult brief. In passing, we may recall that Gilbert Burns, after many years of unsuccessful farming, took on a factor's job in 1804.

The year 1776 had 'a winter locked in ice'.[18] It brought William Burnes to the end of the road at Mount Oliphant, and his tenancy ended Whitsun 1777. He was able to secure an honourable clearance with a mortage on the Alloway cottage and its several acres which he still held in feu.

The sourness of the Mount Oliphant soil carried over into the reminiscences of Robert and Gilbert. In 1787 Robert wrote: 'the chearless gloom of a hermit with the unceasing moil of a galley-slave, brought me to my sixteenth year' (L.125). About ten years later, Gilbert gave his write-off of the farm in a letter to Mrs Dunlop, later published in the Currie biography:

> Mount Oliphant, the farm my father possessed in the parish of Ayr, is almost the very poorest soil I know of in a state of cultivation. A stronger proof of this I cannot give, than that, notwithstanding the extraordinary rise in the value of lands in Scotland, it was, after a considerable sum laid out in improving it by the proprietor, let, a few years ago, five pounds per annum lower than the rent paid for it by my father thirty years ago.

We are not given any details of the 'improvements' made by the later proprietor – one may suspect that they were cosmetic, stopping short of any effective liming and draining. In his 1828 biography of Burns, J.G. Lockhart introduced a new adjective to describe the soil – 'ungrateful' – effectively putting an authoritative stamp of agreement on Gilbert's condemnation. These decrials gave Mount Oliphant the reputation of a jinx farm, particularly as Robert's memory became increasingly idolized in Scotland and beyond. The plain fact is that Mount Oliphant's soil, long over-exploited and neglected, had little to be 'grateful' for. In the letter quoted, Gilbert also mentioned the loss of some of his father's cattle by accidents and disease. The cattle diseases were not described, but a farm would acquire a bad reputation once brucellosis, bovine tuberculosis or anthrax struck. Unless a beast killed by anthrax is quickly incinerated on the spot, the soil remains infective for decades. But in the eighteenth century the unfortunate beast would be butchered for food, not burned.

In retrospect, we can only say that Mount Oliphant was *potentially* a satisfactory farm, noting today's widespread distribution of its same Glenalmond and Glenpark Series soils in south-western Ayrshire sustaining attractive farms. Tile under-drainage and correction of acidity form essential parts of the picture. Glenalmond soils are extensive to the south of Mount Oliphant as far as the towns of Crosshill and Straiton, and again south-westerly right down to the valleys of the Milton, Chapelton and Lady Burns. There are large areas of Glenpark Series soil in the valley of the Doon and to the north in the lower Ayr valley.

LUCKLESS LOCHLEA

With relief and high hopes the Burns family moved to a larger farm, Lochlea, on Whitsun 1777. Robert was then seventeen years of age and Gilbert eighteen months his junior. Their father was aged fifty-six and in poor health. The Lochlea farm comprised some 130 acres, on undulating country about two miles north-east of Tarbolton with an elevation of about 300 feet. Lochlea had an even more clayey subsoil than had much of Mount Oliphant, and this, coupled with a higher rainfall, meant that the natural drainage was even more imperfect.

The leasing arrangement that William Burnes entered into points to an odd blend of hard-headedness and naivety in his make-up. Evidently he had grasped the importance of at least two tied issues – long lease and liming. The agreed-upon term was thirty-eight years, implying William's belief that the farm would secure the future for his sons, or alternatively become a good proposition later for a lease transfer. The agreement required the landlord, David Maclure, to provide and spread 100 bolls of Cairnhill lime per acre initially, and to finance the purchase of lime for William to spread as a second dressing.[19] (A boll is an old volume measure that seems to have varied in place and time. Assuming here that it was equal to four bushels, and as a ton by volume equals 40 bushels, 100 bolls of lime would be 10 tons by volume.) The latter comprised twelve tons of limestone for each acre, with coals to burn it. As twelve tons of limestone would burn down to seven tons of oxide lime (if it were reasonably pure), a liming programme of 10 tons followed by 7 tons was a fairly thorough one for a moderately clayey soil. Another condition agreed upon required Maclure to enclose and subdivide the farm. So far, so good.

If the foregoing terms reveal William Burnes as the shrewd bargainer, other parts of the agreement indicate something to the contrary. For a start, the rental was about twice the Mount Oliphant figure, and events were to prove it onerous. Another aspect of the deal, inexplicably unusual and foolish, was the absence of any written lease document. There seems to have been shilly-shallying from the start, with a first 'bargain' superseded by a second, and neither covered by a written memorandum or contract. The first 'bargain' was for a rental of fifteen shillings per acre per annum for eight years and for £1 per acre thereafter. The second, which included the liming and enclosing provisions, was for £1 per acre from the start for the whole lease term. Why no documentation? A likely enough explanation was that Maclure resisted any proposal for a formal lease because he felt, or knew, that his title to the land was far from clear.

The Soil Survey of Scotland has classified the soil of the main area of Lochlea in the Bargour Series (the most important series of the Bargour Association).[20] This soil series is an extensive one in central Ayrshire, extending from its north-eastern limit around Galston in an irregular horse-shoe arc to the start of the flat beach deposits now accommodating Prestwick Airport, and back south and east through Annbank to almost encircle the Tarbolton-Mauchline area. The series is described in detail in *The Soils Round Kilmarnock*.[21] To summarize, it has a light brown sandy clay loam surface to about eight inches, with the tell-tale gleying starting to show up below that depth. At sixteen inches depth the texture stiffens to a clay loam right down to the original till which is struck at three feet. The Burns ploughmen would have appreciated the relative absence of stones after Mount Oliphant. The parent rock of the till is mainly the red sandstone of the Barren Measures – one of the Carboniferous sequences. (The term 'Barren' has no soil fertility implication. Like the flowers that bloom in the spring, it has nothing to do with the case. It signifies the absence of coal found elsewhere in the Measures.) Like the two soil types at Mount Oliphant, the Bargour Series soil is again Brown Forest Soil, and the Macaulay Institute has published full analyses from three locations. The one sampled nearest to Lochlea (less than a mile to the north) reveals a severe depletion of base elements in the topsoil and consequential acidity: pH 5.55.[22] Of necessity, all such chemical assays are modern, reflecting an amelioration due to some liming of the fields – a presumption supported by the high ratio of calcium to magnesium (3.80 to 0.22 milli-equivalents per 100 gms) in the surface soil referred to. Before Maclure's liming programme commenced in 1777 the soil of Lochlea would have been even more acid and base-depleted. If ever a farm needed lime urgently, Lochlea did. Completing the soil picture there, the Survey has delineated two other soil types occupying small depressed patches, and both of very poor quality. They belong to the Brocklie Series and the Dalsangan Series.

Brocklie Series soil has a dark grey sandy loam surface that gives way to heavy clay only a foot down. Gleying is severe, appearing first at eight inches, and the 'poorly drained' categorising is easily understood. It is not a Brown Forest Soil, it is a Surface-water Non-calcareous Gley. The soil of the Dalsangan Series is even poorer. Its natural drainage is described as 'very poor', and it belongs in the Peaty Gley group. The Institute has determined pH figures for six Peaty Gley surfaces and they range down from 5.4 to 3.6 – the latter getting close to the acidity of vinegar. There is little doubt that Brocklie or Dalsangan soil, or both of those, underlaid the site of the 'Miln damb' of the subsequent litigation document. That area of Lochlea, by mutual agreement, was to remain rent-free until Maclure had drained and limed it,[23] but it would appear that he never accomplished that task, let alone the overall liming programme that was tackled grudgingly and pursued in fits and starts.

All seemed to go fairly well for William Burnes and his family during the first few years at Lochlea, with whatever was planted seeming to revel in the newly-limed soil and producing well. They were also important formative years for young Robert, what with his Tarbolton Bachelors' Club, joining the freemasons, learning to play the fiddle with Davie Sillar, and his courtship of Alison Begbie. During the same period he was taking increasing interest in matters agricultural, no doubt so encouraged by reading Jethro Tull's classic work *Horse-hoeing Husbandry* and Adam Dickson's comprehensive *Treatise of Agriculture*, the two volumes of which (1762 and 1769) ran to some 2,000 pages. The earliest of Robert's letters known to us today was written from Lochlea to his Maybole friend William Niven. It carries a postscript stating: 'I have three acres of pretty good flax this season'. Not long after that flax was harvested he agreed to his father's proposal to learn flax-dressing, and went to Irvine for the purpose. It turned into a fiasco. He fell ill with an unidentified malady which was accompanied by a severe bout of depressive illness, and the flax-dressing exercise ceased when the premises were burnt to the ground. On his return to Lochlea after an absence of six months he maintained an interest in flax with some success, winning first prize for his lint seed, harvested in 1782.[24] Flax grows well on slightly acid (pH 6) and moderately heavy soil, and the sandy clay loam of Lochlea would have suited it well. But flax should only be included in a rotation in

128

one year in four, as it is very subject to disease, and needs to be free of weed infestation, both during growth and processing. Is that why we hear no more of flax growing after the 1782 harvest in the Burns story? Perhaps. Robert Chambers recounts that David Sillar told him many years later that the flax castle in Spain was initiated by William Burnes in the fanciful belief that he could become 'entirely a lint farmer'.[25] The last forlorn mention of flax at Lochlea was an item in the sequestration list of May 1783: 'Fourteen bundles of shafe lint'. A best-laid (?) scheme.

For the unlucky William Burnes his relatively happy situation at Lochlea during the first four years there was not to last. Some debts to Maclure led to disastrously costly litigation, and for over a century it was assumed that the blame lay with the tenant, not the landlord. But the judgment was reversed by the discovery of the documentation of most of the legal detail early in the twentieth century. (For the full text see *The Lochlea Litigation*, Burns Chronicle 1935.) The Ayr bank of Douglas, Heron and Co. had failed and the company was putting pressure on its borrowers, one of whom was Maclure. It would appear that as a consequence Maclure became tardy in meeting his obligations for the improvement of Lochlea and William Burnes reacted by witholding some rental payments. To settle the argument the parties resorted to arbitration. It would seem that the dispute was centred on which of the two 'bargains' was operative – the first with fifteen shillings per acre rent and no liming by the landlord, or the second with twenty shillings rent and the liming financed by Maclure.

The arbiters failed to agree and appointed one John Hamilton to act as oversman or umpire, who reduced the sum of £775 claimed by Maclure to £231. Burnes would have paid the latter sum and ended his problem had not one John McAdam put in his oar. McAdam claimed hereditable security of the large estate of which Lochlea was part and brought legal action against all debtor tenants. In response, Burnes took an appeal to the Court of Session but it failed on technical grounds. Acting quickly, Maclure obtained, from the Sheriff-Depute of Ayrshire, a sequestration order on all the Lochlea crops and stock, and in desperation Burnes went back to the Court of Session, this time with a Multipoinding action. (Multipoinding, in old Scots law, was an action brought by the holder of moneys or effects claimed by different persons. Each claimant was summoned to appear and state his grounds of claim. The court then decided on the disposal of the money or effects.) After due deliberation the Court awarded the £231 to the preferred creditor – Douglas, Heron and Co. By that award the sequestration order was blocked, but Burnes's legal costs amounted to more cash than he could raise, and another year of extremely bad weather dashed all hopes for a profitable crop which might have retrieved his fortunes.

The troubled year of 1783 ended. For unrelieved poignancy the close of the Lochlea scene would outrank that of any Verdi opera. A joyless hogmanay brought to William Burnes only the forebodings of what awaited any eighteenth-century debtor, and prescient fears for the future of his mercurial first-born. Those stresses added their destructive power to the worsening tubercular disorder afflicting him. He died on 13 February, 1784.

RETREAT TO MOSSGIEL

Foreseeing the wind-up of the Lochlea tenancy several months before the climax, Robert and Gilbert took the lease of another farm, Mossgiel, in November 1783. They also took the step of formally recording their status, and that of their sisters, as employees of their father and so becoming creditors of the estate. The writer Hilton Brown, with questionable justification, described that step as 'a piece of rather sharp practice'.[26] No more than a pragmatic stratagem, it suggests that a lesson had been learnt from the absence of formal lease documents covering the Lochlea tenancy, but if Maclure and his co-creditors had decided to play hard the brothers were fully entitled to use the same methods. View it how you will, the move enabled the family to transfer some oddments of chattels and stock to Mossgiel.

Mossgiel (entered on Armstrong's 1775 map as 'Mossgill') was about two miles south-east of Lochlea, in Mauchline parish. Its 118 acres commanded an annual rental of £90 in 1783. The owner was the fifth Earl of Loudon, who left the management of his estate to a tacksman, the lawyer Gavin Hamilton; a man whom the Burns brothers regarded – with every justification – as a good friend. Mossgiel is on the north-west outskirts of the town of Mauchline, and while usually described as an upland farm with its elevation around 550 feet it is more correctly placed in the Lowland Transition Zone. Slopes are moderately steep, and the annual rainfall would be around 45 inches. The Soil Survey of Scotland has identified two soil types within the boundaries – the Bargour Series on the lower north-east side and the Lanfine Series on the higher south-west side.[27]The Bargour Series area is continuous with the area of the same soil at Lochlea, already described. The Bargour soil yields place to Lanfine soil as the elevation increases, and this is evident today on noting that the adjacent railway track disappears from sight below Lanfine soil into the Mossgiel Tunnel.

Lanfine Series soil has some important textural and chemical differences from the adjacent Bargour soil. It developed on reddish brown till of texture ranging from sandy loam to sandy clay loam. The parent rock is a combination of the Old Red Sandstone sedimentary with a proportion of various volcanic rocks. The latter, rich in basic elements such as calcium, magnesium and potassium, add to the potential fertility of soil formed from it. However, as in the case of other Brown Forest Soils already discussed, many centuries of exploitative abuse after deforestation tended to leave the root zone impoverished and acid. Modern analytical findings vary somewhat from place to place, some of them reflecting the early poverty of the soil and others suggesting an intervening history of improvement practices.[28] It is reasonable to assume that in 1784 the Lanfine soil of Mossgiel would have been in the former category (and the Bargour soil there no better than the identical soil at Lochlea prior to Maclure's liming). Even a modest preliminary liming of the soil at Mossgiel would have made the period of the Burns men there a more productive and happier one. The Lanfine soil of Mossgiel would have been the most easily cultivated soil that Robert and Gilbert had so far encountered. It contains few stones, and the brown loam surface changes to sandy loam at 10 inches depth and to coarse sandy loam at 16 inches. However, once again, the natural drainage is imperfect with the texture stiffening to sandy clay loam, and in parts to clay loam, at 27 inches. The tell-tale gleying starts to show about 10 inches down.

Twenty-five-year-old Robert started, repeat *started*, farming operations at Mossgiel with enthusiasm. To quote his own reminiscences:

> I entered on this farm with a full resolution, 'Come, go to, I will be wise!' – I read farming books; I calculated crops; I attended

markets; and in short, in spite of 'the devil, the world and the flesh', I believe I would have been a wise man; but the first year from unfortunately buying in bad seed, the second from a late harvest, we lost half of both our crops: this overset all my wisdom, and I returned 'Like the dog to his vomit, and the sow that was washed to her wallowing in the mire.'

(L.125)

Those colourful words which flowed from the poet's quill are very informative. Virtually all seed on the Scottish market for the 1784 sowing would have been bad seed, produced under the appalling weather conditions of 1782–3. The picture in exposed Ayrshire would have been even worse than that described by John Ramsay for southern Perthshire in 1783:

> in the middle of March a prodigious fall of snow. In many places of this country it lay for a fortnight from two to three feet deep. . . . By reason of snow or rain, very little oats or black victual could be sown here till the middle of April – most piercing cold winds in the end of that month and in May, and of course no vegetation. The barley got a dry but a very cold bed. . . . Exceeding heavy rains in the end of May and beginning of June, which chilled the young corn. Ten days of hot weather about the middle of July, after which torrents of rain attended with cold stormy winds which lasted for six weeks. . . . It looked liker February than the warm month. Hurricane 24th August which blew down a number of trees, and did much mischief to the wheat by breaking the straw. In the middle of September, notwithstanding a fortnight of fine weather, the oats in general green . . . boisterous wet weather to the end of the month. . . . Mornings of the 4th and 13th October frost like mid-winter, the ground being hard under foot till far in the day, and ice on the ponds as thick as a crown-piece. It whitened the late corn and prevented its filling. . . . Melancholy at that season to see stooks and sheaves white with snow and stiffened with frost. . . . In the high countries [corn] covered with snow and not cut down till well in November . . . to beginning of December very deep snow and the frost so intense that it threatened to set the mills.[29]

In the light of such information about the 1783 weather, we can be certain that plenty of seed corn of low-germination performance would have hit the Scottish market in 1784. Robert was right. He was also right about losses due to the late harvest in the following year.

We have no statistical record of Mauchline weather in 1785, but the England and Wales weather tables published in 1972 by H.H. Lamb[30] would be indicative of trends for south-west Scotland. Lamb's Table, App. V.33, lists the quarterly rainfall of all the years since 1727 in terms of the percentage of the 1916–1950 average. Whereas the respective winter-spring-summer-autumn percentage figures for 1784 are 59-99-133-59, those for the year 1785 are 59-27-109-113. These reveal that while 1785 had a very much drier spring than 1784, the autumn was markedly wetter, enforcing a late and difficult harvest.

Robert Burns was uncommunicative about Mossgiel conditions from 1786 on. We know why of course – writing and publishing poetry, plans for emigration, the rapturous Highland Mary and Jean Armour happenings, and the Edinburgh adventures were major diversions. Gilbert's reminiscences tell us a bit more:

> The farm of Mossgiel lies very high, and mostly on a cold wet bottom. The first four years [1784–8] that we were on the farm were very frosty, and the spring was very late. Our crops in consequence were very unprofitable; and, notwithstanding our utmost diligence and economy, we found ourselves obliged to give up our bargain, with the loss of a considerable part of our original stock.
>
> (Letter to Mrs Dunlop, published by Currie, 1800)

Gilbert's reference to giving up 'our bargain' probably refers to the final abandonment of Mossgiel in 1797 when there was a lease break – a year after Robert's death.

Robert and Gilbert were not doing a paint job on their reputations as farmers in blaming the weather for their misfortunes. Modern research into past climate reveals that the 80s decade of the eighteenth century was one of the several year clusters of severe weather that occurred within the longer 'Little Ice Age' of 1550 to 1850. There had already been several of these interludes of deterioration of climate, each lasting a few years, notable instances being around 1607–8, 1684 and 1740. Lamb's tabulation gives the *average* winter temperature for 1684 as *minus* 1.2 decrees C. That year is identifiable as that of the calamitous freeze at Exmoor, described so vividly in *Lorna Doone*, Chapter 42. It was followed by a group of climate-related crop failures in Scotland in the 'King William Years' (1689–1702), these playing a significant part in the moves for the Union with England, made urgent through the dread of starvation. The cause of these subordinate cycles in the overall pattern of climate fluctuation seems to involve the incidence of extensive slow-moving anticyclones ('blocking highs') drifting from west to east from the Atlantic. Their slow-advancing fronts sweep cold air southwards from northern latitudes, and as they tend to be cloud-free they bring extremes of weather, with frosts particularly severe and prolonged. The factors triggering these phenomena are not clearly understood, but sun-spot cycles, major volcanic eruptions and even planet alignments have been postulated.[31] Whatever natural laws operated, it is clear that Murphy's Law played its part in the coincidence of the later Lochlea and early Mossgiel years for the Burns men with the arrival of one of these extreme weather year clusters.

Seemingly minor 'asides' in the written record of the doings of the Burns brothers can be significant in this discussion of their farming conditions. One of these is Gilbert's account of hearing what motivated Robert to write *Death and Dr Hornbook* after a mason-meeting in Tarbolton early in 1785: 'These circumstances he related to me when he repeated the verses to me the next afternoon, as I was holding the plough and he was letting the water off the field beside me.' Really now! Pools of water in the path of the plough at Mossgiel? One can imagine the horses' hooves squelching in the mud and the plough-shoe playing havoc with whatever crumb structure the unlimed soil might have once possessed. Evidently no stone-and-brushwood drains had been put down in the Mossgiel subsoil, even though these would have been a top-priority improvement on that farm. The Lanfine Series soil absorbs rainwater into its light-textured upper layers very readily. But, checked in its further vertical descent by the clay bottom, this water is prone to move laterally and emerge in the form of springs at lower levels, there causing (in the Bargour soil) serious intermittent water-logging, if not actual swamp conditions. This problem had been widespread in farmlands throughout Scotland and the cure was well known – stone drains taken to the heads of all springs.[32] Neglected, the lower pastures would become dominated by sedges, tussock grass, Yorkshire fog and other swamp-tolerant plants of poor feed value. On soil improvements effected by the Burns brothers at Mossgiel the record is silent. It is probably silent because no such steps were ever taken.

One may wonder why a man of Gavin Hamilton's experience and goodwill failed to persuade the owner of Mossgiel to allocate capital for the long-term improvement of the land. But the owner, James Campbell, fifth Earl of Loudon, was in no position to continue the programme set in train by his late cousin John, the fourth Earl (1705–82). John had been an enthusiast for the improvement of his Ayrshire estate, having planted more than a million trees as well as constructing roads and improving the land.[33] But his successor James, with no more than a military background, brought with him to the earldom a load of personal and financial trouble. His wife Flora (n. M'Leod) had died in 1780 soon after giving birth to their only daughter, and the appalling weather of 1782 and 1783 brought his worsening financial situation to a state of crisis. Deeply distressed, he took his own life with a pistol-shot in April 1786 – the very time when the personal problems of Robert Burns were piling up and Mossgiel was proving to be demonstrably unprofitable. Moved to deep sympathy for Isabella M'Leod, sister of the Earl's wife, in her double bereavement, he wrote a two-stanza dirge; one that reads today more as a silhouette of his own depressed state than as an effective source of consolation for unhappy Isabella:

> Raving winds around her blowing,
> Yellow leaves the woodlands strowing,
> By a river hoarsely roaring
> Isabella stray'd deploring.
> Farewell, hours that late did measure
> Sunshine days of joy and pleasure;
> Hail, thou gloomy night of sorrow,
> Cheerless night that knows no morrow.
>
> O'er the Past too fondly wandering,
> On the hopeless Future pondering,
> Chilly Grief my life-blood freezes,
> Fell Despair my fancy seizes.
> Life, thou soul of every blessing,
> Load to Misery most distressing,

> Gladly how would I resign thee,
> And to dark Oblivion join thee!

(K.207)

The Earl's distressed heirs were forced to auction off a substantial fraction of the estate, including Mauchline Mains, Haugh Miln, east, west and south Mossgiel.[34] (East Mossgiel was the Burns farm.) With their credit rating low after Lochlea, any prospect of Robert and Gilbert raising a loan had now become very dim. For Robert, farming as a source of livelihood had lost its appeal and migration to the West Indies became the goal – the goal which was to be put aside by his extraordinarily sudden rise to fame as a poet, and his decision to go to Edinburgh.

TO ELLISLAND – VIA EDINBURGH

Robert Burns, on his borrowed pony, left Mossgiel late in November 1786, never to return to Ayrshire as a participating farmer. Gilbert took over the Mossgiel farm and battled on until the 1797 lease break, never having made the grade financially, even with the aid of a personal loan of £180 from Robert, provided in 1788. After a ride lasting two days, Robert Burns was in Edinburgh.

Burns entered a very different world when he came to Edinburgh to find himself fêted and lionized as the creator of the Kilmarnock volume of poems. He came from an Ayrshire community which was still very much in the iron grip of Knox's dogma and discipline to mix with liberated and progressive personalities in club and fashionable drawing-room. From now on, kirk satires would only lash dead lions. Mice, lice and daisies had played their part in launching him to fame but they had served their poetic turn and were to stay in the past. Mixing with James Johnson and David Herd awakened a new enthusiasm for the captivating folksong art of his country. He was also to discover that Scottish women could be as stimulating intellectually as they could be flesh-wise. (One of Burns's remarks when he first came to Edinburgh, was, that between the men of rustic life and the polite world he observed little difference – that in the former, though unpolished by fashion, and unenlightened by science, he had found much observation and much intelligence – but a refined and accomplished woman was a being almost new to him, and of which he had formed but a very inadequate idea. Cromek's *Reliques of R.B.*)

As he no longer had to spin out seven pounds a year spending money he felt free to share the cost of touring the Highlands by coach. The change exposed him to the seductiveness of port wine, a drink which was to remain his favourite to his last days. Extensive touring of eastern lands from the Borders to Moray Firth had shown him that not all Scottish soils were heavy and water-logged. But did he now look ahead to becoming a more enthusiastic and efficient farmer? The answer has to be no. If anything, he tended to turn away from the prospect of returning to the soil, even though he now mixed with prominent enthusiasts for agricultural improvement. Among their number were the Duke of Gordon, Lord Hailes, and James Burnett, Lord Monboddo. The law lords were prominently represented in the circle of land improvers. Lord Hailes had long advocated long leases and wrote them for the tenants of his excellent East Lothian properties,[35] and Lord Monboddo had made his Kincardineshire tenancies the envy of all around, even against his own financial interests – he is reported as never having cleared more than £300 annually as a landlord.[36] Monboddo, when in Edinburgh, held fortnightly 'learned suppers' where Burns enjoyed rounds of discussion with the capital's erudite. But whether the poet was more interested in his genial host's progressive farming ideas than in his attractive (but ill-starred) daughter, Elizabeth Burnett, is open to doubt. ('There has not been anything nearly like her in all the combinations of Beauty, Grace and Goodness the great Creator has formed, since Milton's Eve on the first day of her existence' L.68.)

Few young men of Burns's day, or indeed before or since his day, would have been subjected to such an avalanche of advice as Robert encountered between November 1786 and March 1788. Through it all he must have been in a state of painful indecision about his long-term future, as, understandably, he carried to Edinburgh a bias against farming, coupled with doubts about the only alternative which seemed to be available – the Excise service. Even a few weeks before leaving Ayrshire he had confessed to Robert Aiken: 'I have been feeling all the various rotations and movements within, respecting the Excise' (L.53). His peace of mind was not helped when influential friends did their best to talk down the Excise notion and advise a future in farming. After only six weeks in Edinburgh he wrote to John Ballantine about the offer of a lease of a Nithsdale farm by Patrick Miller:

> Some life-rented, embittering Recollections whisper me that I will be happier anywhere than in my old neighbourhood, but Mr Miller is no judge of land; and though I dare say he means to favour me, yet he may give me, in his opinion, an advantageous bargain that may ruin me.
>
> (L.77)

J. De L. Ferguson, writing in 1931, was highly critical of Burns's influential friends, Mrs Dunlop, the Earl of Glencairn and others, in advising the Bard to forget about the Excise and return to farming.[37] Ferguson's opinion appears to have been based on an uncritical acceptance of Burns's eventual denigration of Miller and his farm. It is a view difficult to justify. More about that later.

We can be confident of one clear resolve emerging from Burns's tours and contacts with new acquaintances: if he were to return to farming it would be on the morning side of Scotland's great mountains. Let the farmers battling with their muddy Ayrshire rigs go on seeing the moon rising over the Cummock hills – he could do without that pleasure from now on.

Had Miller's estate been in Kyle or Carrick an offer would probably have received scant consideration. But a farm in beautiful Nithsdale was another matter, and as Robert's financial returns from the Edinburgh edition assumed reality, Miller's offer was seen in a more favourable light. Miller was genuinely interested in the young poet's future and he was a generous man. Even before the publication of the Edinburgh edition was announced Robert told Ballantine:

> An unknown hand left ten guineas for the Ayrshire Bard in Mr Sibbald's hand, which I got. I have since discovered my generous unknown friend to be Patrick Miller Esq., brother of the Justice Clerk; and drank a glass of claret with him by invitation at his own house yesternight.
>
> (L.63)

We may well assume that the offer of a Dalswinton farm tenancy was first made on that occasion. But soon the mental tug-o-war – Excise versus farming – was to be on with a vengeance. The tours of 1787 brought not only the sight of productive farms east of the Uplands and Highlands, but also a meeting with Robert Graham, twelfth Laird of Fintry, who had recently been made a Commissioner of Excise. An Excise job was probably discussed, but the first positive move to that goal was made on Robert's behalf by Dr Alexander Wood, the surgeon who treated his injured knee late in 1787. On learning his patient's ambition for an Excise career, Wood approached the Commission and a preliminary listing was made.

With exemplary patience, Patrick Miller had waited more than a year for a definite answer to his proposition when Burns at last arranged to go to Nithsdale, late in February 1788, with an experienced farmer friend John Tennant to inspect the Dalswinton farms. Three were on offer: Ellisland on the west bank of the Nith, Foregirth on the east bank about a mile and a half to the east, and Bankhead on the east bank just across the river from Friars Carse. The latter two farms were on low ground, tending flat, while Ellisland was on mainly high ground, light-textured but stony. Tennant was enthusiastic about the farms, but whether he preferred Ellisland to the other two is not recorded. All we know is that Burns settled for the pleasant elevated terraces of Ellisland, with their attractive apple and shade trees, in preference to the flatter meadows of the other two. Miller's factor Cunningham (father of the biographer), who accompanied Tennant and Burns on their tour of inspection, is on record as having remarked: 'Mister Burns, you have made a poet's, not a farmer's, choice.'[38] Mister Burns had decided that he had found the place that he had visualized in responding to Patrick Miller a year before:

there is nothing I wish for more than to resume the Plough. Indolence and Innatention to business I have sometimes been guilty of, but I thank my God, Dissipation or Extravagance have never been part of my character. If therefore, Sir, you could fix me in any sequester'd romantic spot, and let me have such a Lease as by care and industry I might live in humble decency, and have a spare hour now and then to write out an idle rhyme . . . I am afraid, Sir, to dwell on the idea, lest Fortune have not such happiness in store for me.

(L.100)

Burns's mind must have been in a whirl during those early months of 1788. His amorous affair with Clarinda had been pursued with sustained intensity, as well as the briefer but more consequential one with Jenny Clow. Although in pain with an injured knee, he rode off to Glasgow in February to visit Richard Brown and witness at first hand the joys of newlywed existence. On the way back he called on Mrs Dunlop, spending with her two days which were probably two days of high-pressure indoctrination on the virtues of a farming life. Back in Mauchline he was to be confronted with a tale of financial woe from Gilbert, and advanced him £180 out of his new-found wealth. Later in February he rescued his very-pregnant and abandoned Jean, setting her up in a room in Mauchline and conducting his notorious 'horse-litter' exercise with her. It was then back to Edinburgh for 'racking shop accounts with Creech', negotiating an Excise commission, and resuming his rapturous association with Clarinda. One wonders how he found time to reach agreement with Patrick Miller and sign the Ellisland lease by 18 March. Back in Mauchline, he married his Jean, and during April and May he was taking Excise instructions under James Findlay.

It would appear that during that same period Burns was able to squeeze in some farming preliminaries. He enquired about hiring two man-servants through a friend at Brownhill on March 31 (L.232) and in May he informed Ainslie that he was 'horribly busy, buying and preparing for that farming business' (L.243). We are not given details of his projected farming programme, nor of what he bought, but a cart to be drawn by Jenny Geddes would have been a likely item. He would need that to take personal effects to Ellisland, certainly to take the plough which (according to Cunningham) a friend had given him as a wedding present. A young man similarly placed today would be buying a small truck or utility.

Let us try to visualize the scene on 12 June 1788 as tired Jenny Geddes took Robert Burns on the last leg of his lonely trek from Mauchline to his new farm. At last the Nith was crossed at Auldgirth and the valley broadened. Robert may have felt like a pioneer, but he was hardly that. Bronze Age people had lived there, leaving only a stone circle at the spot where the Nith made a sharp turn to the left. A little further on was Friars Carse, long ago farmed by the industrious monks of Melrose and now owned by the Riddells whom Burns was yet to meet. Just across the river Red John Comyn had held sway until the blade of Robert the Bruce obliged him to quit the sphere. At last Ellisland farm came into view, displaying a green crop which must have (prematurely) pleased Robert's eye (and hungry Jenny Geddes' too, for a different reason), but as Ellisland had no usable buildings they had to keep on going as far as the Isle where Mr and Mrs Cullie had agreed to put them up.

The Cullie couple were to be Robert's hosts until December when a Mr Newal lent him his temporarily vacated home and where at last Jean was able to join him. The intervening five months with the elderly rustic Cullies were certainly a miserable period for Burns, judging from some lines they provoked:

> I've dwindled down to mere existence;
> Wi' nae converse but Gallowa' bodies
> Wi' nae kend face but Jenny Geddes.
>
> (*Epistle to Hugh Parker*, K.222)

A severe attack of influenza at that time added to his melancholy: 'I am scarce able to hold up my head with this fashionable influenza, which is just now the rage hereabouts' (L.273). He did not exaggerate – there was indeed a 'flu' pandemic in 1788.[39] The Isle period may well be seen as a five-month minus in the life of Burns, but it was a timeless plus for the world in the lovely lyric it inspired – *Of A' the Airts the Wind Can Blaw*.

The building of a dwelling house, byre, barn and stable at Ellisland was a priority requirement. The lease specified: 'which dwelling house the said Robert Burns becomes bound to finish and complete during the course of the ensuing summer'. Good intentions, yes. But Thomas Boyd, the architect-builder, made slow progress. With the summer long over, and by mid-winter still without his house, Burns lost patience and wrote to Boyd in the strongest terms: 'For God's sake let me but within the shell of it' (L.313). His annoyance was understandable, with travelling time wasted every day and only makeshift facilities for dairy work. It was not until May 1789 that the Bard and his family finally moved into residence at Ellisland.

In the autumn of 1788 Burns and his hired hands harvested the crop which had been sown by David Cullie. Cullie, well past his prime, had decided to give up farming and it is likely that he had made a patchy job of the spring sowing. The planting was almost certainly one of oats, the only cereal worth growing on the acid unlimed soil. The crop was a poor one and it was harvested under difficult weather conditions. (See Letter 272, and one to Mrs Dunlop of 5 September in Ferguson's Addendum, Vol. I, p. 381.) The relative failure of that first harvest seems to have planted in the mind of Burns the dual *idée fixe*: that the farm was likely to fail and the Excise was to be his salvation. As early as 10 September, with the first harvest not even finished, he wrote to Ainslie: 'I hope for the best: but I have my Excise Commission in my pocket; I don't care three skips of a Cur-dog for the up-and-down gambols of Fortune' (L.279).

At least two hundred and fifty of Burns's letters written during the Ellisland years are available for our perusal today. Among them one might expect to find some details of his plans and programmes for tillage, liming, sowing, stocking, harvesting and marketing. But on those topics the record is frustratingly sterile. Instead we encounter a recurring jeremiad about his 'bad bargain', almost invariably followed up by an optimistic reference to the Excise back-up.

Hero-worshipping Mrs Dunlop did her best to ensure a good agricultural future for Robert Burns. She had given him a heifer as a wedding present (according to Cunningham) and her son the Major followed up with the gift of another young cow ('the finest Quey in Ayrshire': L.285). She even saw the young farmer as a potential Professor of Agriculture, joining with Dr Moore in recommending him to Sir William Pulteney – who had given £1,250 to Edinburgh University to establish the first Chair in Agriculture and Rural Economy. (The appointee to this, the first Chair of Agriculture in Britain, was Dr Coventry. He was appointed in 1790. It was characteristic of the progressive policies of Scottish universities. Glasgow created the first British Chairs in Natural Philosophy (1760); and Engineering (1840).) We need hardly be surprised to learn that Robert saw this appointment as 'an unattainable object' (L.351). He had freely admitted his limited expertise to James Smith in 1787: 'Farming, the only thing of which I know anything, and heaven above knows but little do I understand of that' (L.113). In her efforts to steer her protégé away from the Excise, however, in her settled life at Dunlop she failed to envisage a ploy foreign to her kindly nature – skulduggery. The letter which Robert wrote to Excise Commissioner Graham on 10 September 1788 (L.269) is enough to make any bardolater fidgety on reading it. After enlarging on the worn-out poverty of Ellisland and the loan he made to rescue Gilbert he went straight to the point:

> There is one way by which I might be enabled to extricate myself from this embarrassment, a scheme which I hope and am certain is in your power to effectuate. – I live here, Sir, in the very centre of a country Excise-Division; the present Officer lately lived on a farm which he rented in my nearest neighbourhood; and as the gentleman, owing to some legacies, is quite opulent, a removal could do him no manner of injury; and on a month's warning, to give me a little time to look over my Instructions, I would not be afraid to enter on business. – I do not know the name of his Division, as I have not yet got acquainted with any of Dumfries Excise People; but his own name is Leonard Smith. . . . When I think how and on what I have written to you, Sir, I shudder at my own Hardiesse.

In other words, please sack Leonard Smith and let me have his job because I need the money. Perhaps even more ethically questionable than the request was Graham's response – he agreed! He sent Burns a letter to take to Collector Mitchell in Dumfries, and on 27 October 1789 the new appointee was formally sworn into the Excise service. The salary was £50 a year plus perquisites, the latter comprising generous incentive commissions. But he really was to earn that salary, riding thirty or forty miles on each of four, or more often five, days of the week in all weathers, completing detailed and exacting paper-work each night on his return, and all that on top of the 'management' of his farm. Day-to-day farm supervision became Jean's responsibility. She had been taught to make butter and cheese back in Mauchline by Robert's mother and sisters, but field operations and farm-hand supervision were another matter. To put the issue simply, it was not the way to run a farm.

Commentators on Burns, with monotonous persistence, tend to accept the poet's write-off of the Ellisland venture as a 'ruinous bargain' without questioning the set-up in any depth. To a great extent the reputation of Patrick Miller has been caught in the same pejorative net, and that is unfortunate and unjust. But today we are not wholly dependent on scraps of information from a remote past in attempting to make a judgement on the Ellisland farm of

1788–91. For a start, we can evaluate the supposedly infertile soil in the light of scientific findings.

The soil of Ellisland is markedly different to that of Mount Oliphant, Lochlea and Mossgiel. The late Pleistocene glaciation brought a till layer to Nithsdale as it had to Kyle, but the deposited material was to be greatly modified by subsequent processes. Like the Merry Monarch, Britain's ice age took 'an unconscionable time dying' on the slopes east of the Uplands. The ice sheet first decayed to leave only well-defined separate glaciers in the valleys of the Nith, Cairn, Annan and other rivers.[40] With the slow warming of the climate the glaciers ceased their downward flow and broke up to leave great blocks of dead ice, particularly in areas where the valleys broadened. The final disposition of the till was determined by the flow of melt-water which was augmented by torrential rain. The numerous blocks of stagnant ice forced this water to flow in new paths around and below them, in many cases with little conformity to the pre-existing river and burn courses. The flows could be extremely turbulent, eroding and re-depositing the till and shattered rock to form the elongated mounds called kames, and broader areas called kame terraces. The last surviving ice blocks, well imbedded, left depressions in the ground which have been called kettles. (Some of these persisted as little lochs; others were to fill with basin peat in subsequent centuries.) Ellisland is a mile or so within the area of the Nith valley where it becomes markedly broader – an area corresponding roughly to that of the underlying Permian sandstone which extends up from Dumfries – and this area experienced the full force of the melt-water turbulence. It is a classical 'fluvio-glacial' area. The glacial retreat features of mid-Nithsdale have been mapped in detail by J.C. Stone.[41] His published map shows two kames within the Ellisland area and several more in the immediate vicinity. Also mapped are two small kettles on the property and more of these on the land between Ellisland and Friars Carse. The turbulent melt-waters influenced the nature of the soil profoundly. A high proportion of the original clay was washed free and carried downstream to settle on the Solway sea-bed while sand and gravel fractions travelled only moderate distances, and least mobile of all were the chunks of Ordovician-Silurian rock (the main parent rock of the Ellisland soil). And so were laid down the stony, gravelly terraces of Ellisland and of many farms to the east, to await the natural afforestation that later millenia were to bring.

Part of Ellisland was holm (alluvial), deposited by the water of the Nith quite recently in terms of geological time. In area it accounted for one of the six inclosures specified in the Miller-Burns lease and would probably have been of some twenty-five or thirty acres. Alluvial areas can vary relatively rapidly with time. Since the days of Burns, Ellisland has gained a new alluvial strip up to fifty feet in width alongside the 'red scaur' bank described by Lockhart in 1828. That feature is no longer to be seen, having been obliterated by erosion and the slumping of loose material from above. (A 'red scaur' may still be seen, however, about three hundred yards upstream.) The scaur was a cliff-face exposure of the original till, below the zone of fluvio-glacial disturbance. At the cliff edge above was a walking path much used by Burns when he took time off for solitary relaxation and reflection.

The high ground fluvo-glacial soil of Ellisland has been classified by the Soil Survey as belonging to the Yarrow Series. In 1971 the Macaulay Institute made detailed mechanical and chemical analyses of samples from a Yarrow Series profile taken at Bellfield, a mile or so downstream from Ellisland. The soil details of both locations accord well.[42] The cultivated zone (to about 8 inches) is a brown sandy loam with a moderate humus content. Its clay content is 7 per cent, sufficient to give the soil a blocky crumb structure and friability. The sand content rises from 58 per cent in this top layer to 68 per cent in the layer underlying it to a depth of 16 inches. Almost pure sand and gravel, with no clay at all, are next encountered. Greywacke stones of varying size are abundant at all depths sampled. Texture-wise the soil is attractive, and certainly the most easily cultivated soil that Robert Burns ever put to the plough. The bigger stones at or near the surface would have been an initial handicap but most of them would have been easily dislodged for removal. The very open nature of the soil, persisting to an appreciable depth, limits its water-holding capacity, and with an annual precipitation around the modest 35-inch figure it could cause a drought problem during an occasional period of failed rainfall. On the other hand, the soil would never require artificial under-drainage.

A 1971 chemical analysis reveals a satisfactory level of essential plant nutrient elements, the high surface figures for calcium and phosphate reflecting the benign fertilizing routines of the nine-teenth and twentieth centuries. A high ratio of calcium to magnesium (28.5 to 0.7 milli-equivalents per 100 gms.) makes it clear that ample liming has been carried out, in fact it has brought the pH up to 6.5 – close to neutrality.[42] But what was the situation when Burns took over in 1788? As an unimproved Brown Forest Soil it would have been quite acid, with a root zone seriously depleted of essential elements by many years of unrelieved exploitation.

The Ellisland venture got away to a bad start for Patrick Miller as well as for Burns. Miller's reminiscences, set down in a letter many years later (24 September 1810) tell a rather sorry tale:

> When I purchased this estate about five and twenty years ago, I had not seen it. It was in the most miserable state of exhaustion, and all the tenants in poverty. . . . When I went to view my purchase, I was so disgusted for eight or ten days that I never meant to return to this county.[43]

Patrick Miller had overlooked one elementary rule of property buying – by closing his deal sight unseen. This seems odd for a hard-headed banker (he had become a director of the Bank of Scotland) but he was a man prone to embark impulsively on unusual ventures. He became an enthusiastic experimenter on paddle-wheel propulsion of boats, extending this to steam power in collaboration with William Symington. He had sunk £30,000 into this project before pulling out and leaving Symington unsubsidized, but the project had been visionary and an important milestone in the world's technological advancement.[44] Despite his inauspicious start in paying £25,000 for the 5,000-acre Dalswinton estate without first looking it over, Miller went on to become one of the significant 'improvers' in Scotland's Agrarian Revolution.[45] He went on to exploit the procedures which were proving successful on many Scottish estates: experimenting with livestock crosses, new pasture plants and soil improvement. He introduced one of the bent grasses, fiorin (Agrostis stolonifera), to his pastures. He was not to be spared criticism for this because fiorin, while well suited to low damp pastures, could be regarded as a weed when it escapes to good grassland.

In 1788 Patrick Miller was still very much the tyro in farming matters, and he would have been very dependent on the promptings of his tenant-to-be for guidance on progressive husbandry. The lease which was eventually signed is more notable for its flowery legal jargon on incidental formalities than for its potential for farming success. The agreement was reached in that early period when Miller was motivated to act generously towards the much-admired poet who obviously needed help in achieving a secure future. For this reason, Burns could almost certainly have asked for more and got more. He could have made out a convincing case for a longer period of initial concessional rental. Three years was an unduly short period: six to eight years would have been appropriate on such a run-down farm and would probably have been granted for the asking. But an even more serious defect was the lack of a clause covering a compulsory liming schedule.[46]

Burns should have known about the importance of liming, if only by recalling the emphasis it had been given at Lochlea. Then again, in his diary of his recent Border tour he referred to various attractive farms from time to time, but he seemed to assume that their productivity was based on the natural excellence of the soil, rather than what had been done to it. A few questions asked would have put him on the right track and he certainly had opportunities to ask questions. He had dined once at the Duns Farmers' Club and twice at the Kelso Farmers' Club. It must have been common knowledge in such circles that William Dawson had been carting lime twenty miles, to make his estates at Harperton, Frogden and Graden show-places of luxuriant fields and fat livestock[47] – such strategies soon becoming talked about and copied by neighbours. (William Dawson (1734–1815) of Berwickshire was one of the most famous of Scotland's agricultural improvers. He came to be regarded as the Father of Agriculture in his area of influence.)

In the Miller-Burns lease the words lime or liming do not occur once. It is hardly believable that Miller would have rejected a proposition for at least an initial lime programme for Ellisland, covering the cost by a direct advance or by lowering and extending the concessional rent period, for, after all, it would have been in his own interests as well as his tenant's. The omission was all the more unfortunate because of the modest lime requirement of Ellisland's light Yarrow Series soil. Although we cannot go back in time to measure its pH, we can be certain that when Burns first farmed that neglected Brown Forest Soil it would have been very acid. But the low clay and humus content involved a correspondingly low lime requirement for a given lift of pH value, in fact a quarter of the amount per acre that Lochlea's Bargour Series soil needed should have sufficed. As little as two tons per acre would have meant far better crop yields and pasture quality, particularly with the stimulation of the soil-enriching clovers long held back by soil acidity. Closeburn lime had to be brought only six miles, but the only lime ever carted by Burns (Letters 223, 306) seems to have been for his builder's mortar and wall plaster. The 'plaisterers' and other tradesmen were still working in the Ellisland house in June 1789 (L.347).

In fairness to Miller and Burns, it may be pointed out that there is just a possibility that liming was not entirely out of mind in the framing of the lease, even though it was not spelled out. Under the lease terms Miller was to provide £300 to cover the cost of the buildings and enclosure dykes, and it was further specified that any money left over was to be expended 'in the improvement of the farm as to him [the tenant] shall deem most expedient'. This reads as though Burns was expected to do better than simply break even on the costs of building and enclosing. But was, in fact, any money left over? Evidently not, as Burns still owed his contractor Boyd some of his money as late as June 1791 (L.458). Ramsay of Ochtertyre, who dropped in on Burns in 1790, later wrote: 'I was much pleased with his *uxor Sabina qualis*, and the poet's modest mansion, so unlike the habitation of ordinary rustics'.[48] We need only smile in passing at Ramsay's waggish praise of Jean with a Latin simile, but his comment on the 'modest mansion' could be significant in the funding context. It does suggest that the poet had let himself go a bit when it came tò the design and cost of the dwelling. A pity. No money for lime.

Admirers determined to place Burns in the best light as an efficient farmer have repeatedly put forward the absolving view that he came to Ellisland new to Nithsdale land and its needs, and unaware of the benefits that a good liming programme could bring, but he could hardly have persisted in such a state of ignorance, as he was soon to strike up a close friendship with his neighbour Robert Riddell of Friars Carse. Riddell was one of the countryside's notable agricultural improvers, later to receive a silver medal from the Dumfriesshire Agricultural Society in recognition of his achievements. He wrote the *Introduction to the Agricultural Account of*

Dumfriesshire, printed in Singer's *Account of the Agriculture* of that county in 1812 – eighteen years after Riddell's death. In that *Introduction* he laid emphasis on the benefits to be gained by liming in Nithsdale and Annandale, and one cannot believe that he failed to press this point with Burns the newcomer. (Riddell's *Introduction* is readily accessible in J.M. Wood's *Robert Burns and the Riddell Family*, reprinted as an appendix.)

Commentators in general agree that the rental provisions of the Miller-Burns lease were reasonable, if not generous. The term was for seventy-six years with three breaks, and therefore conducive to long-term improvement by the tenant. The annual rental was on the generous side – £50 rising to £70 – apart from the shortness of the concessional rent period. For 170 acres the figures convert to just under six shillings, rising to eight shillings and three pence, per acre (Hilton Brown's figure). On prevailing rentals in the neighbourhood we need not doubt Allan Cunningham's figures: 'Much of the ground in Nithsdale was leased at seven, ten, and some fields of more than ordinary richness at fifteen, shillings an acre.' As part of Ellisland was rich holm it must be agreed that the rent asked by Miller was by no means excessive, and Burns would have had no qualms about it at the time of signing. He could not have forgotten that Provost Fergusson ('my father's generous master') had charged William Burnes ten shillings for unimproved land on the Carrick Border. After that, the Lochlea rent had been fifteen rising to twenty shillings (although subject to liming provisions) and that of Mossgiel fifteen shillings. But even at its moderate level, Burns seemed to be struggling to raise the Ellisland rent from the start, and by late 1791 he was disparaging Miller in a letter to Cleghorn, referring to 'the long faces made to a haughty Laird, or still more haughty Factor, when rents are demanded & money, Alas, not to be had!' (L.473).

Not much more can be told of the farming operations of Burns at Ellisland because details from primary sources are, like the longitude of a famous sark, sorely scanty. The harvest of 1789, the second to be gathered in but the first sown by the poet, was again poor, being late and badly affected by the weather. Confirming the latter, Chambers quotes from a letter from an un-named Sanquhar correspondent, dated as late as 21 October: 'While much was cut, very little was yet got in, owing to the bad weather.' Immediately after that harvest Burns took up his duties as an Excise officer and

Ellisland dropped back into the status of a hobby farm. It was a very ill and fatigued tenant who battled through his Excise rounds during the winter that followed, but in the spring of 1790 he was able to sow another crop. We have no precise details of the harvest of autumn 1790, but the fact that a kirn party was held at Ellisland suggests that the harvest was a good one, or at least one not to be ashamed of. (The kirn is the last handful of grain cut down on the harvest-field. Traditionally, when the kirn was taken the farmer went immediately to his highest ground to give three cheers, or 'cry the kirn', so informing his neighbours. Jamieson: *Dictionary of the Scottish Language*.) That party was later described by Robert Ainslie, who had dropped in, in a letter to Mrs M'Lehose. Clearly, there had been much dancing and merriment at Ellisland that night.

Mrs Carswell awards the Bard 'a bumper crop – "the finest the land had carried this twenty years"', seeming to quote from an unstated source of information. Barke extrapolated the Carswell assertion: 'It had been a successful harvest: by far the best that had ever been garnered from the stony acres of Ellisland since man had first attempted to crop its dour unyielding soil.'[49] These assessments may have some factual basis, but the Burns letters available to us are silent on the matter. And, bumper crop or poor crop, Burns at this very time was planning to abandon farming, hopefully by sub-letting to Gilbert. But Miller refused to vary the lease clause which disallowed sub-letting, and there the matter rested for the time being. Another crop was sown in the spring of 1791 and the poet would have hung on and harvested it in the autumn had not another character entered the Ellisland scene. This was John Morin of Laggan, who had approached Miller with an offer to buy Ellisland for the sum of £1,900. Miller was keen to accept, even offering Burns 'some little consideration' for the lease. The offer was accepted of course, and one may wonder which of the two parties was the more inwardly jubilant – Burns who was barely managing to pay his rent and which was going to rise from £50 to £70 the ensuing November, or Miller who was glad to see the last of a tenant who seemed not to share his enthusiasm for farming improvement, or indeed for farming. It was quite a tidy arrangement for Miller, as Ellisland was the only part of his Dalswinton estate on the west bank of the river, and only accessible by a roundabout trip through Auldgirth. The termination clause appended to the lease document is dated 10 September 1791, although verbal agreement must have been reached a month or so earlier.

And so the 1791 cereal crop was auctioned still standing in August. A passage in a letter from Burns to Thomas Sloan, dated 1 September, is rather elusive in its significance: 'I sold my crop this day se'ennight, & sold it well: a guinea an acre, on an average, above value' (L.466). Did he mean that the crop was really thinner than it looked? Were the bidders better predicters of the new season's grain prices than the grower? Or was it an oblique put-down of Ellisland's productivity to garnish his case for quitting? We will never know. Livestock and equipment were later sold by auction and the family moved to Dumfries, where Burns had been appointed by the Excise to a foot-walk position. The date of the move was probably late November or early December.

Of Burns' finances at this time we have little detail. Jean was later to state:

> We did not come empty-handed to Dumfries. The Ellisland sale was a very good one, and was well attended. A cow in her first calf brought eighteen guineas, and the purchaser never rued his bargain. Two other cows brought good prices. They had been presented by Mrs Dunlop of Dunlop.[50]

Jean's memory for these few details was probably reliable, even though at the time of relating them a lot of soap had passed under the wedding ring. The three beautiful Ayrshire cows that Jean remembered so well would have been the pride of the Ellisland herd. Discerning bidders would have seen them as exceptional breeding stock, and competed for them keenly. There would have been additional livestock up for sale, as William Clark in his *Recollections* stated that Burns had nine or ten cows, four horses and some sheep. There were enough ewes to warrant Jean making ewe-milk cheeses; indeed in the previous January there were enough of these cheeses to prompt Robert to send one to Peter Hill in Edinburgh as a gift (L.440). There were also hens, with a surplus of eggs to give away (L.393).

With the 'consideration' for the lease added, the cash returns from the Ellisland wind-up would have been far from trivial; in fact the proceeds of the sale of the implements and of the increased herd would have exceeded the original outlay for such items. Burns was able to depart with all farming debts paid, apart from the minor items of ten shillings owed to the *Dumfries Journal* for the final sale advertisement[51] (still unpaid twenty months later), and an account from Patrick Miller for 'one pound fourteen shillings for dilapidations in thatch, glass and slating.'[52] That parting-shot account would suggest that Miller had become thoroughly disillusioned with the poetic protégé he had wanted to set up in comfort four years earlier. The Excise *pis aller* which had so quickly subverted his benevolent plan must have been a source of considerable annoyance to him.

Allan Cunningham, whose biography of the Bard appeared in 1834, claimed that Burns left behind at Ellisland only his favourite putting-stone and 'three hundred pounds of his money, sunk beyond redemption.' The putting-stone bit may be true but the rest is nonsense. In his first letter to Mrs Dunlop from Dumfries, announcing his move, Burns wrote: 'I have got rid of my farm with little, if any loss.' In reading that, perhaps Mrs Dunlop turned her thoughts to the value of her generous gifts to Burns, really 'sunk beyond redemption' at Ellisland.

CODA

A summarized recapitulation of the rueful story of the Burns men as farmers, with some probing of cause and effect, is now offered. By the 1760s the Agrarian Revolution was making real headway, led from the eastern side from the Border lands to even as far north as Caithness. The south-west, remoter from the pioneering centres of improvement, and plagued by heavier soil and excessive rainfall, made slower progress. Both east and west shared the problem of stony land, but the east led the way in turning the problem round – by clearing the stones and piling them up as enclosure dykes. The same may be said of other vital reform items such as long leases, liming and turnips for winter feed. A new social class, the tenant farmers, was emerging. Some of those tenants would have been confident in their first venture, others vague about problems of unimproved acid soils prone to waterlogging and the chance of raising each half year the target rental – a rental that had been edged up to the limit of what the market could stand at the time of signing the lease. The rent levels were so poised that one or two seasons of bad weather would mean crushing debts for the impecunious, and possible eviction. Tenants who started with assets nil or almost nil were either very courageous or starry-eyed. In their ranks we find William Burnes, signing his formidable Mount Oliphant lease in the year 1765.

The soil of Mount Oliphant was potentially productive, but it was to remain only potentially productive until it was drained and its acidity corrected. These improvements were never to be effected during William Burnes's tenancy. An initial cash allowance covered only livestock and implements, and the purchase of hundreds of cartloads of lime, even if William knew of the need for it, was out of the question. The landlord and his heirs were either unaware of the need for liming or were unwilling to make that kind of investment in their land asset. A ruinous bargain? Indeed it was.

Things started quite differently at Lochlea. Maclure the landlord either knew about the need to correct the soil acidity or William Burnes had learnt about it and insisted on a good liming schedule. It worked, and Lochlea began to produce well, but after four years Maclure became the victim of financial troubles and began to dodge his contractual obligations to his tenant. Disputes led to costly litigation through the lack of any clarifying lease document, and the consequent legal expenses incurred by the unfortunate tenant over three years, coupled with loss of production through bad weather, brought insolvency. The death of William Burnes brought the sad affair to an end. In many ways the Lochlea venture was a *good* bargain, but it was flawed by a ruinous deficiency – of a single document.

In many ways the Mossgiel chapter was a recapitulation of the drift to stalemate which characterized Mount Oliphant, but along an even more insidious and discouraging path. Because of the aristocratic owner's money problems there was no initial subsidy, and bad seasons caused serious early setbacks which debarred expenditure on essential soil improvement. Robert moved out after three years and Gilbert struggled on hopelessly for a further ten, finally leaving heavily in debt to Robert's deceased estate.

Finally, Ellisland. Summarizing the Ellisland story is difficult because of its complexity and controversy, and the paucity of wholly credible contemporary records. The guide to a clear understanding lies in the following statement:

Robt. Burness; a man who had little art in making money, and still less in keeping it; but was however a man of some sense, a great deal of honesty, and unbounded goodwill to every creature – rational or irrational.

Those are not words intruded by some pontifying wiseacre – they are those used by Burns by way of self-introduction for his Common Place Book of 1783–5.

The Ellisland venture differed materially from the previous three in that a useful amount of capital was available at the start. How much capital? In addition to Patrick Miller's £300 for building, enclosing and improving, Burns had what was left of Creech's payments, less the £180 advance to rescue Gilbert at Mossgiel. Robert Heron, in his Burns *Memoir* of 1797, stated that:

> Mr Creech has obligingly informed me, that the whole sum paid to the poet for the copy-right, and for the subscription copies of his book, amounted to nearly eleven hundred pounds. Of this sum, indeed, the expences of printing the edition for the subscribers, were to be deducted.

Elsewhere in his *Memoir*, Heron presumed that the clear profit would have been at least seven hundred pounds. That figure accords with a passage in a letter from William Nicol to John Lewars: 'he certainly told me that he received £600 for the first Edinburgh edition, and £100 afterwards for the copyright.' Robert Chambers' estimate of the net return was £520, and Dr Currie's was £500. The figure continues to descend as we peruse Robert's own letters. He told the Earl of Glencairn in February 1788 that after deducting Gilbert's £180 he was left with 'about £200' (L.192), and to Mrs Dunlop in his letter of 25 March 1789 he wrote: 'By Mr Creech, who has at last settled amicably & as fairly as could have been expected, with me, I clear about 440 or 450£' (L.324).

Why the variation? To Robert, was the honesty he wrote about, like Nanki-Poo's modified rapture, a contractile quality? The answer seems to lie not in any lack of honesty in the computations, but in the approach to making them. The net returns could well have been about £700, but early progress payments from Creech probably suffered an insidious attrition process in the hectic Edinburgh days, with details of spending either forgotten or considered to be legitimate costs associated with publication. (The paternity suit settlement for May Cameron would probably have equalled or exceeded the equivalent of a half-year's rent for Ellisland.) In any event, it seems clear that not more than about £270, in addition to Miller's £300, were available to Burns to get started at Ellisland, and to pay rent falling due before sales of produce could cover it. The sum was far from large but it would have been enough for many a young man – other than Robert Burns. For him it turned out to be not enough, and one can doubt whether adding Gilbert's £180 would have changed the ending. If money talks, all it ever seemed to say to Robert was goodbye. He did not even await his first harvest to buy 'fifteen yards of black silk' for Jean (L.262) and a *cask* of whisky for himself. (It is possible that the cask of whisky was a gift. But Burns's letter about it to Tennant the distiller (L.291) contains no expression of thanks. It reads more as a tribute from a very satisfied customer.) Ever generous, he helped friends in need with loans and he paid for the clothing, and finally the funeral, of his young brother. The cumulative postal cost of hundreds of un-franked letters from Ellisland, at the rate of four pence per sheet, would have been substantial. He almost certainly over-spent on his house, leaving no funds for the improvement of the fields (except for some grass seed: L.336). Even when the Excise salary came along, equalling his rent exactly, he remained short of cash. His substantial account with Peter Hill for books remained unpaid until the receipt of the final auction money. The dream of 'a sequester'd romantic spot' had become a distressing nightmare.

The Ellisland tenancy was more *a bargain ruined* than *a ruinous bargain*. Burns was too easily diverted to matters other than farming, some admirable in their way, others less than admirable, and taking the Excise job was the ultimate diversion. His frequent admissions of indolence in his letters probably had some factual basis, but his illnesses and injuries must be considered in that context. It would appear that his most unfortunate trait was an indifferent attitude to soil improvement, an attitude which played a major role in debarring agricultural success. J.A. Symon, the specialist agricultural historian, states bluntly that Burns, unlike his landlord Miller, could not rank as an improver.[53] It was not that he was unaware of Scotland's Agrarian Revolution – in fact he made a point of including its leaders among the great men of his country in his Lochlea period poem *The Vision*:

Some teach to meliorate the plain,
With tillage-skill;
And some instruct the shepherd-train,
Blythe o'er the hill.

(K.62)

If that final crop of 1791 had in fact been a good one, it would almost certainly have been one of oats, the cereal more tolerant of acid soil than barley or wheat, planted in an enclosure helped along with cattle dung for several years. But the full potential of Ellisland would not have been reached in only three years of half-hearted farming, as each enclosure in turn needed the tonic effet of up to four years of ley pasture, first limed to correct acidity and bring on ample clover growth. Such leys ploughed in with their accumulated dung would have become fields ready for sowings of wheat, barley, oats, turnips or potatoes, any one of which would then have given excellent yields under reasonable weather conditions.

Burns must have realized that his failure to make Ellisland a success stemmed from his own state of mind and body. Had it been simply a matter of 'dour unyielding' or 'stubborn' soil and a shortage of development capital he would never have considered unloading his 'ruinous bargain' on to the shoulders of his even more hard-up brother Gilbert (L.324, L.419).

It would be interesting to learn precisely what steps were taken by his successor Morin to make Ellisland demonstrably productive, but such details are probably lost to the record. However, we know that Morin paid £1,900 for the property in 1791 and sold it for £4430 in 1805, and the probing commentator need note little more than that outcome. Not all of that price increase – 133 per cent – is to be attributed to war-time inflation as during that same period the price of oatmeal, an economic pointer, increased only from about eighteen to twenty-seven shillings a quarter – a rise of only fifty per cent.[54]

Burns's 'sequester'd romantic spot' – Ellisland of the years 1788 to 1791 – can make no claim to fame for enriching its tenant. It enriched others. Just call to mind *Tam o' Shanter*, *Flow Gently, Sweet Afton*, *John Anderson My Jo*, *Ye Banks and Braes o' Bonie Doon* and *Auld Lang Syne*.

Chapter Five

WHEN 'CATCH THE THIEF!' RESOUNDS ALOUD

(K.321)

Burns appears to have been sensitive to the wave of censure falling on plagiarism in the later eighteenth century. In his *Wounded Hare* poem (K.259) the version in his Second Common Place Book includes a stanza expressing fears for the 'little lives' of the doe's hapless nurslings, a word picture which seems to have been lifted from Pope's *Windsor Forest*: 'They fall, and leave their little lives in air', describing the death of larks killed by the gun of the fowler. Evidently Burns had second thoughts about using the expression and omitted the containing stanza in the 1793 edition of his poems. Need he have worried? He was familiar with the poetry of Oliver Goldsmith and possibly took to heart the message of the satirical *A New Simile in the Manner of Swift*. In that witty satire Goldsmith likened contemporary poets to the ancient god Mercury, whose feathered head suggested a feather-brain, and whose serpent-encircled staff symbolized a venomous quill. He proceeded to a postscript with the lines:

> Moreover Merc'ry had a failing:
> Well! What of that? Out with it – stealing;
> In which all modern bards agree,
> Being each as great a thief as he.

Goldsmith was being merely observant. With the flowering of Augustan scholarship and its concentration on the Greek and Roman classics, a new and extensive reservoir of themes and phrases had been discovered, and even Milton, Dryden and Pope were accused of raiding the classics and offering lifted ideas as their own. Thomas Gray (1716–71) became the special target of Wordsworth for this type of plagiarism. On this, Roger Lonsdale,[1] a modern editor of Gray's works, quotes Wordsworth:

> if I were to pluck out of Gray's tail all the feathers which, I know, belong to other Birds he would be left very bare indeed.

Lonsdale follows on with a discerning comment:

> His threat to remove Gray's borrowed feathers itself alludes to a famous passage in Horace (Epistles I.iii) which adapts a fable of Aesop to describe a plagiarist poet as a crow who disguises himself as a peacock until he is stripped of his false plumage.

This is an amusing exposure of a plagiarism sequence – Wordsworth stealing a theme from Horace which had been appropriated from Aesop, to lend colour to his charge against Gray. The message is that he who would seek to expose plagiarism in the words of others is well advised to watch his own.

Just how serious is the offence of plagiarism? This is not always an easy question to answer, as there is an ill-defined zone between two extremes. For instance, it would be absurd to feel required to state the Biblical source every time one says, or writes about, the crumbs from the rich man's table, an eye for an eye, casting pearls before swine or a labourer being worthy of his hire. The same applies to numerous passages from Shakespeare and from many other authors and poets, Burns himself included. In other words, simple familiarity and repetition have made numerous borrowings from the huge literary stockpile of the past common property. The only tarnishing hazard they create lies in their overuse, infecting a composition with clichés. However, the appropriation of another writer's inventive passages in such a way as to allow them to stand as one's own is literary theft, attracting, on discovery, opprobium if copyright is inapplicable or both opprobium and legal penalty if copyright has been materially breached. Immunity from such penalties lies in acknowledgment, with authorization when applicable. However, between extremes there is that misty zone of borderline plagiarism; typically of brief passages or themes of which the origin is often unfamiliar.

If poets and prose writers are in honour bound to avoid the use of every phrase or theme previously used by others, their task would be worrisome and their output lessened. Borrowing has even been accorded an element of approval:

> He writeth best who stealeth best all things both great and small for the great mind that used them first from nature stole them all.[2]

It would seem that Milton held similar views, but with an important qualification:

> For such kind of borrowing as this, if it be not bettered by the borrower, among good writers is accounted plagiary.[3]

Taking note of such expressed indulgences, or *ab initio*, T.S. Eliot was later to assert:

> Immature poets imitate, mature poets steal, bad poets deface what they take, and good poets make it into something better, or at least something different.[4]

In other words, absolution is to be accorded the poet who succeeds in raising the contextual standard of the borrowed expression or theme. If he uses conscientious restraint the inheritor may be seen as paying a compliment to the known or unknown originator, whose work in no sense suffers loss. Like Portia's quality of mercy, the borrowing 'is twice bless'd; It blesseth him that gives and him that takes'. (But when acknowledgment is added it is thrice bless'd.) In prose writing, a due acknowledgment is made either contextually or by a formal reference, but such devices are unsuited to poetry. Instead, the poet uses parenthesis – inverted commas or bracketing.

Burns habitually used parenthesis when he included a borrowed passage in his verse. For instance, in Fergusson's *A Drink Eclogue*, Brandy's first line spoken to Whisky is:

> Black be your fa', ye cotter loun mislear'd!

In stanza XVI of *Address to the Deil*, Burns inserted the line:

> (Black be your fa')

His parenthesis indicates acknowledgment of a borrowing. The brackets can have no other significance. But like other poets, Burns omitted to indicate what seem to be *trivial* borrowings.

Ferreting out a poet's recyclings is a popular pastime for 'parallel-spotters', to quote the tag used by Roger Lonsdale in the study cited *supra*. It can add to our understanding of a poet's work but loses its worthiness if it is pursued only to level plagiarism accusations. A quick check through Kinsley's monumental *Commentary* volume on Burns reveals about ninety 'Cf.' reminders identifying Ramsay, about fifty each for Pope, Thomson and Fergusson, twenty or so each for Milton, Shakespeare, Young and Dryden, plus one to a dozen for each of about forty other sources or parallels. Yet never once does Kinsley level a charge of plagiarism; he only broadens our knowledge of the background which helped to make Burns the poet that he is.

The fact that Burns knew no Greek and very little Latin would have shielded him from the temptations which had beset the earlier Augustans. He even tended to be scornful of such sources, laying himself open to a different charge – inverted snobbery. In the *Epistle to J. Lapraik* (K.57) he rather labours the point in four stanzas, one of which is:

> A set o' dull, conceited Hashes,
> Confuse their brains in Colledge-classes!
> They gang in Stirks, and come out Asses,
>   Plain truth to speak;
> An' syne they think to climb Parnassus
>   By dint o' Greek!

On the other hand, in Burns's *Sketch* (K.82) we discern an element of approval rather than scorn as he saw the resources of the ancients put to good use by poets he admired:

> In Homer's craft Jock Milton thrives;
> Eschylus' pen Will Shakespeare drives;
> Wee Pope, the knurlin, 'till him rives
>   Horatian fame;
> In thy sweet sang, Barbauld, survives
>   E'en Sappho's flame.

Burns appears to have found use for short passages and themes discovered in the poems of some of his more recent predecessors, but not to the extent of warranting his labelling as a plagiarist. The Miltonic indulgence – raising the level of poetic merit – stands to his defence repeatedly. Take for instance stanza VII of *Man was Made to Mourn, a Dirge* (K.64):

> Many and sharp the num'rous Ills
>   Inwoven with our frame!
> More pointed still we make ourselves,
>   Regret, Remorse and Shame!
> And Man, whose heav'n-erected face,

> The smiles of love adorn,
> Man's inhumanity to Man
> Makes countless thousands mourn!

The final two lines appear to have been inspired by either of two passages in Dr Edward Young's *Night Thoughts* – a very long blank verse sequence divided into nine Nights (filling 317 pages in my edition). To illustrate the point, both sets of relevant lines are now quoted, with some context:

> Ambition fires ambition; love of gain
> Strikes, like a pestilence, from breast to breast;
> Riot, pride, perfidy, blue vapours breathe;
> And inhumanity is caught from man –
> From smiling man. A slight, a single glance,
> And shot at random, often has brought home
> A sudden fever, to the throbbing heart,
> Of envy, rancour, or impure desire.
>
> (Night V)

and further:

> Shall truth be silent because folly frowns?
> Turn the world's history; what find we there,
> But fortune's sports, or nature's cruel claims;
> Or woman's artifice, or man's revenge,
> And endless inhumanities on man?
> Fame's trumpet seldom sounds, but, like the knell,
> It brings bad tidings: how it hourly blows
> Man's misadventures round the list'ning world!
>
> (Night VIII)

We may note how Burns made 'Man's inhumanity to Man' and its consequence a powerful climax to his eight lines, developing the theme progressively to the end of the dirge and deploring the ruthless exploitation of the low-born under a class system he can in no way change – the only relief coming with death, 'the poor man's dearest friend'. Such incisive emphasis does not leap forth from Young's brilliant but ramifying lines. An idea source? Yes. Plagiarism? Not at all.

The issue is less straightforward on the question of *theme models*. Almost every writer on the poetry of Burns seems to have been

Edward Young LLD. After Joseph Highmore. *The Poetical Works of Edward Young*, Ward, Lock & Co, London, n.d.

unable to resist pointing out that the model for *The Holy Fair*
(K.70) was *Leith Races*, for *To a Mountain Daisy* (K.92) it was *Ode to
the Gowdspink*, for *The Twa Dogs* (K.71) it was *Mutual Complaint of
Plainstanes and Causey* – all three models by Robert Fergusson. The
trouble about this kind of sleuthing lies is not knowing where to
stop, and in never being certain that the source claimed was in fact
the source. For example, an even better theme model for *The Twa
Dogs* than *Plainstanes and Causey* can be postulated. There is nothing
about dogs in Fergusson's poem; it is a dialogue about the feelings
of a roadway subjected to the rumbling wheels of rich men's
carriages and those of a footpath for pedestrians. The parallel ends
there. For a more obvious source of the two-dog theme we need
only look at Pope's *Bounce to Fop*. Bounce was Pope's own Great
Dane and Fop was Lady Suffolk's lap-dog, and in an imaginary
letter Bounce compares his lifestyle with Fop's. And it is quite
certain that Burns had read Pope's works at an early period in his
life, long before he discovered Fergusson's. (As *Bounce to Fop* is a
little-known poem – it appears in no school-use anthology, for very
obvious reasons – the full text is given in Appendix B.) Then again,
are we really tied to this 'model' business? Burns was quite capable
of working out a theme *ab initio*, and any connection with earlier
poems of others could have been simply coincidental. Who really
knows?

The technical poetic field of metrical and rhyming formulae barely
touches the issue of plagiarism for, after all, any poet is fully entitled
to copy any pre-existing poetic structure, be it Shakespearean
sonnet, triolet or limerick. But if he fails to do the job well he may
not escape criticism for his copying of a formula which he has
admired in others but in which he lacks the special word-handling
talent to bring it off. An early form which Burns used with spectacular success is 'standart habby'. This metre-rhyme structure
appears to have been invented in the late sixteenth century by
Robert Sempill whose poem *Elegy on Habbie Simpson, the Piper of
Kilbarchan* gave the form its name. Allan Ramsay (1686–1757) sent
his friend William Hamilton of Gilbertfield an *Epistle* of eleven
stanzas in that form, one of which is:

> May I be licket wi' a bittle,
> Gin of your numbers I think little,
> Ye're never rugget, shan, nor kittle,

Robert Fergusson. Ogburn, after Runciman. *The Works of Robert Fergusson*, S.A. and H. Oddy, London, 1807.

> But blyth an' gabby;
> An' hit the spirit to a tittle,
> O' standart Habby.

and from that point onwards the term became fixed in poetic nomenclature. One doesn't have to read much Burns verse to recognize its engaging metrical form in many of his highly successful poems: *To a Mouse*, *Address to the Deil*, *The Vision*, and many more. But Burns saw merit in other forms for other needs, and his ability in utilizing them underlines his versatility.

From his earliest poetic years, Burns looked to the Augustans for style and concepts, and this inspirational source tended to become more prominent in his post-Edinburgh years. He did not hide this fact. In September 1788 he told Margaret Chalmers:

> I very lately, to wit, since harvest began, wrote a poem [To Graham of Fintry], not in imitation, but in the manner of Pope's Moral Epistles. It is only a short essay, just to try the strength of my Muse's pinion in that way.
>
> (L.272)

One may assume that Fintry was appropriately impressed by the flattering lines – successfully aimed at patronage – and Burns returned to Popean styles from time to time, both for substantial efforts in rhyming couplets, and for smart epigrams and epitaphs. How well he succeeded may be judged from the following passage:

> Be sure yourself and your own reach to know,
> How far your genius, taste, and learning go;
> Launch not beyond your depth, but be discreet,
> And mark the point where sense and dulness meet.
> O Dulness! portion of the truly blest!
> Calm sheltered haven of eternal rest!
> Thy sons ne'er madden in the fierce extremes
> Of Fortune's polar frost, or torrid beams.
> Some have at first for wits, then poets pass'd
> Turn'd critics next, and proved plain fools at last.
> Some neither can for wits nor critics pass,
> As heavy mules are neither horse nor ass.
> Critics – appalled, I venture on the name,
> Those cut-throat bandits in the paths of fame:
> Bloody dissectors, worse than ten Monroes;
> He hacks to teach, they mangle to expose.

Readers familiar with the works of both Pope and Burns will quickly see through – and, hopefully, forgive – this irreverent interweaving of four lines of Pope, four lines of Burns, four more lines of Pope, and a final four lines of Burns. (Pope – Essay on Criticism, 48–51; Burns – K.335, 56–59; Pope – Essay on Criticism, 36–39; Burns – K.335, 37–40. Alexander Monro (secundus) was Professor of Anatomy at Edinburgh at the time Burns wrote the lines.)

The manoeuvre illustrates how Burns drew inspiration from Pope for one class of his output – a class which earned him little fame. Further examples of Burns treading in the footprints of Pope are not hard to find, and while he achieved some success at times he never really matched the deftness of his English idol for sheer economy of words and the ability to sustain a rapier-point satire with unfailing fecundity through many major works. Burns even trod the dangerous ground of the Alexandrine wind-up (an additional foot in the final line):

> That, placed by thee upon the wished-for height,
> Where Man and Nature fairer in her sight,
> My Muse may imp her wing for some sublimer flight.
>
> (To Graham of Fintry, K.230)

Evidently Pope's warning had not been taken:

> A needless Alexandrine ends the song
> That, like a wounded snake, drags its slow length along.
>
> (An Essay on Criticism, 356–7)

Burns reveals some kinship with Pope in the abbreviated format of epigram and epitaph. While he had some noteworthy successes in this area, he was rather too ready to fall back on black humour and bad taste for his message. Heron clearly had that trait in mind in referring to Burns's 'misanthropical malignity' as the Dumfries years advanced. It needed the unique satiric gift of Pope to create such a hilarious two-liner as was inscribed on the collar of the dog he gave the Prince of Wales – to entrap the over-curious:

> I am his Highness' dog at Kew;
> Pray tell me, sir, whose dog are you?

Burns's rhymed couplets acquired freshness and brilliance when he felt free to break away from fashionable Augustan English and perfuse his pentametric lines with his native language. This liberation gave us the delightful *The Brigs of Ayr* (K.120), written in 1786 and first published in the edition of 1787. Greater triumph followed his dropping back to tetrametric couplets plus Lallans for *Tam o' Shanter*. His self-appointed mentors Henry Mackenzie and John Moore tiresomely entreated Burns to put aside the vulgar tongue, revealing that *they* were the Philistines in the disputation.

There is an innate poetic beauty in many Scots words, particularly in disyllabics such as meikle, lyart, billie, cranreuch, aiblins and asklent. The English equivalents of these would simply

Alexander Pope. H. Worthington, after I. Richardson. *The Works of Alexander Pope*, ed William Roscoe, Longman, Brown et al., London 1847. *Courtesy of The State Library of Victoria.*

have flattened the poetry in Burns's charming creations. Who would believe that the beautiful *Of A' the Airts the Wind Can Blaw* would have been such a success if Burns, in some roundabout way, had to make do with 'directions', or even 'azimuths', to replace 'airts'? And as for 'hurdies' in *Tam*, the only replacements available are 'buttocks' or 'backside'. Dreadful thought.

Burns was drawn to imitate Pope; he did not plagiarize Pope. The plagiarism issue came to the fore with the publication of the four-volume centenary work *The Poetry of Robert Burns* in 1896, by Henley and Henderson.[5] (William Ernest Henley (1849–1903), born in Gloucester, had an established literary reputation. He was the author of several books and plays and of the defiant song *Invictus*. He had been editor of several literary periodicals, and was a close friend of, and collaborator with, R.L. Stevenson. In his spare time he wrote poetry; some of it good.)

W.E. Henley, who clearly had dominated the editorial duumvir, contributed the controversial *Essay* in the fourth volume, and opened a literary hornet's nest with unflattering comments on Scotland and the Scots of Burns's day, and with accusations of 'pilfering' by Burns. He left his readers in no doubt of his admiration of Burns as a vernacular poet:

> When he used the dialect which he had babbled in his
> babyhood, and spoken as a boy and youth and man – the
> tongue, too, in which the chief exemplars and ruling influences of
> his poetical life had wrought, he at once revealed himself for its
> greatest master since Dunbar.

He also emphasized that the 1884–6 period was Burns's most creative:

> it was at Mossgiel that he did nearly all his best and strongest
> work. The revelation once made, he stayed not in his course, but
> wrote masterpiece after masterpiece, with a rapidity, an
> assurance, a command of means, a brilliancy of effect, which
> made his achievement one of the most remarkable in English
> letters.

Few Burnsians would disagree. Henley also paid tribute to the poet's remarkable gift of humour:

> For the master-quality of Burns, the quality which has gone, and

will ever go, the furthest to make him universally and perennially acceptable – acceptable in Melbourne (say) a hundred years hence as in Mauchline a hundred years syne – is humour.

(The aptness of this prophecy for me and fellow-Melbournians, as the centenary of the Centenary Edition fast aproaches, is indeed evident. R.H.F.)
So far, so good. No pack-drill yet. But it became another story when Henley got going on Burns's source material, first on the English language poets:

> He read Pope, Shenstone, Beattie, Goldsmith, Gray, and the rest, with so much enthusiasm that one learned Editor has made an interesting little list of pilferings from the works of these distinguished beings.

Either not anticipating the reception awaiting his remarks, or anticipating a fuss and not caring, Henley moved on to the song lyrics which became Burns's dominating poetical interest after the Edinburgh break:

> He never boggles at appropriation, so that some of his songs are the oddest conceivable mixture of Burns, Burns's original, and somebody Burns has pillaged. Take, for instance, that arch and fresh and charming thing *For the Sake of Somebody*.

Following the trail, Henley saw that song's origin in 'a poor enough botch by Allan Ramsay' of an earlier poem (which he prints) but he concedes some reinstatement of Burns:

> Yet, despite the pilferings and the hints, it were as idle to pretend that *Somebody*, as it stands, is not Burns, as it were foolish to assert that Burns would have written *Somebody* without a certain unknown ancestor.

But it was not so much the 'pilfering' charges that upset the world of Henley's 'common Burnsites' as the tone of his numerous biographical and historical assertions. He had much to say about the peasantry of Scotland ('lewd, grimy, ribald') and maintained that Burns was ever one of them. He described old Scotland as 'a place out of which the Whigs crushed the taste for everything but fornication and theology'. He rummaged the Highland Mary legend coldly. He described the kirk's sway as 'a narrowing and perverted influence'. He saw *The Cotter's Saturday Night* as a sentimental and untrue picture, and much more in like vein, for which see the full text of the essay.

Henley did not have to wait very long for the angry reaction of numerous reviewers at home and abroad, and the late-January speech-makers dealt roughly with him. Dr John D. Ross[6] was even moved to publish a book in which he assembled a collection of trenchant reviews and speeches, contending in his Preface:

> There is only one redeeming feature about the Essay – and only one – it was not written by a Scotsman. Thank Heaven for that! No countryman of Burns would be guilty of laying such filth before the world.

It is obvious that Dr Ross had not seen the very long two-instalment review in the influential weekly *The Bulletin* – the periodical which had, in seventeen stormy years from its inception, emerged as Australia's potent voice of independence, never hesitating to assail privilege, smugness and hypocrisy without mercy, but ever ready to give due prominence to talent newly discovered in cultural and other fields. (The founder-owners, J.F. Archibald and J. Haynes, had earlier lost a libel action brought against them. The damages awarded were trivial, but as they could not pay the costs they were arrested and imprisoned for a brief term.) *The Bulletin* has been recently dubbed *The Journalistic Javelin.*[7] As its review on Henley and Henderson's work includes the most savage attack on Burns and his songs ever printed, and as it seems to have received no attention from Burns commentators outside Australia, some extracts, at length, are now quoted:

> From an Unsigned Review in *The Bulletin* (Sydney), 23 October and 4 November 1897.

> About the middle of last century was born to a decent Scottish laboring family a son whom they called Robert. His surname was Burns. . . . He was a capable fellow, and he probably knew pretty nearly how good or how bad his verses were. The average Scotchman does not know how good or how bad Burns's verses are, and he does not know how much Burns plagiarized. . . Burns amuses and interests, but he can rarely elevate or inspire anyone save a Scotchman. Burns inspires a Scotchman less because he is a poet than because he is

Scotch. . . . The 'Centenary' editors are influenced in spite of themselves by the Burns *mana* – by the thought present all the time at the back of their heads that they are dealing with England's envy and Scotia's pride. But their illusion seems the least that is possible to Scotchmen. They call the lap-dog for which Burns wrote an epitaph 'a little beast'; they talk of 'the cad in Burns' – O sacred Haggis! – and expose a billet-seeking democrat writing slushy verses in honour of Lord President Dundas. . . . The chief value of the 'Centenary' lies in the evidence it provides for exactly estimating Burns's rank as a poet. It has always been known or guessed that he was scarcely ever a completely original writer; but detailed proof was hard to come at. . . . By dint of brains and industry, Henley and Henderson have placed Burns's plagiarisms more clearly before the world than ever they were placed before. They were particularly fortunate in discovering in the British Museum the Herd MS, of which Burns made large use in compiling the songs attributed to him. . . . His earlier poems are Fergusson plus his own vitality; his later poems represent his own skill and taste plus the vitality of a hundred unknown balladists. . . . Burns never put more humour in five verses than Alexander Ross put into 'Woo'd, and Married, and a''. He never put as much pathos in a ballad as William Hamilton put into 'The Braes of Yarrow', or Allan Cunningham put into 'She's Gane to Dwall in Heaven'. He never put more tender sentiment in a song than Hogg put into 'When the Kye Comes [sic] Hame'. . . . Burns the songster was an inspired vamper, tinker, mender, and little more. . . . Of 252 songs in the collection attributed to Burns, 36 of the best contain so little of him that they should forthwith be struck out of his book. About 104 are more or less vamped – generally more – and practically do not belong to Burns either. The remaining 112 comprise those which are indubitably by Burns. . . . And these 112 are, with some notable exceptions, the weakest lot in the whole collection. . . . In any case, hapless Caledonia need not mourn for laurels reft and banners torn. The credit which is taken from Burns is merely transferred to Scotland . . .

It must be remembered that Burns himself, though he was not over-squeamish regarding his plagiarisms – as when he palmed off 'Behold the Hour' on Clarinda as his own – never claimed

credit for many of the verses which his eulogists attribute to him.
If he did, he might have claimed credit for a Clean-Steal like
'The Dusty Miller'. [Burns's words and the Herd MS version
quoted.] In the same Clean-Steal category are 'The Primrose'
(ravished from Thomas Carew [Now known to be by Herrick,
not Carew. (Kinsley III, 429)] – Burns himself calls it an 'old
English song, which I dare say is but little known' – wherefore
he ravished); 'Bonie Dundee'; 'Whistle an' I'll Come to You,
My Lad'; 'Landlady Count the Lawin'; 'Laddie, Lie Near Me';
'We're a' Noddin'; and some two-score more. In these cases if
Burns had not forcibly annexed the whole of his originals, he
annexed so much of idea, phrase and rhythmus that the song
would be nothing without them.

The Clean-Steal class slides imperceptibly into the Neat-
Vamp class, in which Burns contributes so much that the
product is practically a new song. An example is 'A Red, Red
Rose' – [Burns's verses quoted, plus one from the blackletter
ballad 'The Wanton Wife of Castle Gate']. In this class come
many of the songs by which Burns is best known and
loved – some 108 in all. Included are 'The Birks of Aberfeldie',
'M'Pherson's Farewell', 'It was a' for Our Rightful King', 'The
Silver Tassie', 'John Anderson My Jo', 'O Were my Love' (first
verse Burns, second and best old), and many others. . . .

In the Neat-Vamp class of Burns's songs the Derivative class
merges. Just where one class begins and the other ends is a
matter for individual taste to determine. An example of the
Derived song is 'Auld Lang Syne'. [Burns's first verse and
Chorus quoted, plus the same of the old ballad of the same
name.]

The writer's classification of the whole body of Burns's songs
goes thus:

Burns's Very-Own (as far as we know), for which he takes 100
per cent of what credit there is (and these include all the
numerous worthless items gathered by editors' devotion): 151
songs. Clean-Steals, for which Burns takes 0 to 25 per cent of
the credit: 50 songs. Neat-Vamps and Derivatives, for which
Burns takes from 25 to 75 per cent of the credit: 108 songs.

After one has diligently sifted wheat from chaff all through
Henley's fat third volume, the typical Very-Own song stands out
distinctly from the typical Clean-Steal or Neat-Vamp.

Examples . . .

> *One of Burns's very own songs*
> Where, brave angry winter's storms,
>   The lofty Ochils rise,
> Far in their shade my Peggy's charms
>   First blest my wondering eyes:
> etc.
>
> *Showing some old balladist's freedom and intensity.*
> Ay waukin, O,
>   Waukin still and weary;
> Sleep I can get nane
>   For thinking on my dearie.

Surely everybody can see the difference between this Burns paste and the Old-Balladist diamond! And the sluggish flow, the flat form, the empty idea, and the artificial trope tinselling the trite sentiment – these are all thoroughly characteristic of Burns when he wrote right out of his own head. The sincerity, the ring, the intensity (either of pathos or humour), the charm and the power – these are always the property of the rough, so-joyous, so-sad old rhymers from whom the song Burns borrowed. Often his sympathy gave their work a better form; but theirs was the living fire. The young Burns had fire, too; the elder Burns had flashes of it; but it was not the divine fire that those earlier Titans stole from Heaven [and much more in a similar vein filling the prominent inside front cover page – 'The Red Page', reserved for literary topics – in each of two issues of *The Bulletin*].

The review reflected a key component of the policy of *The Bulletin* – to be provocative; to assail *hauteur* and smugness in any field. However, it reads more as an opportunistic and unjustifiable assault on the capability and honesty of Burns, and it does less than justice to Henley and Henderson in purporting to be a fair review of their massive and useful publication. It is a perverse blend of a few truths, many sneering half-truths and plain untruths.

The jibe at 'a billet-seeking democrat writing slushy verses in honour of Lord President Dundas' is quite unfair, revealing ignorance of the background circumstances. Burns was pressed to

173

write the poem by his advocate friend Charles Hay and was not at all happy with the result. Of it he wrote 'these kind of subjects are much hackneyed; and besides, the wailings of the rhyming tribe over the ashes of the Great are damnably suspicious and out of all character for sincerity' (L.164).

The Red Page writer was correct in down-grading *Where Braving Angry Winter's Storms*, but unfair in setting it up against the superb old *Ay Waukin O*. The first-named song was written by Burns as a compliment to Margaret Chalmers, who disliked it and objected to its publication. It was not just a bad song: it was the swan song for its writer's connubial hopes in Peggy's direction. Later he was to write 'These English songs gravel me to death. I have not that command of English that I have of my native tongue. In fact, I think that my ideas are more barren in English than in Scotish' (L.644). But Burns evidently believed that a song honouring a lady of social standing should be in English to accord with her fashionable standards, and thereby walked into a trap he knew to exist.

The reviewer was not in error in exposing an element of plagiarism in one, and only one, instance – in 'palming off *Behold the Hour* on Clarinda'. It was obviously based on verses published in 1774 in the *Edinburgh Magazine*, and Burns omitted to mention that fact to its recipient. Years later, Thomson told him that he was keen to include the air 'Oran gaoil' in his *Select Collection*, and Burns, finding that *Behold the Hour* would fit it, sent him the lyric as his own (L.583).

The numerous charges of plagiarism levelled by the Red Page would hardly have been printed had the writer bothered to read the correspondence about so much of the specified lyric material. The pejorative terms 'Clean-Steal' and 'Neat-Vamp', and the assertions of 'per cent of the credit' claimed by Burns, are meaningless and an unjustified slur on his reputation. Henley had not used such terms – they are the reviewer's fictions and have no sensible bearing on the issue of plagiarism. What misunderstanding on lyric origins still exists is due to the slackness of later song publishers in their ascriptions. What Burns signed as his own, as derived songs, and as songs entirely or almost entirely by others, is made clear in *The Scots Musical Museum*. He used the code letters, R, B, or X for his own songs. Those coded Z were pre-existing songs for which Burns provided revised or new verses, in some cases with no more than the chorus retained. He used code D for Dr Blacklock's, and code T for 'Balloon' Tytler's lyrics (L.280, 285).

The reviewer went astray in writing off *Dusty Miller, Bonie Dundee*, and *Landlady Count the Lawin* as Clean-Steals, as they appear in *The Museum* unsigned. *Laddie Lie Near Me* was a song never sent to Johnson by Burns. (Burns included this song in his *Remarks on Scottish Songs and Ballads*, prefixing it 'This song is by Dr Blacklock.) The Neat-Vamp condemnation is equally hollow. The songs *Silver Tassie* and *It Was a' For Our Rightful King* were published unsigned. *M'Pherson's Farewell* and the immortal *Auld Lang Syne* were correctly signed Z. *John Anderson* was signed B with the fullest justification. For the reviewer to write off that masterpiece as a Neat-Vamp is probably his most blatant blunder. The title is all that is left of an old and very bawdy song in Burns's superb lyric, and its B signature stands as the hall-mark of the genius behind its creation. *The Red, Red Rose* is one of the few borderline cases, but Burns died before seeing Johnson's proof sheets of the 1796 volume, and one may well assume that he would have corrected the B coding to Z had he been given the opportunity. The songs only published by George Thomson in his *Select Collection* can hardly be brought into any plagiarism argument, as Burns left all editorial detail to that editor.

The identity of the review writer was never revealed. It could have been the Red Page editor himself, A.G. Stephens, a minor poet and, by reputation, a not-infallible critic.[8] Alternatively, the lone hand, or perhaps the collaboration, of the associate editor James Edmond[9] may be suspected. He had spent six years in New Zealand where he could have picked up the unfamiliar Maori word *mana*, which means supernatural power or prestige. (The word had not progressed beyond the Addendum in the 1975 *The Concise Oxford Dictionary*.) Whoever it was, his assumption that the word 'kye' was a singular noun in the title of the Ettrick Shepherd's beautiful ballad points to no real familiarity with Scottish song.

The inevitable – and presumably hoped for – reaction to the Red Page review duly came in protesting letters, for which the editor found space in generous amount. The first printed was signed 'MacParritch',[10] the sender sarcastically and briefly expressing regret that the songs he was brought up on were written by an imposter! This was followed by several article-size letters from

George Black, an Edinburgh-born, tempestuous, radical member of the New South Wales parliament. (George Mure ('Baldy') Black was a colourful character. His various occupations had included billiard-marking, country journalism, poetry writing, book-keeping and politics. He was a spirited open-air speech-maker and a clever pamphleteer. In his political career he rose to ministerial rank in 1915. His personal life was florid. He took up with a married woman, fought her husband, and fathered twelve children with her. Breaking with her he found another married woman whom he married after she was divorced. After her death he married again and had four more children. *Australian Dictionary of Biography* Vol. 7. M.U. Press.) Black had mustered all his rhetorical resources, and his string of charges in apt phraseology was printed in paragraphs alternating with responses by the reviewer, equally apt.[11] The latter rested his case thus:

> If George Black does not get every Caledonian vote in the Gibbs electorate at the coming contest, then there is no gratitude in Scotchmen. [Black was defeated in the election of April 1898.] To shield the national idol's clay feet he has recklessly exposed his own body. A beautiful specimen of Henley's 'Common Burnsite'.

The journalistic wrangle was brought down to earth by the intervention of Joseph Furphy, who used the pen-name Tom Collins. He was at that time little known as a writer, but rose to fame a few years later – incidentally, through the sponsorship of the Red Page editor, A.G. Stephens – with the writing of the delightfully humorous novel *Such is Life* (1903). In his Red Page letter of 12 March, Tom Collins dismissed the plagiarism row as secondary and trivial, pointing out that the real worth of Burns stemmed from his courage, vision and integrity, and emphasizing:

> the valuable deodorant contributed to Christianity by 'Holy Willie's Prayer', 'Address to the Unco Guid', 'The Kirk's Alarm' &c. Now name another English-speaking citizen who, single-handed, has successfully gibbetted abuses of such solidity and sanctity, or who has indicated vital truths so far in advance of his own time. This is the province of the Poet proper.[12]

The irascible 'Baldy Black' was not satisfied. He renewed his attack on *The Bulletin* and its Red Page reviewer with the publishing of his book *In Defence of Robert Burns* in 1901.[13] His text is marred by intemperate abuse of *The Bulletin* ('the plush-breeched flunkey of letters'), of the review ('the peevish maunderings of the literary homunculus') and of the reviewer ('Monsieur Frangipani'; 'Sir Know-all'; 'this second-rate tinker in criticism'; 'Sir Oracle'; 'the bilious critic'; 'an unshaven scribe with an inky fore-finger in a dingy back room'), descending to an ethical literary plane far lower than his victim's. He was also in error on some important points, as in asserting that Burns probably never heard of the Herd MS, and the value of the book is lessened by a good deal of irrelevant padding. The book attracted little notice in Australia and less beyond Australia.

This chapter approaches its conclusion with a recapitulation of an earlier remark directed at Wordsworth: 'The message is that he who would seek to expose plagiarism in the words of others is well advised to watch his own'. Then note one observation by the anonymous reviewer in the Red Page:

> In any case hapless Caledonia need not mourn for
> laurels reft and banners torn.

In Smollett's post-Culloden poem *The Tears of Scotland* are the lines:

> Mourn, hapless Caledonia, mourn
> Thy banished peace, thy laurels torn!

Chapter Six

THE LOVELY DEARS

(K.45)

In genial Burns Club circles, particularly in the treatment of the annual climactic Immortal Memory oration, there is the tendency – arguably with its merits – to regard the sex life of Scotland's Bard as a topic out of bounds, or at best acceptable for the odd throw-away comment in lighter vein. Fair enough. In such company Burns is regarded as a mutual friend, long-departed but immortal, and the sexual doings of a friend are traditionally regarded as private matters. However, in the colder field of biography and cultural appraisal such niceties are obstructive, particularly in the case of a man like Burns whose wild oat sowings often surfaced in his poetic and prose creativity. Having to bypass Puysange's Dictum may from some Burns worshippers draw critical fire, but in assessing the whole person, due attention must be paid to transgressions as well as high flights of character and genius. (Puysange's Dictum: 'Thou shalt not offend against the notions of thy neighbour.' J.B. Cabell: *The High Place.*) One sideline to be shunned is moralizing, but outside of that the requirement to be sought is the whole truth.

Dr J.L. Hughes, the bardolater consummate, found his response to the libidinous revelations in the life story of his hero in rigorous expurgation. He made his stance clear from the outset in the Preface to his 1922 book *The Real Robert Burns*: 'Only the good in the lives of great men should be recorded in their biographies.'[1] Would Dr Hughes have advocated revision of the Bible, to exclude bits like Chapter 11 of II Samuel?

Dr Hughes devoted a long chapter headed *Burns a Revealer of True Love* to the poet's amours, rapturously describing pure associations with Alison Begbie, Jean Armour, Mary Campbell and a few others, claiming that Burns genuinely and reverently loved those young ladies, and never in a 'fleshly' way. The names Elizabeth Paton, May Cameron, Jenny Clow and Anna Park are tendentiously excluded from the whole book. But one cannot believe that the author was unaware of the significance of the latter four lasses in the life of Burns, as details were there for the reading in biographies already published. Sometimes there are situations in which expurgation itself can amount to misrepresentation and distortion.

The great Wordsworth, in his published *Letter to a Friend of Robert Burns*, written from Rydal Mount in 1816, said of authors 'Our business is with their books, – to understand and enjoy them.' That ever-worshipped poet, with only one recorded amorous lapse (at age 22 in France), had made a commendable point for luminaries like himself. But when sexual adventures play a major role in a famous life, expurgation never stems the flow of exaggerated scandals down collateral gutters of time. It merely plays into the hands of the nudge-wink magpies that Burns scholars at times have to cope with at gatherings. Exaggeration characterizes the 'inside knowledge' of these sages, who invariably know little of Burns's life and less of his poetry. He is typically credited with two dozen or more bastards, left scattered along the Burns trail of old Scotland.

A quasi-expurgatory treatment has been evident in much of the early biographical handling of the Burns story. What could be described as the 'abbreviated smother' has been used, the most notorious example being Dr James Currie's comment on Burns's alcohol intake and its suggested consequence in the sexual area:

> He who suffers the pollution of inebriation, how shall he escape
> other pollution? But let us refrain from the mention of errors
> over which delicacy and humanity draw the veil.[2]

Posterity was left hardly guessing at Currie's meaning of 'other pollution'. The spectre of venereal disease was flashed into the scene, and almost certainly erroneously, as quite apart from the fact that alcoholic excess is liable to operate against sexual performance, there is just no record of Burns ever having been the customer of a prostitute. His advice to his young brother William on the matter persuasively reflects his credo:

> Whoring has ninety nine chances in a hundred to bring on a
> man the most nauseous & excruciating diseases to which Human
> nature is liable; are disease & an impaired constitution trifling
> considerations? All this independant of the criminality of it.
>
> (L.391)

John G. Lockhart fell back on Currie's style of brevity in his otherwise detailed biography of 1828, drawing on this passage in Heron's *Memoir* of 1797 and sustaining the libel:

> Too many of his hours were now spent at the tables of persons who delighted to urge conviviality to drunkenness – in the tavern – and in the brothel.

Instead of checking and refuting the last four of Heron's words, Lockhart, as did Currie, used the abbreviated smother technique by adding:

> It would be idle now to attempt passing over these things in silence; but it would serve no useful purpose to dwell on them.[3]

These small serves of obloquy, however, satisfied both their credulous deliverers and, for a century or more, like-minded readers:

> One half-pint bottle serves them both to dine
> And is at once their vinegar and wine.
> (Pope: Second Satire of the Second Book of Horace)

In the verifiable account of the life of Burns there is indeed vinegar and wine, but imagined whoring intrudes a flavour that is spurious, unfair and objectionable.

Currie's yen for expurgatory nicety is exemplified in his published text of Burns's autobiographical letter to Dr Moore. Young Robert had formed a close friendship with the sailor Richard Brown during his stay in Irvine, and of him he wrote:

> He was the only man I ever saw who was a greater fool than myself when *woman* was the presiding star; but he spoke of a certain fashionable failing with levity, which hitherto I had regarded with horror. Here his friendship did me a mischief; and the consequence was, that soon after I resumed the plough, I wrote the *welcome* enclosed.
>
> (L.125)

Currie changed the phrase 'a certain fashionable failing' to 'illicit love'. Why? The first part of Burns's assertion implies that Brown was somewhat *gauche* in his approach to heterosexual intercourse: the part following – 'he spoke of a certain fashionable failing with levity' – implies a familiar approach to the alternative activity. But homosexuality, quite freely discussed today, would then have been a sensitive topic (sodomy being a capital offence at the time) so Currie eliminated it with his alteration. The change gave Brown the wrong message. Seeing only the Currie version, many years later, he protested 'Illicit love! . . . levity of a sailor! When I first knew Burns he had nothing to learn in that respect' (quoted in a footnote by Henley). The 'mischief' caused by Brown's friendship reads as a strong adverse reaction to the 'horror' – strengthening the normal urge and leading to its satisfaction with Liz Paton not long afterwards. Alan Dent hints at a homosexual tinge in the Brown-Burns association[4] but his case is vague and unconvincing.

Some writers have resorted to an exonerative approach when dealing with the erotic adventures of Burns. L.P. Hartley, in his novel *The Go-Between*, observed that: 'The past is a foreign country – they do things differently there.' The past applicable here is the eighteenth century; more specifically Scotland's late eighteenth century. The impression offered is that fornication was then more unrestrained and acceptable than in modern times. Two factors really put any such comparison beyond our reach. The first is the discontinuance of the merciless activity of the kirk's 'houghmagandie pack', leading, when successful, to public rebuke from the pulpit and the fining of the male party. The second is the prevention of pregnancy by female-initiative contraception, a procedure which gradually from its introduction by Place's method in 1823[5] has made ex-nuptial coition less consequential, at least in terms of what may be visible later. Today's statistician figures for ex-nuptial births – typically around 12 per cent in advanced societies, and on the increase – give an incomplete picture of present-day extramarital indulgence. However, an associated statistical comparison is available: one with a tragic bearing on our topic. It is that of maternal mortality in childbirth.

Statistics for maternal obstetric death in the eighteenth century are available for some maternity hospitals. The British Lying-in Hospital, London, had a maternal death rate of 2.4 per hundred confinements in the period 1748 to 1758, that figure improving only to 1.7 in the period 1779 to 1788.[6] The Dublin Lying-in Hospital had 2.7 deaths per hundred in 1768.[7] For modern times, that sad statistic has been reduced to well below one in 2,000, and no doubt it will improve further.

As first pregnancies are more hazardous than the second, third or fourth, the old figures would have been even more melancholy for primigravidae had they been separately recorded. In the countryside, far away from good hospitals, all the maternal death rate figures would have been higher, with care left in the hands of midwives unable to cope with dangerous developments. All too many expectant mothers died from complications such as pre-existing heart disease, diabetes or severe anaemia, and developing abnormalities for which caesarian delivery is mandatory today would have been usually fatal. Even after apparently successful birth, post-partum complications such as haemorrhage and puerperal infection took all too many lives. The perils of pregnancy have traditionally been a price accepted by the married woman for the blessings of home and family and for expected support in old age, but for the single girl the hazard stood uncompensated and magnified. In disgrace, she was liable to be thrown on her own resources and unable to keep a job, and then placed in a life-threatening situation through exposure, malnutrition and infection. When we look at the maternal death-rate figure prevailing today it is clear that embarking on pregnancy is now safer than acquiring a driver's licence and using it: for those harking back to sadder centuries 'the plaintive numbers flow for old, unhappy, far-off things'.

In rural Scotland in the days of Burns, the severity of the statistical death rate facing pregnant unmarried girls, certainly not less than 2 per cent and perhaps double that figure, may not have been common knowledge, particularly for the girls themselves. Robert Burns, basically a caring man, could also have been ignorant of the tragic percentage, but were he not we must assume that his reputedly strong passions swept the risk factor from his mind as the prospect of gratification took over. Peer pressure undoubtedly played a part in his opportunist attitude to sexual conquest. He and fellow-fornicators James Smith and John Richmond constituted the Mauchline 'Court of Equity', with its satirical rules for regulating fornication. That court existed only in verse. Whose verse? Not hard to guess (K.109). Burns initiated a recorded five, possibly six, pregnancies in unmarried girls and in two instances there are grounds for suspecting consequential maternal death.

Burns's attitude to sexual success was typically one of light bravado, expressed in verse or colourful prose. He marked the first occasion, involving Liz Paton, by writing and publishing his defiant satire *Epistle to J. Rankine* (K.47). His second inspired a prose extravaganza in the style of Sterne's *Tristram Shandy*,[8] sent to John Arnot. With sustained metaphor, that letter of April 1786 described in detail the defloration of Jean Armour by its writer, who followed on with an account of subsequent flight to dodge the legal consequences:

> whilst I was vigourously pressing on the siege; had carried the counterscarp, & made a practicable breach behind the curtin in the gorge of the very principal bastion; nay, having mastered the covered way, I had found means to slip a choice detachment into the very citadel; while I had nothing less in view than displaying my victorious banners on the top of the walls – Heaven & Earth must I 'remember'! [borrowed, a little inaccurately, from Hamlet: I.2, 142–3. The correct parenthesis is: 'Heaven and earth!/Must I remember?'] my damned Star wheeled about to the zenith, by whose baleful rays Fortune took the alarm, & pouring in her forces on all quarters, front, flank, & rear, I was utterly routed, my baggage lost, my military chest in the hands of the enemy; & your poor devil of a humble servant, commander in chief forsooth, was obliged to scamper away, without either arms or honours of war, except his bare bayonet & cartridge-pouch; nor in all probability had he escaped even with them, had he not made shift to hide them under the lap of his military cloak.
>
> (L.29)

All would agree that the above writing was brilliantly contrived. What is lacking – and let us sustain the warfare metaphor – is any mention of 'enemy casualties'. Fortunately, Jean Armour emerged from the 'engagement' with only her reputation damaged, and, subsequently, a pregnancy that ended safely. Can anyone confidently say the same for Mary Campbell, and for Anna Park?

Concerning the life and death of Mary Campbell, who has frequently been referred to as Highland Mary, we have very few firmly established facts, but there seems to be no reason for doubting the traditional account of her having been the elder daughter of Archibald and Agnes Campbell of Auchamore, in Dunoon parish. Mary, as an attractive young woman, is next discovered at Mauchline in the role of nursemaid to Gavin Hamilton's young son Alexander (according to Mrs Todd, Gavin's sister), and it may be presumed that Burns first met her in that situation. Mary's posthumous image ranges down from the sublime one of the Mariolatrous following, prominent in the nineteenth century, which would equate her with Bice Portinari (Dante's 'Beatrice' and revered inspirer) to that of the somewhat less immaculate young woman described by Joseph Train (1779–1852) as a mistress of James Montgomerie, brother to Lord Eglington – even when she was in Hamilton's employ. But at least we can have some confidence in the only prose passage written about her by Burns himself, as the annotation to his song *Highland Lassie, O* (K.107) in the interleaved *Scots Musical Museum*. That page is now missing, but it was available to Cromek for his *Reliques* in 1808, and the annotation runs:

> This was a compositon of mine in very early life, before I was known at all in the world. My Highland lassie was a warm-hearted, charming young creature as ever blessed a man with generous love. After a pretty long tract of the most ardent reciprocal attachment, we met by appointment, on the second Sunday of May, in a sequestered spot by the Banks of Ayr, where we spent the day in taking a farewell, before she should embark for the West-Highlands, to arrange matters among her friends for our projected change of life. At the close of Autumn följning she crossed the sea to meet me at Greenock, where she had scarce landed when she was seized with a malignant fever, which hurried my dear girl to the grave in a few days, before I could even hear of her illness.[9]

Although Isabella Burns in later years stated that her brother turned to Mary Campbell only after his rejection by the Armours in March 1786, we must not assume uncritically that the attachment had not commenced earlier. Had Burns been doubling upon his amours he would hardly have told his fifteen-year-old sister about it. The time of the commencement of the association is entirely dependent on the quantitative meaning of 'a pretty long tract of the most ardent reciprocal attachment', prior to the second Sunday in May. Burns's graphic reference to 'generous love', coupled with what we know of his unrestrained sexual philosophy – he advised his young brother to 'try for intimacy as soon as you feel the first symptoms of the passion' (L.337) – leaves us in little doubt that Mary was already pregnant on that significant spring Sunday.

Whether the famous inscribed Bibles were exchanged on that specific occasion or earlier is uncertain, but the day of parting has been the assumed time on the basis of Cromek's flowery footnote:

The lovers stood on each side of a small purling brook; they laved their hands in its limpid stream, and holding a Bible between them, pronounced their vows to be faithful to each other.

However, as a more practical issue, if what Burns and Mary inscribed amounted to a declaration of marriage it was technically bigamous. An equivalent written declaration by Burns and Jean Armour existed; retaining its validity in Scots law despite its mutilation by lawyer Aiken to mollify Jean's angry parents.

The documented statement that Mary Campbell died at Greenock in the spring following from a malignant fever adds weight to the supposition that she was by then well advanced in pregnancy, particularly if that fever was the typhus rampant at the time in Greenock. There is quite a high survival rate for *uncomplicated* typhus in young people, but typhus supervening in advanced pregnancy would have meant almost certain death in 1786. The 1920 exhumation and examination of the human remains in Mary's grave – a grave that was found to contain three adult skulls and what appeared to be the base of an infant's coffin – neither confirm nor rule out pregnancy as a factor in Mary's death, but twentieth-century biographers have been drawn to the positive conclusion on the basis of the overall picture. Franklin Bliss Snyder, in his much-praised biography of Burns published in 1932,[10] favoured the retrospective finding of pregnancy. Scotland's Maurice Lindsay later gave all known factors exhaustive examination, and concluded that 'no other interpretation really appears to make sense'.[11]

The complete absence of confirmatory documentation of Mary's conditon by Burns himself is explainable. He would have kept the exchange of Bibles and vows secret, as later leakage of the story would hardly have helped the prospects of being granted the bachelor's certificate he planned to claim from the kirk. Furthermore, from late July 1786 onwards he was being harried by Mr Armour who was incensed over *his* daughter's confessed pregnancy, and had word got out that another girl was also pregnant to the offender it could have added fuel to the legal fire that Armour had kindled with a writ *in meditatione fugae* – even blowing it up to the fiercer flame of bigamy, a felony. Burns's letters to Mary Campbell would tell us much today had they been preserved, but they are said to have been destroyed by her father, who, (in Maurice Lindsay's words), 'came to execrate the very name of Burns.' Why? That reaction by Mary's father would not have been so savagely rancorous had his daughter simply died of a fatal fever which just unluckily had ended an innocent romantic attachment. The same parental hatred of his daughter's seducer would be enough to explain the almost complete obliteration of names from the end-papers of Mary's Bible (now in the Burns monument at Ayr).

Burns's vacillatory treatment of Jean Armour during two years from early 1786 may have *started* with the honourable intentions implied by a written declaration of marriage, and as a genuine love match. After all, his grilling over the Liz Paton affair could have helped to change his outlook in the course of a year and a half after writing, on 13 September 1784, his summarized philosophy on marriage:

> to have a woman to lye with when one pleases, without running any risk of the cursed expence of bastards and all the other concomitants of that species of Smuggling. These are solid views of matrimony.
>
> (To J. Tennant jnr, L.18)

Not exactly the romantic approach. Burns may have believed that his marriage contract had really been rendered null and void when the lawyer Aiken mutilated the document, and there is no reason to doubt that he was genuinely heart-broken and distracted during the period of hiding that followed. It is equally likely that he had every intention of emigrating to Jamaica, with or without Mary Campbell. But the publication of his Kilmarnock book and his move to Edinburgh, pocketing a bachelor certificate, seemed to have put an end both to emigration plans and any romantic and warmly lovable image with which he had previously invested Jean Armour. But regardless of whether any of that image was re-created or not, on a return visit to Mauchline in June 1787 the now-famous poet indulged his sex drive once more with Jean, now the mother of his twin boy and girl. When her second pregnancy became evident her parents reacted savagely and heartlessly, turning her out of house and home. To his undying credit, William Muir of Tarbolton sheltered and supported her during this unhappy period of her life. Amid the stresses of those circumstances, her baby girl died in October 'by careless murdering mischance' – according to Burns (L.146).

The next recorded sexual engagement between Robert Burns and Jean Armour has horrified all admirers of the poet. Very late in that second pregnancy, with most of his Edinburgh business terminating, Burns came back to Mauchline facing up to the task of deciding on his future. His plans, as outlined in a letter to Ainslie, definitely excluded marriage with Jean, but, seemingly, not sexual intercourse:

> Jean I found banished like a martyr – forlorn, destitute, and
> friendless; all for the good old cause: I have reconciled her to her
> fate: I have reconciled her to her mother: I have taken her a
> room: I have taken her to my arms: I have given her a
> mahogany bed: I have given her a guinea; and I have f——d her
> till she rejoiced with joy unspeakable and full of glory. But – as I
> always am on every occasion – I have been prudent and cautious
> to an astounding degree; I swore her, privately and solemnly,
> never to attempt any claim on me as a husband, even though
> anyone should persuade her she had such a claim, which she has
> not, neither during my life, nor after my death. She did all this
> like a good girl, and I took the opportunity of some dry
> horselitter, and gave her such a thundering scalade that
> electrified the very marrow of her bones. O, what a peacemaker
> is a guid weel-willy pintle! It is the mediator, the guarantee, the
> umpire, the bond of union, the solemn league and covenant, the
> plenipotentiary, the Aaron's rod, the Jacob's staff, the prophet
> Elisha's pot of oil, the Ahasuerus' sceptre, the sword of mercy,
> the philosopher's stone, the horn of plenty, and the Tree of Life
> between Man and Woman.

> (L.215)

This letter tells us a good deal about Robert Burns. It reflects his familiarity with the Old Testament, which he admired and studied ardently. (Ahasuerus, literally 'lion-king', was an honorific title bestowed on three different warrior kings. They are referred to in Daniel IX,1; Ezra IV,6 and throughout Esther.) The letter also, once more, reveals Burns's flair for expressive prose and imaginative metaphor, for what could have been more apt than his selection of 'thundering scalade'? A scalade, or scalado, is an old military term for an assault against a high fortress or similar elevated structure. As the occasion was only about ten days prior to Jean being delivered of twin babies, her bodily configuration at the time could hardly have inspired a more descriptive metaphor. However, on the negative side, more than one biographer has caustically condemned Burns for his timing of the event – as causing or contributing to the early death of the twins born soon after. True it is that obstetricians advise against sexual intercourse during the last few weeks of pregnancy, but there is no absolute case for blaming Burns for the sad outcome. The matter is examined more fully in Appendix C.

Value judgments on the 'horse-litter' episode should not be our concern: it was a matter involving only Burns and Jean Armour. On the other hand, the describing of details for the amusement of a third party, Robert Ainslie, was tasteless. Ainslie kept the letter for many years. It was, of course, a letter worth keeping as an example of one of Burns's special skills – the writing of highly expressive prose. Rather less than admirable was the manner of the letter's release to the world at large. Instead of passing it to a responsible archive, Ainslie allowed it to reach the hands of the editor of the 1827 *Merry Muses of Caledonia*, Scotland's underground bawdy collage of the day, therein to be valued less for its literary qualities than for its titillating potential. The precise extent of Ainslie's involvement in the publication is unknown, but if it was deliberate it reveals him in a bad light. One might have expected a greater degree of sensitivity in a man who became a kirk elder and the author of two religous books. J. De L. Ferguson, in winding up his brief biographical note appended to *The Letters of Robert Burns*, did not resist adding a sarcastic comment about Ainslie's 'piety' in that context.[12] Allan Cunningham published the letter in his Burns biography of 1834, omitting the section describing the sexual performance. Many later writers on Burns, with historical rigour prevailing, have published the complete letter.

We may presume that in her later years as a widow living in Dumfries, nobody was so insensitive as to bring to Jean's notice the explicit lines printed in *The Merry Muses* seven years before her death. If for no other reason, it would have taken her thoughts back to an agonizing period in her life. She must have been desperately lonely and distressed around the time the letter was written; going into labour for her second twins on 2 or 3 March 1788 without their father having checked up on her welfare since 23 of February – the day he arrived back from Paisley and Glasgow and immured her in an upstairs Mauchline room. Back in Mossgiel he wrote to Clarinda: 'I am disgusted with her; I cannot endure her . . . I have done with her, and she with me' (L.210). Soon afterwards he was in Nithsdale. On 3 March, the day Jean gave birth, he wrote the long indecent letter to Ainslie, stating in it that he had just returned from Miller's farm. Obviously the letter-writing task had taken precedence over riding to Mauchline from Mossgiel to see how Jean was faring. On 6 March he wrote to Clarinda again, mentioning that 'yesterday I dined at a friend's at some distance' (L.217), still unaware of the birth of the twins. On 7 March he had still not bothered to see Jean, as is known from his letter to his sailor friend Brown, of that date, in which he related in smart nautical terms:

I found Jean – with her cargo well laid in; but unfortunately moor'd, almost at the mercy of wind and tide; I have towed her into convenient harbour where she may lie snug till she unload; and have taken the command myself – not ostensibly, but for a time, in secret.

(L.220)

Snug? Hardly the right word to describe her miserable situation. She was incommunicado with, and ignored by, the man respons-ible for her plight. The anticipated 'unloading' mentioned to Brown had already taken place – four days before the letter was written, and one of the newborn twin girls, with only three more days to live, must have been visibly failing. Poor Jean. When the bardolaters make their move to have Robert of Mossgiel canonized, the events of a few weeks early in 1788 will make the task of the *advocatus diaboli* a very brief one.

The high-flown epistolary gush to Clarinda was again turned on by 14 March, with the writer of it back in Edinburgh. Perhaps by then he knew about Jean and the death of the weaker twin girl: perhaps he didn't. All we know is that in a further dozen letters to friends written between then and early April he omitted all mention of Jean, but kept harping on 'a load of care'. At last on

7 April he dropped a hint to Margaret Chalmers about marriage plans:

> I have lately made some sacrifices for which were I viva voce with you to paint the situation and recount the circumstances, you would applaud me.

(L.235)

One is allowed to wonder what the 'sacrifices' were. Abandonment of bachelor independence and Clarinda?

At some time between Jean's first and second pregnancies, Burns, for good measure, was confronted with yet another parentage quandary that he had initiated during the earlier part of his Edinburgh sojourn. When he arrived at Dumfries on the way back from the Borders tour in June 1787 he received good news and bad news. The good news was that he was to be honoured with the freedom of the burgh. The bad news was in a letter waiting there for him, dated 26 May, written on behalf of an illiterate servant girl May (or Meg) Cameron by one Mrs James Hogg of the Canongate. (The date of this letter is conjectural. Its reference to the 1787 visit to Dumfries follows Wallace-Chambers. Ferguson tentatively placed it in 1788, when Burns arrived in Dumfriesshire to take up residence.) The message of the letter was that the girl was 'in trouble', friendless, homeless and destitute.[13] Burns's response was to write to Ainslie asking him to 'send for the wench and give her ten or twelve shillings, and advise her to some country friends', and adjuring him not to 'meddle with her as a *Piece*'. Whether Ainslie complied with his request is not known, but the eventual response by May, presumably through her Canongate helper, was the issue of a writ *in meditatione fugae* demanding security for the support of an expected child.[14] History was repeating itself for Burns. It was a serious matter, for in Scots law if such a writ was ignored the next step would be arrest and imprisonment until the money was lodged *judicio sisti*. Wisely, Burns paid up and the writ was discharged in the terms of a document dated 15 August. There is no further recorded information about May Cameron, unless one cares to infer that she was the girl referred to by Burns, six years later, in a letter to George Thomson. In it he intruded a brief comment about his surprise when 'a Highland wench in the Cowgate bore me three bastards at a birth' (L.586). Robert Fitzhugh[15] supports the view that the reference was indeed to May Cameron; James Kinsley dismisses the described incident as fictitious.[16]

Burns married Jean Armour in April 1788, presumably by the traditional procedure of mutual declaration. A Justice of the Peace later fined him for the irregularity, and that remedy evidently satisfied the Mauchline minister, Dr Auld, after he sighted the relevant documentation (L.251). Burns followed up with quite a few explanatory letters to friends, generally adding to his praise of Jean and her Miltonic 'wood-note wild' a rather tasteless apologia about her limited education. A passage in his letter to Margaret Chalmers is typical:

> This was not in consequence of the attachment of romance perhaps; but I had a long and much-loved fellow-creature's happiness or misery in my determination, and I durst not trifle with so important a deposite. Nor have I any cause to repent it. If I have not got polite tattle, modish manners, and fashionable dress, I am not sickened and disgusted with the multiform curse of boarding-school affectation; and I have got the handsomest figure, the sweetest temper, the soundest constitution, and the kindest heart in the county . . . although she scarcely ever in her life, except the Old and New Testament, and the Psalms of David in metre, spent five minutes together on either prose or verse.
>
> (L.272)

Even if the unexpected union smacked of a shotgun wedding, with a novel difference – the groom aiming the metaphorical gun at himself – Burns's choice of Jean as his wife was probably the soundest choice of any he made in his whole life. She proved to be the quintessence of womanhood, giving her man loyalty, industry, tolerance – and a well-spaced succession of children. In addition to the surviving twin Robert (b. 3.9.1786) she safely delivered Francis Wallace (b. 18.8.1789), William Nicol (b. 9.4.1791), Elizabeth Riddell (b. 21.11.1792), James Glencairn (b. 12.8.1794) and Maxwell (b. 25.7.1796 – the day of his father's funeral). One hesitates to attribute the happy spacing of these births to their father's amorous abstention – the more likely reason is to be sought in nature's own kindly contraceptive, unfailing and ample lactation hormone.

Yet another Edinburgh pre-marital indiscretion was to catch up with the poet nearly four years after the initial event. A girl named Jenny Clow had borne him a baby son in November 1788, just at the time when the run-down Ellisland farm was demanding much capital and attention. Burns offered to take the infant, but just how poor Jean (pregnant again) would have coped with the extra unsought burden is open to doubt. Jenny herself solved that difficulty for the time being by refusing to give up her baby. But some three years later, only a few days after Burns had sold up at Ellisland and moved to Dumfries, he received a letter from Clarinda. Clarinda, disillusioned after her ardent lover's abrupt termination of their ecstatic romance, was in no mood to pull her verbal punches, and her letter demonstrates that she was no dullard with her pen when some gentle sarcasm was in order:

> Sir, – I take the liberty of addressing a few lines in behalf of your old acquaintance, Jenny Clow, who, to all appearance, is at this moment dying. Obliged, from all the symptoms of a rapid decay to quit her service, she is gone to a room almost without common necessaries, untended and unmourned. In circumstances so distressing, to whom can she so naturally look for aid as to the father of her child, the man for whose sake she suffered many a bad and anxious night, shut from the world, with no other companion than *guilt* and solitude? You now have an opportunity to evince you indeed possess these fine feelings you have delineated, so as to claim the just admiration of your country. I am convinced I need add nothing further to persuade you to act as every consideration of humanity, as well as gratitude, must dictate.
> I am, Sir, your sincere well-wisher.
> A.M. [Agnes M'Lehose] (Nov. 1791)[17]

It would appear that the letter touched a raw nerve, but in an effort to present an image of dignity, Burns, in his reply, switched his style of expression from the first to the third person. After elaborating his esteem for his old love in some flowery prose and a line of poetry he got to the main point:

> By the way, I have this moment a letter from her, with a paragraph or two conceived in so stately a style, that I would not pardon it in any created being except herself; but, as the subject interests me much, I shall answer it to you, as I do not know her

present address. I am sure she must have told you of a girl, Jenny Clow, who had the misfortune to make me a father, with contrition I own it, contrary to the laws of our most excellent constitution, in our holy Presbyterian hierarchy.

Mrs M—— tells me a tale of the poor girl's distress that makes my very heart weep blood. I will trust that your goodness will apologise to your delicacy for me, when I beg of you, for Heaven's sake, to send a porter to the poor woman – Mrs M., it seems, knows where she is to be found – with five shillings in my name; and, as I shall be in Edinburgh on Tuesday first, for certain, make the poor wench leave a line for me, before Tuesday, at Mr Mackay's White Hart Inn, Grassmarket, where I shall put up; and before I am two hours in town, I shall see the poor girl, and try what is to be done for her relief. I would have taken my boy from her long ago, but she would never consent. &c.

(L.483)

We have no further information about Jenny Clow and her son. It may be presumed that action followed words, with Burns, then on an annual salary of £70, making some sort of *ad hoc* provision for Jenny's relief. One may wonder whether soft-hearted Jean became involved in the rescue operation, or indeed whether she was ever told about the sorry business. But she certainly was to become deeply involved in the last of her husband's unworthy sexual affairs, he being at the time a formally married man and the incident unambiguously marking his graduation from fornicator to adulterer status. The girl involved was Anna Park.

The date would have been around late June 1790, when Burns was actively working for the Excise and obliged to spend much of his time away from Ellisland farm. The Anna Park affair was described by Dr McNaught as 'the most grievous error of Burns's life'.[18] To place the Bard in a less unfavourable light (Cunningham started it off) many early writers hinted that the beautiful blonde Anna, barmaid at the Globe Inn and niece of the proprietor's wife, tended to be over-free with sexual favours to customers – without a shred of supporting evidence. All that can be said for certain is that Burns, a happily married man conducting his religious services to his Ellisland household, did get Anna pregnant, and that a baby daughter was born on 31 March 1791. Several weeks later angelic

Jean, lactating generously for her baby William Nicol Burns, took over the added task of breast-feeding and rearing the little girl. What had happened to Anna Park is a mystery as the written record cuts off at that point, but interested biographers of recent years (including Robert Fitzhugh, James Kinsley, Hugh Douglas, D. McNaught and Robert Ford) are inclined to accept the view that she died in childbirth. Others (William Wallace, Maurice Lindsay) simply quote two alternative traditional accounts – death in childbirth, and marriage to a soldier and death in childbirth later on. That second anecdotal account is likely to be no more than a composite garbling of two reports – of Anna dying in childbirth or soon after, and of *her daughter* later marrying a soldier (which she did).

In trying to unravel the story of Anna's fate it is important to bear in mind the time lapse of ten or more days between the birth and the fostering, with Anna herself managing the feeding of her infant. In such a period a powerful bonding between mother and baby develops. What event broke that bond? The probably answer is death – death from puerperal infection, or milk fever as it was once called.

Before the twentieth century was to usher in a clear under-standing of paths of bacterial infection and the blessings of chemotherapy and antibiotics, puerperal infection was the great scourge of early motherhood, claiming its victims by the thousand. When a virulent organism gained access to a lying-in hospital in the bad old days there could be a mortality rate for mothers of up to fifty per cent. That tragic situation persisted until the campaign by the Hungarian obstetrician Ignaz Semmelweiss (1818–65) slowly brought recognition of the underlying cause – the lack of even elementary hygiene in the hospitals, and, in particular, the unwashed hands of the doctors!

All things considered, it would appear that Burns, to his dismay, unexpectedly found himself responsible for the continuing survival of a baby girl whose mother had tragically died, and took the only course that was open to him – to own up and take his new daughter to his wife to carry on with the breast-feeding. 'Had that refreshment been denied', little Elizabeth, like young Strephon, might have died. To Jean's everlasting credit it was not denied.

Mention of Anna Park is conspicuously absent in all of Burns's extant letters, and he wrote only one poem (a song lyric) of which

Anna was clearly the heroine. He kept it under wraps for more than two years, but eventually, when proposing lyrics for an air under discussion, he informed Thomson:

> I have made one, a good while ago, which I think, is the best love-song I ever composed in my life; but in its *original* state, is not quite a lady's song.

(L.557)

Evidently Thomson thought it not quite a lady's song even in the toned-down form in which he received it, as he passed it over for his *Select Collection*. Literally, he didn't want a bar of it. Unless one accepts the word 'love' in its crude sense to mean physical union, it cannot be called a love-song:

> Yestreen I had a pint o' wine,
> A place where body saw na;
> Yestreen lay on this breast o' mine
> The gowden locks of Anna.
> The hungry Jew in wilderness
> Rejoicing o'er his manna,
> Was naething to my hiney bliss
> Upon the lips of Anna. –
>
> Ye Monarchs take the East and West
> Frae Indus to Savannah!
> Gie me within my straining grasp
> The melting form of Anna. –
> There I'll despise Imperial charms,
> An Empress or Sultana,
> While dying raptures in her arms
> I give and take with Anna!!!
>
> Awa, thou flaunting god o' day!
> Awa, thou pale Diana!
> Ilk star, gae hide thy twinkling ray!
> When I'm to meet my Anna. –
> Come, in thy raven plumage, Night;
> Sun, moon and stars withdrawn a';
> And bring an angel pen to write
> My transports wi' my Anna. –

(K.320)

These verses (and a similar fourth verse added later) clearly celebrate the raptures of an initial event without even a passing thought spared for consequences. The stars addressed were given a very different context to the lingering one that ushered in the anniversary of the day Mary Campbell died. (See 'Thou Lingering Star with Lessening Ray'. K.274) Guilt and remorse over Anna were to arrive quite a bit later, but arrive they surely did. Burns always seemed to turn to Ainslie when he needed a confidant about sexual triumphs or their bad outcome, and some nine or ten months after Anna's *accouchement* he wailed:

> Can you minister to a mind diseased? [It is a strange coincidence that this quotation refers to Lady Macbeth, indirectly guilty of murder. *Macbeth*, V. 3. 40.] Can you, amid the horrors of penitence, regret, remorse, headache, nausea, and all the rest of the damned hounds of hell that beset a poor wretch who has been guilty of the sin of drunkenness – can you speak peace to a troubled soul? . . . here I must sit, a monument of the vengeance laid up in store for the wicked, slowly counting every chick of the clock as it slowly, slowly numbers over these lazy scoundrels of hours, who, damn them! are ranked up before me, every one at his neighbour's backside, to pour on my devoted head – and there is none to pity me. My wife scolds me, my business torments me, and my sins come staring me in the face, every one telling a more bitter tale than his fellow.
>
> (L.482)

Why such abject misery? It would seem that 'the horrors of penitence, regret, remorse' had driven him to the bottle. Remorse over what? His earlier treatment of Jean? No, that had been put to rights by marriage. His lapses with May Cameron and Jenny Clow? Hardly. Miss Cameron had been paid off, and similar compensation for Miss Clow was pending. His rather indifferent farming performance? Surely not. He had unloaded Ellisland 'at little or no loss'. His Muse had not fled – with *Tam o' Shanter* such a rip-roaring success only recently. The explanation staring us in the face is the Anna Park calamity, in which a few blissful moments had been paid for in the cruel currency of death and humiliation. It was to be the last of Burns's sexual transgressions.

Throughout his life Burns clung obstinately to a rationalizing philosophy about sexual performance, never loath to off-load his prime responsibility heavenwards. It was probably as early as his Irvine period when he wrote:

> Thou know'st that Thou hast formed me,
> With Passions wild and strong;
> And list'ning to their witching voice
> Has often led me wrong.

(K.13)

and in *The Vision*, one of his finest Mossgiel poems, the same theme reappeared:

> But yet the light that led astray,
> Was light from Heaven.

(K.62)

He left God-implanted passions out of the argument when he invoked the comparison between killing in war and procreation, first in the Mossgiel poem *Nature's Law*:

> Let other heroes boast their scars,
> The marks of sturt and strife;
> And other poets sing of wars,
> The plagues of human life;
>
> Shame fa' the fun; wi' sword and gun
> To slap mankind like lumber!
> I sing his name, and nobler fame,
> Wha multiplies our number.

(K.126)

and later (1795 or 1796) in Dumfires:

> I murder hate by field or flood,
> Tho' glory's name may screen us;
> In wars at home I'll spend my blood,
> Life-giving wars of Venus:
> The deities that I adore
> Are social peace and plenty;
> I'm better pleased *to make one more*,
> Than be the death of twenty. –

(K.534)

That line of argument suited Burns down to the ground, as:

To observations which ourselves we make,
We grow more partial for the observer's sake;
(Pope: *Moral Essays*, Ep. 1, 11–12.)

but it has lost a good deal of its eloquence in modern times with
our planet suffering sorely from a plague of people.

Burns earned well-merited and immortal fame for his many
magnificent love songs and, by superficial inference, he has been
traditionally accorded the posthumous status of the celebrated
lover, in the loftiest sense. To a limited extent this may be justified,
but there was always a dichotomy in his stance on love. Let
whoever wishes to accept the offered image of the creator of *Of A'
the Airts, John Anderson* and *Bonny Wee Thing* do so, but a confession
he made is worth keeping in mind:

> but however I may deal in fiction, under my Poetic Licence, I
> sacredly stick to truth in Prose.

(L.274)

Very well, let's have some more of his Prose:

> The welfare & happiness of the beloved Object is the first &
> inviolate sentiment that pervades my soul; & whatever pleasures
> I might wish for, or whatever might be the raptures they would
> give me, yet, if they interfere & clash with that first principle, it
> is having these pleasures at a dishonest price, & Justice forbids,
> & Generosity disdains the purchase! *As to the herd of the Sex, who
> are good for little or nothing else, I have made no such agreement with
> myself*; but where the Parties are capable of, & the Passion is, the
> true Divinity of love – the man who can act otherwise than I have
> laid down, is a Villain! [Italics mine]

(L.646)

When writing to George Thomson, Burns tended to be open and
uninhibited as the collaboration progressed. In the above passage
he made clear to Thomson, and to posterity, his sexual philosophy
with unique clarity. His women were class A or class B. In A were
those he loved or respected, accepting due responsibility for their
continuing welfare. Those in B, 'the herd of the sex', stood only as
a reserve to be drawn upon opportunistically for libidinous
gratification. There is no problem in finding Liz Paton, May
Cameron, Jenny Clow and Anna Park in class B, but what of Mary

Campbell, Jean Armour and Clarinda? Mary's classification has to remain unresolved. Jean suffered some to-and-from shuffling but seemed to make it to class A eventually. The brief affair with Clarinda calls for its own exclusive pigeonhole, one accommodating a sort of A–B hybrid. True, sentiments of great eloquence in *Ae Fond Kiss* sound with a genuine ring, but the history of the attachment suggests that the greatly admired lyric owes less to reality than to the Muse.

In the works of some of the later and less restrained writers we find a questioning of the very existence of 'the true divinity of love' in the life of Robert Burns. Angellier made no bones about it, asserting that Burns was never in love.[19] Hilton Brown considered that 'in his sexual life Burns was something of an animal'.[20] No writer eulogized the Burns love songs more forcefully than did Christina Keith, but, in referring to his dealings with Peggy Chalmers and Maria Riddell, she claimed that Burns's purpose in love was 'merely animal'.[21] Burns had much to say about love in his verses, but it would seem that his endless striving for poetic creativity crowded out that special progression to mutual affection discovered by lovers, leaving the sexual animal unsatisfied but poised to break bounds as opportunities arose. Whether such assertions are true, or unjust to the memory of Burns, it would seem that in matters amorous he did have trouble in striking a balance. Blaise Pascal had found words for the separateness of heart and head – 'Le coeur a ses raisons que le raison ne connaît point' ('The heart has its reasons, of which reason knows absolutely nothing.' *Pensées* IV, 277). But Burns, from his earliest creative years to his latest, insisted that for him love and verse-making were intangibly combined. In 1783, his salad days, he wrote:

> For my own part I never had the least thought or inclination of turning Poet till I got once heartily in love, and then Rhyme and Song were, in a manner, the spontaneous language of my heart.
>
> (First Common Place Book)

And to George Thomson in 1794:

> I put myself on a regimen of admiring a fine woman; & in proportion to the adorability of her charms, in proportion you are delighted with my verses.
>
> (L.644)

It must be remembered that the love that stirred the Muse to action for Burns could be Class A or Class B. In Class A the charms of Elison Begbie inspired the early song *On Cessnock Banks* (K.11), with its warm effusions about rogueish een, red lips and white teeth, and, ever respectfully, no descent to features below the waist. In the same class but with maturity of treatment were poetic tributes to Jean and Phyllis McMurdo, Deborah Davies, Elizabeth Burnett, Lesley Baillie, Jessie Lewars and others. For his much more famous and very own Jean Armour we can observe a progression from B to A as the passionate Ayrshire events fade into the past and the marriage brings an enduring and fruitful relationship. Burns was not just striking attitudes when he wrote *Of A' the Airts, O Were I on Parnassus Hill, My Wife's a Winsome Wee Thing* and, with health ebbing in 1795, his fine tribute to his wife in *Their Groves of Sweet Myrtle.* Jean Armour is the great lady of the Burns story. She worshipped her husband, and to her last days suppressed, or made light of, his failings.

For the unwary, the ageless popularity of 'Jean' as a given name can lead to errors in identifying Burns's heroines. The ballad *There Was a Lass and She Was Fair* (K.414), usually titled 'Bonnie Jean', honours Jean McMurdo, not Jean Armour. The context prevents confusion over Jean Ronald in *The Ronalds of the Bennals* (K.40), and the absence of the actual name in *The Blue-eyed Lassie* (K.232), complimenting Jean Jaffrey of Lochmaben, does the same. The poet's use of a pseudonym has minimized confusion in the case of Jean Lorimer, but his use of the name 'Jeanie' in several songs in her praise is somewhat ambiguous.

There is no call to downgrade Burns's relationship with Jean Lorimer, despite the fact that he admired her warmly and invested her with the attractive pseudonym 'Chloris' – the generic name of the greenfinch. He wrote about thirty songs of which she was the acclaimed or inferred heroine. He began that sequence in the role of proxy wooer for a brother exciseman John Gillespie, unsuccessfully. After a failed marriage Jean frequently visited Burns and his wife. From all accounts, unhappy Jean Lorimer, the *Lassie wi' the Lint-white Locks*, was particularly beautiful, but Burns referred quite emphatically to 'the guileless simplicity of Platonic love' when describing the relationship in a letter to George Thomson with the lyric *Craigieburn-wood* that honoured the lady in question (L.644). The 'Platonic' assurance could have much to do with the fact that the Chloris group of lyrics is more notable for quantity than quality. It is quite unfortunate that J.G. Lockhart believed Allan Cunningham's libellous comments on Jean Lorimer and printed them in his 1828 biography:

> The beauty of Chloris . . . has added many charms to Scottish song; but that which has increased the reputation of the poet, has lessened that of the man. Chloris was one of those who believe in the dispensing power of beauty, and thought that love should be under no demure restraint; and it is not wonderful, therefore, that the poet should celebrate the charms of a liberal beauty, who was willing to reward his strains.

Typical Cunningham fantasies. See also Ford[22] on the issue.

Burns's genius-wrought bawdy compositions stand in a class apart. Many of them were written for the amusement of fellow Crochallan Fencibles during the Edinburgh period, although *My Girl She's Airy* and *The Fornicator* are undisguised references to the earlier Lizzie Paton affair. The provenance, merit and importance of Burns's bawdy poems and songs are the subject of a scholarly analysis by R.D.S. Jack in a recently published collection of essays.[23]

For those who cling to a traditional belief that sexuality without procreative intention and church-sealed contract is innately sinful, the Burns story is wide open for moralistic pronouncement. Such standards vary with place and time, but, in an objective assessment, the offence which cannot be shrugged off is indifference to bad consequences. Even so, defenders of Burns have come forward. Shakespeare's Mariana had already said:

> They say, best men are moulded out of faults; and, for the most, become much more the better for being a little bad.
>
> *Measure for Measure*, V. 1. 437–9

No woman in Burns's life understood him better than did Maria Riddell, and soon after his death she wrote of him:

> He was candid and manly in the avowal of his errors, and his avowal was a reparation.

And in further amplification:

I will not, however, undertake to be the apologist of the irregularities even of a man of genius, though I believe it is as certainly understood that genius never was free of irregularities, so that their absolution may in great measure be justly claimed, since it is evident that the world must have continued very stationary in its intellectual requirements had it never given birth to any but men of plain sense. Evenness of conduct, and a due regard to the decorums of the world, have been so rarely seen to move hand in hand with genius, that some have gone so far as to say (though there I cannot wholly acquiesce), that they are even incompatible; but, be it remembered, the frailties that cast their shade over the splendour of superior merit are more conspicuously glaring than where they are the attendants of mere mediocrity. It is only on the gem we are disturbed to see the dust; the pebble may be soiled, and we do not regard it. The eccentric intuitions of genius too often yield the soul to the wild effervescence of desires, always unbounded, and sometimes equally dangerous to the repose of others as fatal to its own.

('Candidior', *Dumfries Journal* August 1796)[24]

An innovative approach to a defence of Burns for his attitude to women appeared in 1982 in Dr William J. Murray's essay entitled *The Women in Burns's Poems and Songs: the Poet as Liberationist.* Illustrating his argument by quoting numerous poetic passages, Murray pointed out that Burns, in a male-dominated age, was unusual in his recognition of the respect and independence due to women as equal partners with men in their daily labour, sexual fulfilment, home organization and pleasures.[25] Murray was right in the points he made, duly emphasizing the fact that Burns lived in days when few women even dreamed of challenging their subservience, and real liberation was not yet even a rushlight on the distant horizon of time. The picture of Burns's relatively happy peasant women contrasts sharply with one drawn for Lily Armstrong by Neil Munro in *Ayrshire Idylls.* When the mother of the hill-farming brothers of Clashlet – Dugald, Paul and John – died, Dugald said to John: 'We need a woman-body here in Clashlet; wool is going down; we cannot afford to depend on housekeepers; you, John, better cast an eye about for a good strong wife.' John quickly found Lily Armstrong, and she proceeded forthwith to unremitting labours of a slave, and with a slave's subservience: 'She died on the verge of forty, prematurely aged and broken – heart and body; and her husband, who had always had some glimmering of the truth, wept maudlin tears upon her grave.'

If Burns's embryonic support for women's liberation is to be recognized as real, it must be recognized also for its limitations and vagueness. The eighteenth century, the one which brought to Scotland the Agrarian and Industrial Revolutions, had uprooted a large fraction of the humbler orders of women from the quiet shelter of the cotter's home where they had long shared with men the fluctuating fortunes of good and bad seasons. As the century advanced, conditions forced growing numbers of young women away from field and dairy into the developing mines and factories as farming returns for the less-favoured often became less than marginal. In those new spheres of occupation, both men and women were mercilessly exploited for cheap labour, but the lot of the women was particularly bad. A print of the period depicts an eleven-year-old girl carrying on her stooped back a hundredweight of coal from the working-face in a Scottish mine.[26] But to Burns, secondary and mining industry seemed to be almost an unknown world; a world anomalously overlooked by one with acclaimed zeal for reform in other directions. It was his radical English contemporary Blake who fired the first armour-piercing word-missile at the dark Satanic mills. Burns seemed to harbour an active dislike for secondary industry – an attitude revealed on his visit to the Carron foundry to kill time on a dull Sunday. He found the place closed, and reacted with a humorous jibe in verse (see *Verses Written on a Window of the Inn at Carron*, K.165). His reaction to the conditions in the lead mine at Wanlockhead was even more negative. He had been invited there by Maria Riddell, and according to that lady, his impressive conversation underground was suddenly terminated by a claustrophobic turn. No poetry.

In the absence of more convincing pleas, commentators from time to time have defended Burns in his sexual ardour by enlarging on his love of children. He certainly did love the children who were fortunate enough to join his family circle, whether sought or unsought. Jean was quoted as saying of her husband that

during the whole time they were living in Dumfries, although often out at convivial meetings till a late hour, he never on one single occasion, however late he might be of coming home, failed in a nightly custom he invariably observed before coming to bed of going into the room where his children slept and satisfying himself that they were all comfortably 'tucked in and sleeping soundly'.[27]

The Reverend James Currie, in the course of a television interview (as reported by Dorothy K. Haynes) observed that 'he never left a bairn. He owned them all, and looked after them. You must admit that.'[28] But in such a defence some qualifications intrude. He 'looked after' Lizzie Paton's daughter by landing her on his mother and Gilbert at Mossgiel. True, he did assign the copyright of the Kilmarnock volume poems to Gilbert for the child's maintenance, but before the copyright yielded any more returns he sold it to Creech. Whatever he did for May Cameron's bairn or bairns was by way of response to a legal writ. He 'looked after' Jenny Clow's little son by trying, unsuccessfully, to encumber his pregnant wife with his care. It took Clarinda's epistolary arm-twisting, years later, to extract some funds from the father for destitute Jenny's relief. The main responsibility for Anna Park's little baby fell squarely on Jean – not so much on 'the rantin dog the daddie o't'. Extra baby-clouts could be bought by the father for a few pence in a few minutes, but it was Jean who had the washing of them for a year or more under very trying domestic conditions. Emphasis on Burns's love of children, and on what he did or did not do for them, is not remotely helpful in any search for redeeming features in the story of his irregular sexual adventures.

A more persuasive defence of Burns would be available had the record revealed that he was simply the handsome victim of infatuated girls who made sexual advances – advances which he, being human, did not always resist. To rephrase the postulate as a question – did a few words from a gifted tongue and some flashes of two big brown eyes amount to a recipe for instant nymphomania? A contributing factor perhaps, but then Burns was not noted for passivity in matters sexual.

Of one thing we can be sure. Burns was a thoughtful and compassionate man and he did not escape the assaults of a pressing conscience in the train of his lapses – reactions that would have deepened the episodes of depressive illness plaguing him from time to time; particularly in his declining years at Dumfries. Had he encountered them, he would have agreed with John Norman's words, written a century before his time:

> You cannot lock conscience out of your closets or counting-houses. . . . The most secret omission or commission can never escape the privy search of conscience, or its judicial censure. It searcheth all the inward parts of the belly.[29]

Chapter Seven

BUT WHY, O' DEATH, BEGIN A TALE?

(K.79)

ASSERTIONS AND ABERRATIONS

Yes indeed. Why of Death – in this case the death of Robert Burns – begin a tale? At the 1979 Conference of the Burns Federation, an impromptu discussion on the cause of the Bard's death closed soon after a delegate asked 'What does it matter how Burns died?'[1] It does matter to those who feel some concern about the contumely settled upon some of his well-meaning contemporaries and early biographers. If some belated justice, be it only Jeddart justice, can be found for such people, it should be sought. (Jeddart Justice. In the seventeenth century one Jennet, a lawyer, proposed to the Scottish Parliament that captured highwaymen be summarily hanged, and tried afterwards! The measure was approved. This type of 'justice', with a slight garbling of the name, became known as 'Jeddart justice'. See W.E. Aytoun on Gilderoy in *The Ballads of Scotland*, 1870.) Apart from that, it is simply wrong that the medical history of Burns, not without its influence in his poetry, should remain biographically untidy.

For some 130 years after his death it was widely believed that Burns died of excessive alcohol intake. The first writer to give currency to the alcohol story was Robert Heron, in publishing his *Memoir of Burns* in 1797.[2] No writer was ever more eulogistic on the exalted mind and poetic genius of his subject than was Heron, describing him as 'an honest, proud, warm-hearted man; of high passions, a sound understanding, a vigorous and excursive imagination'. He was the only writer of an extended biography on Burns who had been well acquainted with him, and accordingly his assertions became widely accepted. But twentieth-century writers have vilified Heron for his description of the declining years of Burns, even though the *Memoir* author laid most of the blame for excessive drinking on the company Burns kept. Of the Ellisland circle he wrote:

With these gentlemen, while disappointments and disgusts continued to multiply upon him in his present situation, he persisted to associate every day more eagerly. His crosses and disappointments drove him every day more and more into dissipation, and his dissipation tended to enhance whatever was disagreeable in the state of his affairs.

Heron then proceeded to a lengthy description of the undimmed output of fine poems and songs during those and subsequent Dumfries years, but noted with justification the trend to 'misanthropical malignity' creeping into some such items. Of the Dumfries period he wrote:

Foolish young men, such as writers' apprentices, young surgeons, merchants' clerks, and his brother excisemen, flocked eagerly about him, and from time to time pressed him to drink with them, that they might enjoy his wicked wit. His friend Nicol made one or two autumnal excursions to Dumfries, and when they met in Dumfries, friendship, and genius, and wanton wit, and good liquor, could never fail to keep Burns and Nicol together, till both the one and the other were as dead drunk as ever Silenus was. . . . [Silenus, son of Pan and Gaia, was the chief satyr. He had noteworthy voluptuous inclinations, and attended Dionysus faithfully.] At last, crippled, emaciated, having the very power of animation wasted by disease, quite broken-hearted by the sense of his errors, and of the hopeless miseries in which he saw himself and his family depressed; with his soul still tremblingly alive to the sense of shame, and to the love of virtue; yet even in the last feebleness, and amid the last agonies of expiring life, yielded readily to any temptation that offered the semblance of intemperate enjoyment, he died at Dumfries, in the summer of the year 1796, while he was yet three or four years under the age of forty.

At least one of those claims is undeniably factual: 'having the very power of animation wasted by disease'.

When Dr James Currie accepted the task of writing an account of the life and works of Burns, the proceeds of which were to be devoted to the welfare of Jean and the children, he had to decide whether or not to make mention of the decline version as published by Heron. At that time, it would have been fitting to omit such distressing details with close relatives still around. But it would appear that the testimony of William Maxwell, friend of and personal physician to Burns, did nothing to encourage either disbelief or complete suppression, nor did the imparted reminiscences of another close friend, John Syme. The result was a compromise account; one which may be seen as a gentler version of the Heron story, but with the *imprimatur* of a definitive biography seeming to give it the status of revealed truth:

> Endowed by nature with great sensibility of nerves, Burns was, in his corporeal, as well as in his mental system, liable to inordinate impressions; to fever of body, as well as of mind. This predispositon to disease, which strict temperance in diet, regular exercise, and sound sleep, might have subdued, habits of a very different nature strengthened and inflamed. Perpetually stimulated by alkohol in one or other of its various forms, the inordinate actions of the circulating system became at length habitual; the process of nutrition was unable to supply the waste, and the powers of life began to fail. Upwards of a year before his death, there was an evident decline in our poet's personal appearance, and though his appetite continued unimpaired, he was himself sensible that his constitution was sinking. In his moments of thought he reflected with the deepest regret on his fatal progress, clearly foreseeing the goal towards which he was hastening, without the strength of mind necessary to stop, or even to slacken his course. His temper now became more irritable and gloomy; he fled from himself into society, often of the lowest kind. And in such company that part of the convivial scene, in which wine increases sensibility and excites benevolence, was hurried over, to reach the succeeding part, over which uncontrouled passion generally presided. He who suffers from pollution of inebriation, how shall he escape other pollution? But let us refrain from the mention of errors over which delicacy and humanity draw the veil. . . .
>
> From October, 1795, to the January following, an accidental complaint confined him to the house. A few days after he began to go abroad, he dined at a tavern, and returned home about three o'clock in a very cold morning, benumbed and intoxicated. This was followed by an attack of rheumatism which confined him about a week. His appetite now began to fail; his hand

shook, and his voice faultered on any exertion or emotion. His pulse became weaker and more rapid, and pain in the larger joints, and in the hands and feet, deprived him of the enjoyment of refreshing sleep. . . .

About the latter end of June he was advised to go into the country, and impatient of medical advice, as well as of every species of controul, he determined for himself to try the effects of bathing in the sea. For this purpose he took up his residence at Brow, in Annandale, about ten miles east of Dumfries, on the shore of the Solway-Firth.

[In three interposed pages is a melancholy account of Burns visiting Maria Riddell who was at that time staying nearby.]

At first Burns imagined that bathing in the sea had been of benefit to him: the pains in his limbs were relieved; but this was immediately followed by a new attack of fever. When brought back to his own house in Dumfries, on the 18th of July, he was no longer able to stand upright. At this time a tremor pervaded his frame; his tongue was parched, and his mind sunk into delirium, when not roused by conversation. On the second and third day the fever increased, and his strength diminished. On the fourth, the sufferings of this great but ill-fated genius were terminated, and a life was closed in which virtue and passion had been at perpetual variance.

A footnote was appended by Currie: 'The particulars respecting the illness and death of Burns, were obligingly furnished by Dr Maxwell, the physician who attended him.'

The Heron-Currie account of decline and death became the widely accepted version, with some writers giving it added effect with undocumented anecdotal additions. Belated efforts by Gilbert Burns to vindicate his brother's character were of little avail. Gilbert edited a new edition of the Currie work in 1828 and took the opportunity of adding Appendix V, in it testifying to his brother's moderation in alcohol consumption, and adding supportive testimonies by Findlater of the Excise, and by Gray teacher at Dumfries Grammar School. Findlater's image of reliability is perhaps a little dimmed by the inscription written by Burns in a gift copy of the *Select Collection*: 'A pledge of rooted Friendship, well watered with many a bottle of good Wine.'

Burns certainly made frequent mention of his drinking in his numerous letters, but the intensity and frequency of his indulgence are difficult to quantify. At the innocuous end of a theoretical range we might see Burns as a prototype Alf Reesling, a fictional character who was seen once in the street under the influence and was forever afterwards referred to as the town drunkard.[3] At the other extreme, had excessive alcohol intake led to gross nutritive imbalance it could have been the cause of liver disease and premature death. But no discerning biographer of repute accepts the latter interpretation any more.

The ineffectiveness of the early defensive disclaimers lay in the absence of any *alternative* medical explanation of the poet's early death. After all, he did die aged only thirty-seven for some very good reason, but the relatively unenlightened state of medical science in the late eighteenth century, and indeed far into the nineteenth century, meant that no convincing alternative to an alcohol-related decline could be offered. The situation is very different now, but in order to tease out a fully acceptable explanation from the tangled medical record of Burns we must treat the stony path of *retrodiagnostics*. (A muted apology is offered to purists for this Latin-Greek neologistic chimaera. But it is high time we had a word for this popular activity, and this one is surely not more reprehensible than television, cosmonaut, or retro-pharyngeal.) At least this is a branch of the medical art which is entirely free of any risk of incurring punitive damages for a mistake. But it involves all the perils of error associated with *a posteriori* deduction, calling to mind the case of Brian Vaux's egg-stealing poodle named George, and his reaction after his master spiked the eggs in the hens' nest with mustard. (George responded by going back to the coop and biting off the heads of all the hens.)[4]

No physician ever put a stethoscope to Robert Burns's chest or placed a clinical thermometer in his mouth. No pathologist checked his erythrocyte sedimentation rate, his blood and urine chemistry, his electrocardiogram, or a swab culture from his throat. The enlightenment on what those things were aimed at, let alone the equipment and technique for carrying them out, was very far in the future in Burns's day. Late eighteenth-century anatomical knowledge, and some aspects of empirical pharmacology, had by then come quite a long way, but diagnosis and treatment were then limited by the prevailing (and then well-reasoned) Boerhaavian theories of 'acrimonious particles' and of faults in the body humours and solids. Doctors of those years are no more to be sneered at and belittled than are the best doctors of today. They were captives of their times, no less than are today's specialists who still fail to save a victim of malignant melanoma that is actively spreading.

No writer, medical or lay, should make pronouncements on the medical history of Burns before reading all his letters, and, concurrently, Buchan's *Domestic Medicine*. The latter remarkable book, written for the lay reader, gives a revealing summary of the state of the medical art in Burns's day. It undoubtedly played a major role in increasing the average life span in Britain, particularly in Scotland. Published first in Edinburgh in 1769, it had gone through twenty-two editions by 1826, not counting numerous pirated editions. As at least 80,000 copies were sold it must have had wide readership in Scotland. Although some of Buchan's ideas were quaint and useless – for instance his advocacy of tobacco smoke enemas – he laid emphasis on health issues now widely endorsed: clean air, clean domestic conditions, sensible clothing, exercise, temperance and a balanced diet of foods free from adulterants. Although bacterial and viral agents were then unknown, Buchan gave much sound advice on the avoidance of infection. He was not obsessed with indiscriminate bleeding, favouring it only for inflammatory states when there was 'a hard, full, quick pulse', a greatly feared symptom in those days, but condemning it as hurtful for 'low, nervous and putrid fevers'. (Johnson mentioned Barry's *System of Physic*. . . . His notion was that pulsation occasions death by attrition; and that, therefore, the way to preserve life is to retard pulsation. . . . Soon after this, he said something very flattering to Mrs Thrale. It concluded by wishing her long life. 'Sir (said I) if Dr Barry's system be true, you have now shortened Mrs Thale's life, perhaps, some minutes, by accelerating her pulsation.' From Boswell's *Life of Johnson*.)

Buchan had little advice to offer on cardiovascular disorders, reflecting the limited understanding of such then prevailing. He advocated cold bathing, preferably in salt water, for relief of rheumatisms and for the violent palpitations attending 'nervous disorders', giving us a significant hint of the source of the self-diagnostic comments and the ultimate disastrous therapy adopted by Burns. It is a fair assumption that well-read Burns was familiar with Buchan's *Domestic Medicine*. Burnsians will remember the poet's dig at Dr Hornbook for his dependence on Buchan (K.55, line 81). The Burns letters, assiduously brought together and published by J. De L. Ferguson in 1931, are the main source of the bard's medical history, but the comments of some contemporaries given to Currie provide important supplementation. A listing of seventy-seven extracts from all available sources was made in 1970 by Professor Robert Fitzhugh and presented as Appendix B in his engaging biography.[5] It is a useful summary, but the commentary added by Dr Stanley Bardwell is disappointingly brief and devoid of differential diagnoses.

The long-standing Heron-Currie alcoholism edifice crashed down like a house of cards after December 1925 when Sir James Crichton-Browne wrote a series of five articles for the *Glasgow Herald* under the heading 'Burns from a New Point of View' (4,5,7,8,9 December). Sir James gave the world of Burns admirers a new Burns, a temperate Burns, a laundered Burns, but a Burns who was in effect a life-long invalid. So enthusiastic was the public reaction that the author consolidated the series in the form of a small book which was published the following year. It was reissued in 1937, the year before the death of its distinguished author. Sir James emphatically rejected the whole notion of an alcoholic decline and death, pronouncing the one and only cause as rheumatic fever terminating as rheumatic endocarditis, and asserting with finality: 'There can be no doubt about it.'

Sir James Crichton-Browne was born in 1840, the son of a Dumfries medical man. He was educated at Dumfries Academy, Trinity College, Glenalmond, and Edinburgh University, qualifying as an L.R.C.S. in 1861 and M.D. in 1862. He began his medical career as a specialist in mental disease (then always referred to as lunacy). Chaining and other means of physical restraint figured prominently in patient management in those days, and for long afterwards. Strange devices were used to prevent masturbation, a practice believed to be responsible for a good deal of madness. Crichton-Browne occupied a succession of administrative posts in asylums, and in 1875 was appointed to the prestigious position of Lord Chancellor's Visitor in Lunacy, a post he held until his retirement in 1922. His services to the nation, which included support of educational and other campaigns, brought him a knighthood in 1886. To those unaware of his limited experience in

Sir James Crichton-Browne. Photograph by Drummond Young. *Courtesy of the National Galleries of Scotland.*

clinical medicine, the retrodiagnosis of rheumatic fever in Burns, pronounced by such an eminent man, came to be regarded as holy writ, and has been blindly reasserted, with occasional minor variations, by a long succession of medical and lay writers ever since.

Dr. H.B. Anderson of Toronto, by an odd Edison-and-Swan type coincidence, independently reached the same conclusion as had Crichton-Browne, although his paper was not published until 1928.[6] Although his dissertation covers a wider field and is free from the emotive interlarding brought in by his Dumfriesian colleague, it has to be criticized for the undocumented symptom of 'shortness of breath' being imposed on Burns, even though he may have progressed to that disability. Some enthusiastic lay successors have imposed a lot more. James Barke has Burns, as a little boy, crying out in the night with rheumatic fever pain. Another highly regarded biographer refers to episodes of angina pectoris in the life of the bard. There is simply no biographical record of such symptoms or signs.

Burns From a New Point of View is not a long book – it has only 92 pages – but it concedes no pauses in the form of chapter breaks as its tide of oracular prose rolls on undisturbed by some very rocky biographical obstacles. The author clearly took his pivotal cue from Burns's own statement: 'Scarcely began to recover the loss of an only daughter & darling child, I became my self the victim of a rheumatic fever, which brought me to the borders of the grave' (L.687 of January 1796 to Cleghorn, repeated in L.688 to Mrs Dunlop). A point which must be now emphasized, and one in which Sir James and his medical successors have failed badly in not noting, is that Burns did not state that he contracted *rheumatic fever* – that highly specific disorder which Burns and his doctor William Maxwell almost certainly never heard of. Burns wrote that he contracted *a rheumatic fever*. That little word 'a' makes a world of difference in the diagnosis. To Burns, it was a fever with accompanying pain in the bones or muscles. There are many such disorders, but with a sort of Alice-in-Wonderland logic it would seem that when Burns used a term it meant just what Sir James chose it to mean. Clearly, Burns finally succumbed in an acutely feverish state, and such an acute climax to some years of chronic disability attracts a presumption of a secondary infection (not mentioned by Sir James) such as *bacterial* endocarditis, or, more probably, pneumonia, the ubiquitous pre-antibiotic killer. If ever a man literally invited an attack of pneumonia, Burns certainly did when in an extremely weakened state he took to sea-bathing in the waters of the Solway Firth, which at that time would have registered no higher on the Fahrenheit scale than the middle fifties. If we presume a terminal pneumonia or a septicaemia, the differential diagnosis field for the preceding painful chronic disorder widens greatly. In surveying that field, full regard must be given to disorders which were common in 1796 but are in the rare or relatively rare category today.

Rheumatic fever with its cardiac damage sequelae had been only rarely and obscurely notated as a precise medical entity prior to an enlightening description being published by W.C. Wells in 1812.[7] Richard Pulteney had published a single case report in 1761 with a description of rheumatic feverish symptoms and heart lesions seen at autopsy, and Matthew Baillie, in his 1793 text on morbid anatomy had mentioned an association of heart disorder and rheumatism. But in the mid-1790s the cardiac involvement in rheumatism had received scant attention in general medical practice. It is little wonder that the term *rheumatic fever* does not occur once in Buchan's *Domestic Medicine* despite its lengthy dissertation on various fevers. Buchan's fevers were acute or ardent, slow or nervous, or intermitting, and within those broad groupings were more specifically the malignant, putrid or spotted fevers, the miliary fevers, etc. There is no doubt that when Burns used the expression 'a rheumatic fever' he was being symptomo-logically descriptive, not pathologically specific. He could not have been the latter.

Let us take an analytical look at *Burns From a New Point of View*. Its author could qualify as the ultimate bardolater in declaring that Burns was 'the best-brained man that Scotland has ever produced', supporting that high-flown assertion with phrenological notions that the medical world had by that time rejected. But Sir James's book was accepted by the world of Burns admirers as giving a new immaculate image to their falsely maligned hero. For that reason the book's inaccuracies seemed not to matter. On page 11 there is a chemical absurdity – 'bicarbonate of iron in the gaseous state' in spa water – and some biographical errors are imbedded in such a generous excipient of romantic adulation that on first reading it one can lose sharp sight in the haze of associations. But the critical reader will find inaccuracies and unwarranted assumptions. For instance, the Ellisland tenancy is described as five years of steady industry, instead of just over three years of waning enthusiasm and disgust, with Burns becoming, in effect, an absentee farmer during the final two years. The 'Dumfries tittle-tattle' is reviled for spawning the story of alcoholic excesses, but accepted uncritically when Dr Maxwell's image, as well as his handkerchief, was bloodied at the scaffold of Louis XVI by an unconfirmed rumour.[8] His savage writing-off of Dr James Currie as 'the arch-calumniator' does not sit easily beside his own assertion that 'Currie retained his Calvinistic prepossessions to the last'. (Currie veered towards unitarianism.) We must readily admit to Sir James having a talent for colourful phraseology, as we may note from his denunciation of 'the lucubrations of a legion of biographical scribblers all blindly following a misguided leader' (i.e. Currie). But Sir James Crichton-Browne did his own share of uncritical leader-following. For instance, about stooped shoulders.

Robert Chambers, writing of events after a lapse of seventy-five years, got the notion that too much hard work and a deficient diet had given young Robert, among other things, stooping shoulders. But wielding the flail, swinging the scythe and guiding the plough would build up shoulder muscles, not collapse them. Many a champion athlete has the inborn characteristic of stooping shoulders. Devoted Burnsians in far-flung places accepted the Chambers comment and gave the 'stoop of the shoulders' specification to commissioned sculptors, evidently preferring to be so guided than by Nasmyth's full-figure sketch of a well set-up, brawny young man, drawn perhaps in 1787. A prominent Burns statue, in consequence, in one Australian city, is more suggestive of a memorial to Quasimodo than to the Scottish Bard. Sir James accepted the stooping shoulders picture and its cause, and made it part of his main thesis. The relevant passage in Chambers runs:

> While still a boy in years he was called upon, by stern necessity, to do, if possible, the work of a man. He undertook and performed this duty; but high motive will not procure exemption from physical evil. By hard labour, thus prematurely undergone, without the support of a sufficient diet, his naturally robust frame was severely injured. Externally, the consequence appeared in the stoop of the shoulders, which never left him, but,

internally, in the more serious form of mental depression, attended by a nervous disorder, which affected the movements of the heart.

Nothing in the subsequent recorded history of the Burns family suggests that any members were victims of malnutrition. Gilbert was to comment later on the absence of 'butcher's meat' in the house, but never once suggested an overall shortage of food. There must have been a good supply of skim milk – a good source of first-class protein and calcium, and every farm had its kail-yard. Kail is a good source of dietary iron and vitamins, and oat grain, consumed as porridge, sowens or brose, surpasses wheat dietetically. Barnyard fowls would have supplemented protein needs with a few eggs, while cockerels and old hens would have gone into the pot. Chambers's report of a physically wrecked body is at odds with prior comments by other writers:

Dr James Currie:

Burns . . . was nearly five feet ten inches in height, and of a form that indicated agility as well as strength.

J.G. Lockhart:

Robert Burns's person, inured to daily toil and continually exposed to all varieties of weather, presented before the usual time every characteristic of robust and vigorous manhood. He says himself that he never feared a competitor in any species of rural exertion; and Gilbert Burns, a man of uncommon bodily strength, adds that neither he nor any labourer he ever saw at work was equal to the youthful poet, either in the cornfield or the severer tasks of the threshing-floor.

Take or leave the next four extracts, according to whether you believe Allan Cunningham, the reputed fabulist, or not.

At Kirkoswald:

Burns engaged heartily in the sports of leaping, dancing, wrestling, putting the stone, and others of the like kind . . . but though he was possessed of great strength, as well as skill, he could never match his young bedfellow John Niven. (i.e., he beat all bar one.)

At Mauchline:

'his well-knit frame, vigorous and active'

At Edinburgh:

'this big-boned, black-browed, brawny stranger'

At Ellisland:

On laying the foundation he took off his hat, and asked a blessing on the home which was to shelter his household gods. I inquired of the man who told me this, if Burns did not put forth his hand and help him in the progress of the work? – 'Ay, that he did mony a time. If he saw us like to be beat wi' a big stane he would cry, "bide a wee!" and come rinning. We soon found out when he put to his hand – he beat a' I ever met for a dour lift.'

Sir Egerton Brydges:

His great beauty was his manly strength.

Maria Riddell:

his form was manly. . . . His figure seemed to bear testimony to his earlier destination and employments. It seemed rather moulded by nature for the rough exercises of agriculture, than for the gentler cultivation of the Belles Lettres.

Carson at Kenmure, writing about a boating party on Loch Ken in 1793:

Mr Gordon, with the assistance of an oar, vaulted from the prow of the little vessel to the beach, and was soon followed in like manner by Mr Syme and myself; thus leaving the venerable pastor of Kells and the bard on board. The former being too feeble to jump, as we had done, to land, expressed a desire to remain in the vessel till Mr Gordon and I returned; upon hearing which, the generous bard instantly slipt into the water, which was, however, so deep as to wet him to the knees. After a short entreaty, he succeeded in getting the clergyman on his shoulders; on observing which, Mr Syme raised his hands, laughed immoderately and exclaimed: 'Well, Mr Burns, of all the men on earth, you are the last that I could have expected to see *priest-ridden*.' We laughed also, but Burns did not seem to enjoy the joke. He made no reply, but carried his load silently through the reeds to land.

The foregoing comments relate to a man (according to Ferguson, a faithful Crichton-Browne follower) whose life-long health record is 'tantamount to chronic invalidism'.[9]

Something is not quite adding up.

Sir James Crichton-Browne, ardently seeking to discredit Currie and Maxwell and throw out the alcohol story, seized on Burns's 'rheumatic fever' phrase triumphantly. Rheumatic fever just had to be the verdict. But in rejecting any self-inflicted suffering he had to start by making William Burnes, by inference, something of an ogre – an insensitive slave-driver who grossly overworked a sickly son. It is hardly the image of the father referred to by Murdoch as 'by far the best of the human race that I ever had the pleasure of being acquainted with'. As rheumatic fever first strikes, in nine cases out of ten, between the ages of five and fifteen years,[10] both Sir James and Dr Anderson felt that they should go back to the tender years to place the first imagined infection. But it was rather unlikely that the highly specific Group A haemolytic streptococcus bacterium would have found its way to lonely Mount Oliphant where visitors were few. Their case would be stronger if the initial throat infection were back-dated all the way to Alloway. So Alloway it had to be.

Crichton-Browne:

> Burns had heart disease of rheumatic origin, which cut him off at
> middle age, and no doubt dated from childhood. In all likelihood
> it was in 'the auld clay biggin', in the damp Ayrshire climate
> and not very weathertight, some 'Janwar blast' blew in the germ
> of lifelong perturbation.

The contemporary evidence? Nil.

And H.B. Anderson:

> A critical review of trustworthy information fortunately furnishes
> a medical history of the long illness that led to his death at
> thirty-seven years of age, which to my mind shows conclusively
> that it was rheumatism and endocarditis which, with almost
> equal certainty, had its inception in his childhood.

Again, the 'in his childhood' evidence? Nil.

Moving on to the adolescent years, Crichton-Browne asserted 'at Mount Oliphant, from his thirteenth to his fifteenth year, the heart trouble was well declared'. For this period we have, for the first time, an eye-witness comment on Robert's health which we may accept with confidence – that of Gilbert Burns. 'He was almost constantly afflicted in the evenings with a dull headache'. To Crichton-Browne, evening headaches confirmed rheumatic heart trouble. In that outstanding medical reference publication *French's Index of Differential Diagnosis* are listed some seventy-odd causes of headache, but the extended sequelae of rheumatic fever is not one of them. On the other hand, the writer of the relevant section, F. Dudley Hart, ascribes specifically *evening* headache either to serious organic disease of the brain and meninges – and this we may confidently pass over in the youthful bard's case – or to eyestrain or mental stress, or to both of course. Try out the eyestrain factor yourself, by reading by the light of one candle Locke's *Essay Concerning Human Understanding* (all its 300,000 words) or Dickson's *A Treatise on Agriculture* (over 2,000 pages in its two volumes), as Burns said he did. With good artificial lighting and readily available optician services as needed, eyestrain headache is uncommon today, but it was a different story in those days. As to mental stress, Burns's letters and other writings leave us in no doubt that throughout his life he was the victim of recurrent pathological depression. (See letters, 3,4,18,29,53,125,168,177,182, 183,184,185,194,226,228,230,233,236, Addenda 5.9.1788,350,374, 378,379,381,388,482,596,616,619,638,705, Common Place Book 1, and Journal of the Border Tour for May 23–4, 1787.)

Common running-mates of recurrent pathological depression are anxiety and psychosomatic disorders. Again and again Burns pleaded this morbid condition – his 'constitutional hypochrondriac taint', his 'languor of spirits', his 'blue-devilism', his 'bedlam passions', his 'evil imaginings and gloomy presages', his 'diseased nervous system', his 'depression of spirits and all the miserable consequences of a deranged nervous system', 'the Hypochondria which I fear worse than the devil', and similar mental tortures. Modern psychiatric findings identify depression as a villain liable to come on the scene wearing any of many pathological masks. Transient episodes of dejection are normal enough in anyone in response to bad circumstances, but in pathological depression the reaction can be out of proportion to the known causes, and indeed often no cause at all can be elicited. Sleep problems, headache, breathlessness without exertion, libido loss, digestive disorders, cardiovascular upsets without identifiable tissue lesions, listlessness, apathy, fatigue out of proportion to physical effort and not relieved by rest, guilt and remorse out of proportion to deeds, are common manifestations of depressive illness.[11] Research in the 1980s has revealed that it is a genetic disorder with possible familial incidence, and we may suspect that Robert's sister Isobel was a victim.[12] Severe depressive illness does not spare the great minds; indeed it seems to fall more heavily on them than on the population at large. Dr Kay Jamieson, Professor of Psychiatry at the University of California, interviewed all accessible recipients of the Queen's Gold Medal for Poetry and found that half of that distinguished group had received treatment for depression.[13] Many poets of the more distant past have been victims of the disorder. Samuel Johnson and William Blake went through periods of severe depression, and William Cowper was so acutely affected that he required institutional care (such as it was in his time).

The whole problem of comprehending the health record of Burns is complicated by numerous references to disorders that are attributable to, or at least were worsened by, his depressive illness. One might have expected that Crichton-Browne, in his day prominent in the psychiatric field, would have brought to bear on the issue a better understanding. He agreed that Burns had 'an inherited predisposition to nervous depression', but in his determination to implant early heart disease into his hero he tendentiously put the cart before the horse; insisting that it was cardiac disturbance that caused the expression of the depression, not vice versa.

Depressive illness tends to be bi-polar – the depression lifting periodically to be replaced by irrational agitation. In such subjects 'there was never a *heich* but there was a *how*', to apply an old Scots saying. It has been claimed that all morbid depression is bi-polar, with the excitement phase varying from severe to near-zero. (There is now a commendable tendency to prefer the term 'bi-polar depression' to the older one of 'manic-depressive psychosis'.) We may point to many such mood swings in Burns. In December 1787, passionately involved with Clarinda, he told Richard Brown 'my Highland durk, that I used to hang beside my crutches, I have gravely moved into a neighbouring closet, the key of which I cannot command, in case of spring-tide paroxysms' (L.168). Soon after, he was to couple his 'hypochondriac imagination' with 'bedlam passions' in a letter to Margaret Chalmers (L.185). In the following March he again told Brown that 'watching [insomnia], fatigue, and a load of Care almost too heavy for my shoulders, have in some degree almost fever'd me . . . I was convulsed with rage a good part of the day' (L.228). In mid-1789 he wrote of his low spirits to Mrs Dunlop: 'I know not of any particular cause for this worst of all my foes besetting me; but for some time my soul has been beclouded with a thickening atmosphere of evil imaginings and gloomy presages' (L.350).

Soon after, he sent her a draft of *The Kirk of Scotland's Garland*. If ever a poem was a manic outburst it was that coarsely abusive tirade against the Ayrshire clergy. It suited Crichton-Browne, and his many followers, to write off John Syme of Ryedale as 'an entirely untrustworthy witness', but it is hard to believe that Syme's account (first published by Sir Walter Scott) of Burns reaching for his sword-cane as an angry reaction to a mild remark is entirely fictitious. Syme was one of the few witnesses to his friend's behaviour who did not shrink from relating incidents revealing extreme and unpleasant mood swings. He told of the poet, in the course of their Galloway tour, becoming enraged after ruining his boots by using brute force to pull them on while they were wet:

> A sick stomach and a head-ach lent their aid, and the man of verse was quite *accablé*. I attempted to reason with him. Mercy on us, how he did fume and rage! Nothing would reinstate him in temper. I tried various expedients, and at last hit on one that succeeded.

Writers on Burns seem not to have discovered the significance of his bi-polar depressive illness on the quality of his poetic output. He would never have been able to write his more brilliant pieces during a *how* – his finest effusions had to await a *heich*. His gloomy theme poems tend to fall into the forgettable class, and suggest that creativity had been held in check by depression. His unique genius was never expressed with the calmly-sustained fecundity of inspiration which never faultered for Pope throughout 800 lines in *The Rape of the Lock*. Burns's greater works are of modest length, each seeming to have arisen from a murky depth with a new wave of spontaneity, like a Trident missile breaking the ocean surface to soar aloft in fiery brilliance. During those episodes of creativity, image became heaped on image, with the brainstorm abating in a perfect relaxed climax. Some would say anticlimax. In that way he gave us *To a Mouse, To a Louse* and *Tam o' Shanter*, to name but three of many such inspired masterpieces.

The long-overdue challenge to the Crichton-Browne interpretation of young Robert's evening headaches was published in 1979. Dr R.S. Gilchrist, in an article disappointingly brief, expressed the view that the evening headaches were simply caused by sinusitis, a manifestation of a catarrhal diathesis that plagued the poet through to his later years.[14] (A diathesis may be defined as an unusual constitutional susceptibility to a particular disorder.) But doubt must be entertained for the sinusitis cause. Dr F. Dudley Hart, in a comprehensive dissertation on headache in French's *Index*, states that chronic sinusitis typically causes morning headache, which tends to disappear during the day.[15] That view is supported by Dr R.J. Johns in his statement that sinusitis pain is usually at its worst when the sufferer wakens and improves during the day with erect posture.[16] Of course, Burns the teenager may have had sinusitis – it is common enough – but the more likely cause of the evening headaches would have been depression and anxiety. Stress hardly ever abated in the Mount Oliphant years; as the factor's threatening letters demanding overdue rent kept arriving; as the father grew more obviously ill; as the farm animals died and weeds crowded the growing oats to leave only a miserably poor crop. With a possible eyestrain factor added we need look no further to account for the evening headaches.

No further health reports on or by Burns are to be found in the documented record until the middle Lochlea period, when he went to Irvine to learn flax-dressing. At Irvine Burns suffered severely from something or other. Whatever it was, morbid depression was certainly a major component, if not the one and only cause of his misery. The first of two reports on this illness is in a letter from Burns to his father, sent from Irvine:

> My health is much about what it was when you were here only my sleep is rather sounder and on the whole I am rather better than otherwise tho it is but by very slow degrees. The weakness of my nerves has so debilitated my mind that I dare not, either review past events, or look forward into futurity; for the least anxiety, or perturbation in my breast, produces most unhappy effects on my whole frame.

> (L.4, of 27.12.1781)

Gloomy thoughts on gladly facing death follow in the letter. If it were a viral or bacterial infection that he contracted there is no evidence to identify it, although smallpox, then getting around in Irvine, has been postulated. (Two people, Marion Hunter and Gilbert Baird, asserted years later that Burns was pock-marked, but such scarring may have been merely acneous.) But we can be quite certain that in the earlier part of his Irvine stay he suffered a very serious bout of depressive illness, probably triggered by the rejection of his epistolary proposal of marriage. The young lady in question has been assumed to have been Alison (or Ellison) Begbie. Within a few days of the writing of the letter quoted, the flax-dressing premises were accidentally burnt to the ground.

The second report on the unidentified Irvine illness appears in the famous autobiographical letter written some years later by Burns to Dr Moore:

> a belle-fille whom I adored and who had pledged her soul to me in the field of matrimony, jilted me with peculiar circumstances of mortification. The finishing evil of this infernal file was my hypochondriac complaint being irritated to such a degree, that for three months I was in a diseased state of body and mind, scarcely to be envied by the hopeless wretches who have just got their mittimus – 'Depart from me, ye Cursed'.

The smallpox theory is almost certainly wrong. Burns would have mentioned such a serious disease had he contracted it. He knew all about smallpox – he had his boys inoculated against it.

It would appear that early in 1782 at Irvine, a new-found and stimulating friendship with Richard Brown, involving long talks and leisurely walks, brought a lifting of the three-month period of depression. Crichton-Browne, as one would anticipate, saw that period of misery as yet another manifestation of cardiac disorder in Burns. But if in fact it was a new reinfection by the highly specific Group A streptococcus, Burns from then on would have been hopelessly ill with rheumatic fever sequelae and utterly unfit for the later sustained demands of farm labour, of heaving heavy stones at Ellisland or wading into the Solway at the head of an armed party to capture a smuggler's vessel.

In this critical study it is important to have a clear understanding of rheumatic fever and its damaging consequences, so some technical details, with some unavoidable medical jargon, are here intruded. The responsible organism, the Group A beta-haemolytic streptococcus, only infects the throat, but from that site its highly potent toxin enters the circulation, first to cause a feverish reaction (which in some cases is quite trivial), and, after the lapse of one to five weeks, inflammation of the collagenous body tissues of the joints, skin and heart. Young subjects may develop chorea (St Vitus' dance) after a latent period of one to six months. The only *permanent* damage is in the heart structures, notably the valves. The latter react by thickening and distorting. The condition never reactivates after the streptococci are cleared from the throat, but any subsequent infection by the specific streptococcus, even many years later, adds a new quota of heart damage. A reaction to the toxin in renewed infection tends to be sharper than in the first infection, the structures involved acting as if hypersensitized. When one or more heart valves becomes so damaged as to fail to close (valvular incompetence) or fail to open adequately (stenosis), seriously deficient circulation is permanently established. Muscle damage in the heart (myocarditis) further diminishes pumping efficiency, and if the toxin affects the containing membranes of the heart the resulting pericarditis can be painful.[17]

At the time that Crichton-Browne was active in the medical field it was believed that rheumatic fever simply reactivated spontaneously from time to time, and was eventually liable to cause death when the progressively worsening heart function brought complete failure. The essential role of reinfection had not been defined. (Today, patients can be protected from subsequent attacks by sustained antibiotic prophylaxis.) Crichton-Browne, using terms such as 'recrudescence', 'exacerbation', 'relapse' and 'a return of rheumatism' saw a worsening of heart disease in nearly all the illnesses suffered by Burns – early in the Mossgiel period, during the first week or two after arrival in Edinburgh, in the winter of 1792, in October 1795, and in February 1796. Had these illnesses been Group A streptococcal reinfections, Burns would have been a hopelessly bed-ridden invalid years before the terminal illness of 1796.

In support of the verdict of long-standing heart disease in Burns, much has been made of a report of 'a bedfellow', which specifies 'previous to his leaving Ayrshire'. (Dr Gilchrist refers it to Ellisland, presumably because it was related by Grierson of Dalgoner, and Dalgoner is not far from Ellisland.) The report states that Burns experienced 'nocturnal faintings and suffocations', from which he gained immediate relief by rising and plunging into a tub of cold water. (This act probably amounted to no more than dunking the head into a water-filled half-barrel, of the type then in use in farm steadings as a family urine receptacle.) This exclusively nocturnal disorder appears to have been a more acute version of the one that Gilbert was to describe as replacing evening headaches 'at a future period of his life' with 'a palpitation of the heart, and a threatening of fainting and suffocation in his bed, in the night time'. Dr Gilchrist was on the right track in identifying this condition as *paroxysmal tachycardia*, but he could have been a bit more explicit for the lay reader. (Paroxysmal describes sudden isolated episodes: tachycardia simply means abnormally rapid heart-beat rate.) In the particular case described for Burns we may go a bit further and settle for a diagnosis of *paroxysmal nocturnal dyspnea*. (Dyspnea is difficult breathing.)

Despite the formidable medical name, the cause of paroxysmal nocturnal dyspnea is readily explainable. Remember that the right side of the heart pumps blood returned to it from all parts of the body *via* the veins, to the lungs. The left side of the heart accepts back that blood from the lungs and sends it on its way, *via* the arteries, to all parts of the body. The right and left heart pumping rates are normally kept in exact balance by sensitive nervous feedback signals, but, if a nervous paroxysm allows a sudden drop of left heart pumping efficiency, the congested left heart cannot adequately cope with the flow of blood being offered to it by the lungs. The lungs will then also congest. The disorder is analogous to a common road traffic situation. Think of Town A receiving a steady volume of traffic from Town B. If some emergency in Town A prevents clearance of the traffic there, there will be a slow-down on the highway and very soon the network of streets in Town B will be congested. The normally open spaces in Town B will become filled with vehicles. In just the same way, the myriad air spaces of the blood-congested lungs are compressed and breathing becomes shallow and difficult. But why only *nocturnal*? Again, the reason is simple. In bed, the body has changed from its pre-retiring vertical position to the horizontal positon, and just because of that the blood returning to the heart from the legs and abdomen loses the restraint of gravitational pull, arriving at the right side heart at a significantly higher pressure than that prevailing with the body upright. This can be a sufficient influence to tip the balance towards difficult breathing in susceptible subjects.[18] The increase in total blood volume during some hours of resting, caused by fluid seeping into the fine blood vessels from the tissues in which they are imbedded, is an added factor in the consequent lung and heart congestion.

It is common knowledge that shortness of breath in response to increased physical exertion is characteristic of established heart or lung defects, and of any other bodily disorder that makes an increased demand on the circulatory system. There is no mention anywhere in Burns's health record that he experienced difficult breathing *in response to physical exertion*, although he probably did in his last months when he was desperately ill. The dyspnea we are told about occurred only in his Ayrshire years, and only when he was settled in bed. That fact rules out established heart disease resulting from rheumatic fever. The occasional nocturnal attacks were almost certainly triggered by episodes of tension and depression. Relief came by standing up to restore the gravitational pull on the rising blood, and in Burns's case we are told that the remedy was assisted by a splash of cold water to the head. If such was indeed the case it could be attributed to vagal stimulation. (The paired vagus nerves, direct from the brain to the heart, restrain the heart-beat rate when stimulated.)

The nocturnal 'palpitations', evidently milder as there is no recorded mention of associated dyspnea, persisted for Burns at least until his Edinburgh sojourn. Of this, we have thoroughly reliable documentation – supplied by none other than Professor Dugald Stewart:

> I should have concluded in favour of his habits of sobriety, from all of him that fell under my own observations. He told me indeed himself, that the weakness of his stomach was such as to deprive him of any merit in his temperance. I was however somewhat alarmed about the effect of his new sedentary and luxurious life, when he confessed to me, the first night he spent in my house after his winter campaign in town, that he had been much disturbed when in bed, by a palpitation at his heart, which he said, was a complaint to which he had of late become subject.

Neither the exclusively nocturnal heart symptoms nor the weak stomach report lend any support to Sir James Crichton-Browne's rheumatic fever assertions. They point to tension and anxiety. A serious knee injury in December 1787, with healing set back by 'an unlucky fall' nine months later, would have brought new quotas of tension and anxiety.

One may well ask why Crichton-Browne omitted consideration, indeed any mention at all, of one of the most deadly illnesses suffered by Burns. Probably because he saw no way of tying it to rheumatic carditis. The illness was described by Burns as 'a most malignant Squinancy', contracted at Ellisland in late 1790. It was undoubtedly *diphtheria*. Dr Mundell, his physician at that time, probably did not become involved, as Burns would have been far too ill to consider riding to Dumfries for a consultation. There is every indication that the diagnosis was a self-diagnosis, and a correct one in the late 1700s. Buchan, in his *Domestic Medicine*, makes a very clear distinction between the Quinsey and the *Malignant* Quinsey. (Quinsey, Quinsy and Squinancy are synonyms.) He deals with them in separate sections in his book. His Quinsey is clearly today's quinsy or peritonsillitis, with its severe swelling of the throat and difficulty in swallowing. It also corresponds to Dr Samuel Johnson's definition – 'a tumid inflammation in the throat'. But Buchan's *Malignant* Quinsey description is plainly of today's diphtheria in all its details:

> Upon looking into the throat, it appears swelled, and of a florid red colour. Pale or ash-coloured spots, however, are here and there interspersed, and sometimes one broad patch or spot, of an irregular figure, and pale white colour, surrounded with florid red, only appears. These whitish spots or sloughs cover so many ulcers.
>
> There is often a degree of delirium, and the face frequently appears bloated, and the inside of the nostrils red and inflamed. The patient complains of a disagreeable putrid smell, and his breath is very offensive.
>
> The putrid ulcerous sore throat [Buchan's alternative name for his malignant quinsey] may be distinguished from the inflammatory [his term for ordinary quinsy] by the vomiting and looseness with which it is generally ushered in; the foul ulcers in the throat covered with a white or livid coat; and by the excessive weakness of the patient; with other symptoms of a putrid fever. . . . If the sloughs cast off in a kindly manner, and

appear clean and florid at the bottom; and if the breathing is soft and free, with a lively colour of the eyes, there is every reason to hope for a salutory crisis.

Above we have a grouping of signs that describes diphtheria, without a shadow of doubt. Pathognomonic of diphtheria are the initial vomiting and fever followed by spreading white coatings in the throat and nasal passages, and the extreme weakness of the patient stemming from the poisoning of muscles, including those of the heart. Buchan's final qualification on conditions for recovery was portentous for patients failing to meet them. There was a mortality rate up to fifty per cent for diphtheria in the bad old days before serum antitoxin was introduced. It can kill by the powerful toxin causing respiratory failure, a fatal heart failure within two or three weeks, or by the onset of bronchopneumonia. It can also kill by airway blockage caused by swelling and the intrusion of the white membrane.[19]

It is no wonder that Burns was to write that 'a most malignant Squinancy . . . had me very near the borders of the grave' in one letter (L.422, to Dalziel) and ' . . . actually brought me to the brink of the grave' in another (L.423, to Mrs Dunlop). He was lucky to have survived. One thing is quite certain – had Burns been already a victim of rheumatic carditis he would never have lived through the ferocious attack on his heart which the potent diphtheric toxin must have mounted. It would appear that Crichton-Browne, unlike Burns's Dr Hornbook, was not 'sae weel acquaint wi' Buchan'; for had he identified the 'most malignant Squinancy' as diphtheria he would surely have modified his very confident diagnosis of well-established rheumatic heart disease in Burns prior to that critical episode.

There is a gap in the recorded medical story of Burns from this time – late 1790 until mid-1794 – apart from the endless rain of depression-based pleadings ('a mind diseased': 'a damned melange of Fretfulness and melancholy': 'low spirits and blue devils': 'plagued with an indigestion': 'blasted with a deep incurable taint of hypochondria' etc.). And well he might have been depressed. He had been subjected to extra stress and anxiety in 1793, fearing for his Excise future when his political indiscretions brought down on his head a departmental inquiry, and though he kept his job, war was depressing trade and he was earning less. Another severe upset was the loss of the friendship of all the Riddells through his drunken high-jinks in January 1794. Those stresses would have exacerbated inborn depression.

In June 1794 Burns told Mrs Dunlop 'my medical friends threaten me with a flying gout'; in September he followed up with 'I am so poorly today as to be scarce able to hold my pen'; in December 'I already begin to feel the stiffening joints of Old Age coming fast o'er my frame'. Could all that have been a picture of a rheumatic fever reinfection, or of a primary infection, with 'stiffening joints' worrying the patient *from June to December*? Not at all. The joint pain from an attack of rheumatic fever lasts for about a week in a third of all cases, and for two to three weeks in most of the rest. Only in rare instances does it extend to seven weeks.[10] Whatever the trouble was, severe depression was a major component. In September 1794 he again wrote to Mrs Dunlop 'I know you are pretty deep read in Medical matters, but I fear you have nothing in the Materia Medica which can heal a diseased spirit' (L.638). His mood is reflected in his winding up of the letter with the vicious verse attacking Walter Riddell: *So Vile was Poor Wat* (K.452).

We have only sparse information on Burns's health in 1795, apart from eloquent complaints about severe toothache in letters of 30 May and 3 July. Evidently he just put up with this – the thought of extraction of abscessed teeth before the days of anaesthetics would deter the bravest. But the smouldering infection would have been debilitating, to say the least. Currie's statement (based on Dr Maxwell's information) that, from October 1795 to the January following, Burns was confined to his house with 'an accidental complaint' is frustratingly vague. The confusion about it is compounded by Josiah Walker recounting that he passed two days with Burns in November 'and observed no unfavourable change in his looks, his spirits, or his appetite'. Walker went on to describe a walk with the Bard 'a considerable way up the beautiful banks of the Nith', and sessions at the inn.[20] J. De L. Ferguson wrote off Walker as an ass. Perhaps he was, but there is no evidence that he was a liar. There are two ways to reconcile his report of Burns's well-being with contrary accounts of failing health, one being that Walker got his dates wrong – not a likely explanation – and the other is that meeting up with an old acquaintance at a time of depression caused by the recent death of a little daughter, brought to Burns a temporary lifting of that depression. The symptoms of the 'accidental complaint' were then tolerated sufficiently to deceive Walker. From that time onwards the letters of Burns describe his sufferings vividly but medical symptoms vaguely. Nevertheless, there are facts to be noted. One of them is that by 31 January 1796 Burns was starting to 'crawl across [his] room', following a bout of what he described as 'a most severe rheumatic fever' (L.688). But neither he nor Dr Maxwell diagnosed *rheumatic fever* – without the all-important indefinite article – neither is it feasible that either of them could have done so. It is a highly specific clinical entity that was then, with virtual certainty, unknown to them, and one that even today demands advanced diagnostic expertise for positive identification. Burns suffering long drawn-out rheumatic pain, on and off from January 1796 until his death in July, does not tally at all with a clinical picture of rheumatic fever. A different diagnosis is needed to account for the long duration, the fluctuation and severity of the pains. He felt well enough to attend a Masonic meeting on 28 January and to pack and despatch a kippered salmon, with a cheery covering note, to Peter Hill in Edinburgh on 29 January. He again attended a Masonic meeting on 14 April, but missed the one on 16 April. Currie's terse summary, from Maxwell's prompting, of the final six months is probably factual. In early February (as assumed from the context) Burns resumed his tavern visits: 'A few days after he began to go abroad, he dined at a tavern, and returned home about three o'clock in a very cold morning, benumbed and intoxicated. This was followed by an attack of rheumatism which confined him about a week.' Then follows a description of decline, with failed appetite, rapid pulse, pain in the larger joints and in the hands and feet, and sleeplessness, right through to July. Lockhart (1828) was later to supplement the Currie account (with no stated provenance) with the remark that 'The course of medicine to which he submitted was violent', implying that it was to the patient's detriment.

The issue of the violent course of medicine is difficult to resolve. One Dr John Thomson, claiming to have known Burns well in Dumfries, wrote, years later, that 'The physician of Robert Burns believed that his liver was diseased, and placed him under a course of mercury', afterwards sending him to Brow for sea bathing. Thomson proceeded to describe how Burns returned home suffering severe dropsy, and soon to die. Writers on Burns (with the exception of Mrs Carswell, and of James Barke in his novel *The Well of the Silent Harp*) tend to ignore the mercury story, and two reasons for so doing may be postulated. The first is that at the time of Burns's death, John Thomson was as yet medically unqualified, being only about sixteen years of age. This is not necessarily a good reason. The second cause for passing over the mercury report is that it raises the unpleasant and iconoclastic spectre of venereal disease; mercury being then, and for long afterwards, a much-used medication for both syphilis and gonorrhea. But it is logical to reject such an interpretation, not only through the complete absence of evidence of infection in Jean, but also from the freedom from neonatal gonococcal blindness and syphilitic stigmata in any of the children. However, these considerations do not rule out the possibility of Dr Maxwell having ordered some mercurial medication, as this was then in use to stimulate liver function, salivation and other excretory paths, and such stimulation was seen as a salutory means of expelling 'acrimonious' particles from the humours to effect cures. Excessive mercurial medication may have hastened the decline of the Bard through characteristic kidney failure, but the question will probably remain unresolved. As John Thomson's assertions are of interest, and have recently come back into the picture from hair analysis, the text is given in Appendix D for the information of those interested.

Never was 'the sad account of fore-bemoaned moan' so sad as in the letters Burns wrote during his last few months.

To George Thomson in April:

Rheumatism, Cold, & Fever have formed, to me, a terrible Trinity in Unity, which makes me close my eyes in misery, & open them without hope.

In the following month:

I now have reason to believe that my complaint is a flying gout: – a damnable business!

To James Johnson in June:

This protracting, slow, consuming illness which hangs over me, will, I doubt much, my ever dear friend, arrest my sun before he has well reached his middle career.

To James Clarke, 26 June:

Still, still the victim of affliction; were you to see the emaciated
figure who now holds the pen to you, you would not know your
old friend . . . Enough of this! 'tis half my disease!

To George Thomson, 4 July:

Besides my inveterate rheumatism, my appetite is quite gone, &
I am so emaciated as to be scarce able to support myself on my
own legs.

To Alex. Cunningham, 7 July:

tortured with an excruciating rheumatism which has nearly
reduced me to the last stage . . . Pale, emaciated, & so feeble as
occasionally to need help from my chair – my spirits fled!
fled! . . . the Medical folks tell me that my last & only chance is
bathing & country quarters & riding.

To Mrs Dunlop, 10 July, asking for renewal of correspondence:

The remembrance yet adds one pulse more to my poor
palpitating heart. Farewell!!!

To James Armour, 18 July (his last letter – he died on 21 July.)

I returned from sea-bathing quarters today, and my medical
friends would almost persuade me that I am better, but I think
and feel that my strength is so gone that the disorder will prove
fatal to me.

Burns was tragically prophetic in that last prediction.

SEEKING THE FACTS, POST-1926

Putting a name to the illness that so prematurely ended the life of
Robert Burns is not a matter for a snap judgement. In 1944,
Dr S. Watson Smith of Bournemouth was moved to protest that
'the unproved verdict [including that of rheumatic fever] has been
copied from book to book . . . with harping reiteration, so as to be
difficult to reverse or efface'. It has been more than copied: it has
been embroidered and extrapolated. To Dr Smith must go the
credit for making the first objectively professional attempt at a
diagnosis consistent with the foggy medical picture of Burns during

the last few months of his life. His verdict was *subacute bacterial endocarditis.*[21] Unlike Crichton-Browne's rheumatic endocarditis, in which no infecting organisms invade the internal tissues of the heart, subacute bacterial endocarditis is caused by any of a wide variety of bacteria, or even parasitic fungi, attacking the vulnerable heart lining and other heart structures, typically causing death by septicaemia a few months later. The fever, arthritic pain and emaciation fit the picture.

Dr Smith dismissed out of hand both the old story of death from drink and the newer one of rheumatic fever attacks terminating in death. But he left important questions unanswered, and to an extent that throws serious doubt on his diagnosis. Bacterial infection of a heart hitherto fairly healthy would be so unlikely that it would fall into the category of rare diseases. Medical students these days are, or should be, routinely warned against diagnosing rare diseases unless the signs, symptoms and history are so obvious and highly specific that they exclude all the alternatives. Dr Stanley Bardwell, in the summation supplied to Professor Robert Fitzhugh in 1970,[22] was unequivocal on the point that a bacterial endocarditis diagnosis was not justified if preceding rheumatic heart disease had been ruled out. Paradoxically, Dr Watson Smith had ruled it out, and there are good reasons for ruling it out. Burns's first 'flying gout' pain evidently struck in June 1794 and continued, on and off, at least to the end of that year – not at all the rheumatic fever picture. Admittedly, there is the possibility that the 'accidental complaint' that started in October 1795, eight months before Burns died, was a first rheumatic fever attack, paving the way for a fatal bacterial endocarditis. But a first rheumatic fever attack at age thirty-seven would be a rare event. With only vague diagnostic detail, and that detail viewed against quite a lot of negating information spanning much of the patient's life span, we can have no more confidence in Dr Watson Smith's conclusions than in Sir James Crichton-Browne's.

We must think again.

THE NET CAST WIDER

It is time that efforts to strain a variety of vague angles into a rheumatic fever syzygy were abandoned. More acceptable alternatives are not that hard to find, particularly if three logical considerations are kept in view. The first is the recognition of the important fact that in the late eighteenth century some serious disorders, rare today and rarely thought about, were rampant, misunderstood and uncontrolled. The second consideration is that down the ages a very common cause of death, not only for the frail elderly but for debilitated young folk also, had been *pneumonia* – a hazard persisting until the relatively recent advent of sulphonamide drugs and antibiotics. Burns's ride to Brow for his chilling dips, as a very sick man, could well have been to a rendezvous with terminal pneumonia. Thirdly, the unfortunate Bard might well have suffered from more than one serious disorder concurrently. After all that, if the reader will still bear with the writer, he will be invited past the doctor's consulting room to the veterinary experts and the vintner's cellar. There are questions: there are answers.

Question one: Can there be named a serious disease, uncommon today but common and unrecognized in the late eighteenth century; a chronically or acutely feverish disease that can persist for years in phases of remission and reappearance if not identified and successfully treated; a disease that often presents with migratory arthralgia ('flying gout')[23] and relapses with same; a disease that causes depression and exacerbates any episodes of constitutional depression; a disease with its peak incidence in males aged thirty to sixty, and that group outnumbering all cases in children and adult females; a disease causing fatigue, lassitude, loss of appetite, headache and wasting; a disease causing spleen and liver enlargement – likely to have led an eighteenth-century doctor into prescribing mercury; and, notably, a disease regularly cited today as a differential diagnosis for feverish rheumatic presentations, including suspected *subacute bacterial endocarditis* (Anderson, T., 1969)?[24] One single disorder embracing such a melancholy grouping of features would be one tying in with all we know about Robert Burns's distress from June 1794 to July 1796. Have medical Burnsians become an extinct subspecies of homo sapiens? One hopes not, but any still around have missed out on a good Brownie point here, as the diagnosis missing for two centuries can be postulated with relative ease. It is *brucellosis*. Anyone greeting this decision with incredulity should talk to an identified sufferer. (I have done just that, and need no further convincing. R.H.F.)

Human brucellosis, or to give it its older and more descriptive name, undulant fever, is a zoonosis; that is to say, a disease of animals transmissible to man. The particular type of brucellosis most liable to be contracted by the human subject in Britain is bovine brucellosis, a cattle disease previously given the name contagious abortion – for the best of reasons – and to follow the infection trail we must begin in the veterinary context. A cow receives infection *via* the mouth or vagina, and if in calf she will typically abort the foetus at about five or six months term. All aborted tissue is heavily infected with Brucella abortus bacilli and should be destroyed immediately and thoroughly. Subsequent discharges carry the bacilli for about two months, allowing venereal spread through the herd by badly controlled service. Milk from infected cows contains the germs and they multiply further in the drawn milk if it is not pasteurized. Consumed raw, infected milk can initiate human brucellosis, for reasons unknown, only in a susceptible minority of consumers. The pasteurization barrier is a fairly effective final line of defence against human infection, making occurrences fairly uncommon in enlightened modern communities. Bovine brucellosis is routinely controlled today by the vaccination of calves, but in the eighteenth century it was rife (Lawrence, J., 1805,[25] and Fleming, G., 1878[26]), and an estimated 98 per cent of all bovine abortions is attributable to the infection. A full description of human brucellosis is given by Harries and Mitman (1951),[27] and its frequent citing as a differential diagnosis in intractable rheumatic and infection states is prominent in French's *Index*.

For those loath to accept for Robert Burns a medical history of brucellosis and terminal pneumonia, displacing the rheumatic fever and bacterial endocarditis hypotheses, let it be emphasized that brucellosis would have been the far more common disease in the eighteenth century, particularly in towns set in dairying districts and receiving plentiful supplies of milk for drinking and adding to the ubiquitous porridge. The distressing course of brucellosis accords well with two years of suffering described by Burns, and his manner of death attracts a strong presumption of terminal pneumonia. The undulant or relapsing nature of brucellosis stems from the unusual ability of the bacillus to enter body cells, an ability shared by the malarial parasite, with re-emergence after remissions causing relapses over a long period if treatment has been ineffective or neglected. Neither brucellosis nor rheumatic carditis would have been known to Dr William Maxwell and his symptomatic treatment of either would have been ineffective. But brucellosis has to be today's preferred diagnosis, both in terms of Burns's scrappy medical history and statistical probability.

The persuasive impact of statistical probability also enforces reservations about diagnosing rarer fatal disorders that also fit the clinical picture. These include chronic myelocytic leukaemia and SLE (systemic lupus erythematosis). The first-named admittedly has its peak incidence in males aged thirty to forty years, and a prognosis of about two years survival untreated.[28] It presents with low-grade fever and rheumatic pain, and eventually a worsening anaemia brings respiratory distress and palpitations. SLE is rarer still, and for every male case there are about four female victims. That said, let us turn our theorizing to a very positive factor claiming attention on the basis of probability, and pose another question.

Question two: Can we point to any likely additional and concurrent pathological factor that made Burns's sufferings worse? The answer is yes – heavy metal poisoning. Mercury, perhaps prescribed by Dr Maxwell to expel 'acrimonious particles from the humours' in the manner of the day, has been already mentioned, with reference directed to Appendix D. However, the absence of acute mental disturbance, characteristic of sustained mercury poisoning, suggests that mercurial administration – if any at all had been prescribed – was moderate. A far more likely heavy metal villain of the piece in the sad Burns drama was *lead*. Overstated? Not at all. The question leads us back to the topic of alcohol consumption by Burns; to a better and fairer understanding of the beliefs of Dr William Maxwell and Dr James Currie; to the ignorance, and in some cases the criminality, of distillers and wine producers in Britain and across the Channel.

In the eighteenth century there was a perilous link between liquor and lead poisoning, and widespread ignorance about it would have diverted the attention of doctors to the rather more innocent ingredient of liquor – alcohol. Dr James Currie's image has become the target of pompous contumely by defenders of Burns because of his *en passant* comments on the consumption of alcoholic liquor and its evil consequences. With monotonous insistence, Currie has been put down as a sanctimonious and proselytizing teetotaller, which he was not. The most that can be said in that context is that he abstained from liquor when suffering flare-ups of his pulmonary tuberculosis.[29] Currie's objurgations were aimed at *excessive* intake of liquor, particularly by men of genius and poetic sensitivity:

> It is the more necessary for them to guard against excess in the use of wine, because on them, its effects, are, physically and morally, in an especial manner injurious. In proportion to its stimulating influence on the system (on which the pleasurable sensations depend) is the debility that ensues; a debility that destroys digestion, and terminates in habitual fever, dropsy, jaundice, paralysis or insanity.

It may be assumed that Dr Maxwell concurred in the above views as he had read Dr Currie's draft and approved it.[30] Poor Maxwell. Posterity has treated him even more harshly than it has Currie. Crichton-Browne called him 'that very haphazard practitioner' and later writers on Burns have used more merciless expressions, such as 'his idiot of a doctor' and 'it was murder', blaming him for the Brow disaster. Professor Thornton questions the presumption that Maxwell ordered the Brow visit for sea bathing, recalling the Currie-Maxwell statement that Burns acted 'impatient of medical advice'.[31] Burns could have simply decided to try out what he had read in Buchan's book.

There is a vital implication in the quoted passage by Currie on the evil effects of an excess consumption of wine. The views would have reflected the medical teaching of the day, and the subsequent experience and observations of Currie and Maxwell would have, for them, reinforced their validity. In modern medical understanding, however, Currie's forebodings were overstated, particularly regarding debility, dropsy and paralysis. But if for Currie's single word 'wine' we substitute 'lead-adulterated liquor', the statement immediately rises to a better order of accuracy. Doctors Currie and Maxwell were right for the wrong reason.

The pernicious practice of using metallic lead, or its oxide litharge, in the making or subsequent 'improvement' of wine must have been widespread in England, Scotland, and on the Continent in Burns's day. Quite often a wine, particularly if made from early-picked grapes, would have turned out to be rather too acid for the popular taste. Somebody discovered that such acidity did not ntuate if the grape juice was fermented in contact with lead, the organic fruit acids dissolving, and combining chemically with, the lead. Alternatively, litharge could be added to the fermented product afterwards with the same result. Another bad thing that could happen in wine-making was secondary fermentation; an intruding mould or bacterium converting the alcohol, to some degree, to acetic acid – the acid of vinegar. Again, lead came to the rescue, combining with the acetic acid to form lead acetate. Lead acetate, also called 'sugar of lead', is sweet tasting, giving the manipulator an added bonus. What a money-spinner!

Not only did the lead eliminate the unwanted acidity; it also brought a clearing of any murkiness.[32] The use of lead was not confined to the wine-makers' premises: it was exploited by importers and distributors who had been landed with faulty wine in casks or already bottled. Any reader needing any further convincing that these deplorable practices happened regularly in Burns's day should not miss reading the classical essay by Dr A. Fothergill (Bath, 1790) exposing and vehemently condemning the evil business. (Relevant extracts are reprinted in Appendix E.)

The use of lead in the wine industry had been exposed in France prior to 1790, and was considered so serious by the French authorities that they brought in the death penalty to stamp it out, but – according to Fothergill – not successfully. The turmoil of Revolution must have hindered the policing of the statute. There seems to have been no serious attempt to stop the evil in Britain; indeed Sir George Baker was denounced as being disloyal to his county when he drew attention to the same vicious practice in cider-making in Devonshire. Even Scotland's Dr Buchan seemed only vaguely informed on the issue, as may be deduced from his *Domestic Medicine* text. He frequently advocated wine or negus as a medicine, but took care to recommend that families prepare their own liquors because of the widespread prevalence of adulteration in the commercial product:

It would be imprudent even to name those things which are daily made use of to render liquors heady. Suffice it to say, that the practice is very common.

Distilled liquor also would often have been hazardous to health through its lead content. Metallic lead is easy to fabricate, and it was undoubtedly widely used for condenser worms. Volatile organic acids would readily be converted to lead compounds in such stills. With whisky stills, licit and illicit, to be numbered in thousands throughout Highland and Lowland Scotland in the eighteenth century, it may be taken as certain that a high proportion of these were more or less amateur-built, and would have had worms made of the easily-coiled lead pipe. The technique had even spread to colonial America, where it came to be blamed for numerous cases of lead poisoning from moonshine liquor.[33]

Lead is not far down the list from arsenic in its toxicity. It has been said that there is a lead poisoning symptom for every letter of the alphabet. The symptoms vary with the rate and duration of intake, and with age and constitutional differences between victims.[34] The earliest and commonest symptom is painful colic with *simultaneous* constipation. Persons more tolerant to lead appear to have better ability for the bowel to resist absorption and expel it in the faeces. In others less favoured, a large proportion of ingested lead passes immediately to the liver, from which some biliary excretion takes place, but the excess, which may be substantial, reaches the systemic blood circulation.[35] It has been found that if more than 2.0 milligrams of lead acetate are absorbed daily in an adult, a progressively increasing body burden of lead accumulates. A defensive reaction of the body is to store the lead in the bones as an inert phosphate of lead, but if the blood level stays at or above 0.1 mg/100 g, lead remains outside the bony depots to wreak clinical mischief.[36] Episodes of raised parathyroid activity tend to cause the release of lead from the bones back into the blood, and this would appear to be responsible for overt symptoms of poisoning following precipitating circumstances such as an infectious disease or an alcoholic debauch.[37]

Symptoms of chronic lead poisoning are multiple and variable. They include severe anaemia (with pallor actually out of proportion to the anaemia), weakness, irritability, headache, weight loss, abdominal pain or colic, loss of appetite, insomnia, muscular incoordination, paralysis in the extremities, joint pain, and a disturbed pulse rate. Lead has special affinity for the fatty compounds of the body, and so interferes with the growth of nerve cells, making the growing child gravely at risk of brain damage. Kidney tissue is vulnerable; therefore nephritis, precipitating harmful toxic states, can eventuate in lead poisoning. It may simulate poliomyelitis, post-diphtheric paralysis, localized neuritis or polyneuritis, *and rheumatic fever*.[38]

There is no doubt that Burns was a habitual wine drinker in his post-Ayrshire years, and on many occasions drank to excess. (Barke, in his six novels, tendentiously has Burns usually quaffing ale, but the message of all available documentation is that for Burns the destination of the nappy was his verse, not his interior.) Defenders of Burns have consistently talked down the significance of his wine consumption, claiming that he was more inclined to hold back at convivial gatherings than to match the intake of his hard-drinking friends. He may have done so at times, but there were many occasions when evidently he did not. Apart from the convivial scene, he was inclined to solitary indulgence, as is made clear from many of his letters. J. De L. Ferguson, a prominent defender of Burns and detractor of Currie, wrote that 'for every apologetic or defiant reference in the letters to drunkenness, there are a dozen or a score to ill health'.[39] A quick check on that point will reveal that the correct ratio is closer to one to two, not one to twelve or twenty. (See letters 42, 72, 108, 112, 117, 127, 174, 182, 186, 191, 195, 209, 214, 216, 217, 291, 306, 316, 323, 440, 463, 482, 485, 501, 506, 529, 539, 584, 592, 600, 608, 618, 629, 631, 657, 678: thirty-six references for comparison with the seventy-six of Fitzhugh's ill-health listing.)

Burns would have been particularly at risk from lead-adulterated wine. He was usually hard-up in his Dumfriesshire years and he would have been on the look-out for cheaper wine, and faulty wines that had been rescued with litharge could have been sold at competitive prices. In his Excise treks he would have been offered sample drinks from a wide variety of sources, many of them dubious, to say the least. We may even cast doubt on his Ellisland cask of whisky. It tasted 'strong' even with 'five waters', suggesting that it was the over-rectified product of an inexpertly-built still, probably fitted with a lead worm.

One does not have to look far to find suspicion of lead poisoning in the documented health record of Burns. He had 'a miserable head-ach and stomach complaint' during his first two weeks in Edinburgh following a convivial party en route. During his Highland tour with his hard-drinking friend Nicol he suffered 'a fit of the colic', severe enough to warrant a pertinent entry in his journal. In December 1789 he wrote of 'the miseries of a diseased nervous sytem' and being 'ill with a nervous head-ach' – severe enough to force him to give up all his Excise work for three weeks, and this undiagnosed disability kept recurring over later years. Glauber's salt was his 'sour-faced old acquaintance', suggesting its habitual use. Was lead causing his constipation? Maybe. He wrote several times of being unable to hold his pen (L.619, 638, 668). This could have been figurative in meaning, but alternatively it could have been literal and a consequence of some peripheral paralysis.

Professor R.D. Thornton, who has in effect restored the reputation of both Currie and Maxwell in two impressive books, entertains no illusions about heavy drinking by Burns in the Dumfriesshire years. He was the first to write of one very hectic drunken escapade, documented in hitherto-buried court records, perpetrated by Burns and his fellow-exciseman John Lewars.[40] There is no doubt that a lot of wine consumed meant a lot of lead poisoning in the late eighteenth century, and Burns might well have been a very susceptible subject.

Old Scotland itself as a country had no bad reputation for shortening the life-span, in fact it was considered that slipping away too soon brought disgrace to the glen. Once the hazards of serious infectious disease had been left behind, the temperate tended to live on and on. Most of the 'Reverends' who were friends of Burns exemplify this: Archibald (died aged 82), Baird (79), Blair (82), Carfrae (80), Lawrie (77) and Skinner (86). Many other steady citizens also performed well in the longevity stakes: James Burness (87), De Peyster (86), Findlater (84), Hill (83), Miller (84), Monboddo (85), William Tytler (81). As for the ladies, we may take note of Clarinda (82), Miss Benson (83), Mrs Dunlop (85), while 'the bony Lass o' Ballochmyle' reached a grand 90. We may read something into the eleventh Earl of Buchan's advice in a letter to Burns of February 1787: 'drink deep of the fountains of Helicon, but beware the Joys that is dedicated to the Jolly God of wine'. It would appear that the Earl proved his point by attaining the age of 87.

Against the above background we may note that, like Burns himself, some hard-drinking contemporaries were relatively short-lived. William Nicol died in 1797 aged 53. His printer friend 'old ˄nful Smellie' died in 1795 aged 45. Robert Riddell, one of the ˄istle' drinking contestants at Friars Carse, died in 1784 aged

39, and his brother Walter died in 1802 aged only 38. William ('Ebenezer') Michie, for whom Burns wrote a mock epitaph when he fell asleep during a spree, also died in 1802 aged 38. Lacking precise details explaining the untimely death of these men, it makes no sense to be dogmatic on the issue, but we know enough to justify suspicion of chronic lead poisoning, at least as a contributing scale-tipping factor.

That's about enough on the gap-bedevilled medical history of Robert Burns, apart from some dismounting generalities. Nothing offered is declared *ex cathedra*; indeed any such pose by a scientist who is not a medical practitioner would be audacious: some would say impertinent. Fair enough, but it is worth remembering that, in far bigger leagues, Pasteur was a chemist and Faraday was a book-binder's apprentice. Overall, one ascendant injunction emerges – beware of the biographer; in particular the medical biographer! Currie and Maxwell got it wrong because of contemporary limitations in the medical art: Crichton-Browne got it wrong, partly because his medical knowledge was dated, but more significantly because his unqualified worship of the Bard interfered with objectivity. Gilchrist, in his forceful but rambling way – not invariably rigorous – demanded new departures but could not cast off a final rheumatic myocarditis mooring line. Must we forever keep searching for the dropped penny under the Crichton-Browne lamppost? A penny can roll a long way in the dark.

If his theses do little more than attract dispassionate and well-reasoned dialectic, the author will be more than satisfied.

> . . . doubt wisely, in strange way
> To stand inquiring right, is not to stray;
> To sleep, or run wrong is. On a huge hill,
> Cragged, and steep, Truth stands, and he that will
> Reach her, about must, and about must go.

> (Donne: *Satire* III, 77–81)

APPENDICES

APPENDIX A

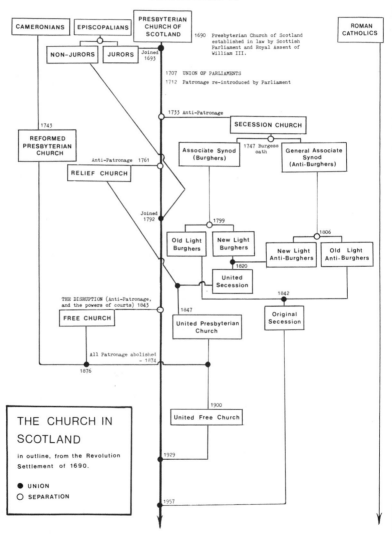

The Church in Scotland. (R.H. Fowler)

APPENDIX B: ALEXANDER POPE'S *BOUNCE TO FOP*

The earthy humour of this highly original Epistle, represented as
written by Pope's Great Dane bitch at Twickenham to Lady
Suffolk's lap-dog, would have delighted Burns. It is highly
probable that it gave him the idea of writing *The Twa Dogs* (K.71).
Note that both poems are set in tetrameric rhymed couplets, and
have stanzas of varying length.

> To thee, sweet Fop, these lines I send,
> Who, though no spaniel, am a friend.
> Though, once my tail in wanton play,
> Now frisking this, and then that way,
> Chanced, with a touch of just the tip,
> To hurt your Lady-lap-dog-ship;
> Yet thence to think I'd bite your head off!
> Sure Bounce is one you never read of.
>
> Fop! you can dance, and make a leg,
> Can fetch and carry, cringe and beg,
> And, (what's the top of all your tricks)
> Can stoop to pick up strings and sticks.
> We country dogs love nobler sport,
> And scorn the pranks of dogs at court.
> Fye, naughty Fop! where'er you come
> To f——t and p——ss about the room,
> To lay your head in every lap,
> And, when they think not of you – snap!
> The worst that envy, or that spite
> E'er said of me, is, I can bite:
> That sturdy vagrants, rogues in rags,
> Who poke at me, can make no brags;
> And that to towze such things as flutter,
> To honest Bounce is bread and butter.
>
> While you, and every courtly fop,
> Fawn on the Devil for a chop,
> I've the humanity to hate
> A butcher, though he brings me meat;

And let me tell you, have a nose,
(Whatever stinking fops suppose)
That under cloth of gold or tissue,
Can smell a plaster, or an issue.

Your pilfering Lord, with simple pride,
May wear a pick-lock at his side;
My master wants no key of state,
For Bounce can keep his house and gate.

When all such dogs have had their days,
As knavish Pams, and fawning Trays;
When pampered Cupids, beastly Veni's,
And motly, squinting Harvequini's,
Shall lick no more their Lady's br——,
But die of looseness, claps, or itch;
Fair Thames from either echoing shore
Shall hear, and dread my manly roar.

See Bounce, like Berecynthia, crowned
With thund'ring offspring all around,
Beneath, beside me, and a top,
A hundred sons! and not one Fop.

Before my children set your beef,
Not one true Bounce will be a thief;
Not one without permission feed,
(Though some of J——'s hungry breed)
But whatsoe'er the father's race,
From me they suck a little grace.
While your fine whelps learn all to steal,
Bred up by hand on chick and veal.

My eldest-born resides not far,
Where shines great Strafford's glittering Star:
My second (child of fortune!) waits
At Burlington's Palladian gates:
A third majestically stalks
(Happiest of Dogs!) in Cobham's walks:
One ushers friends to Bathurst's door;
One fawns, at Oxford's, on the poor.

Nobles, whom arms or arts adorn

Wait for my infants yet unborn.
None but a peer of wit and grace,
Can hope a puppy of my race.

And O! would Fate the bliss decree
To mine (a bliss too great for me)
That two, my tallest sons, might grace
Attending each with stately pace,
Iülus' side, as erst Evander's,
To keep off flatt'rers, spies, and panders,
To let no noble slave come near,
And scare Lord Fannys from his ear:
Then might a royal youth, and true,
Enjoy at least a friend – or two:
A treasure, which, of royal kind,
Few but himself deserve to find.

Then Bounce ('tis all that Bounce can crave)
Shall wag her tail within the grave.

And though no doctors, Whig or Tory ones,
Except the sect of Pythagoreans,
Have immortality assigned
To any beast, but Dryden's hind:
Yet Master Pope, whom truth and sense
Shall call their friend some ages hence,
Though now on loftier themes he sings
Than to bestow a word on kings,
Has sworn by *Sticks* (the poet's oath,
And dread of dogs and poets both)
Man and his works he'll soon renounce,
And roar in numbers worthy Bounce.

APPENDIX C: THE DEATH OF THE SECOND TWINS

Robert Burns has proven sins enough without superadding, by
unprovable supposition, an element of direct accountability for the
neonatal death of Jean Armour's twin baby girls – as a consequence
of the notorious 'scalade' on the 'horselitter'. The first of the pair to
die lived eight days: the second twenty days. Why did they die so
soon?

The first cause of death to eliminate, if possible, is prematurity. Prematurity, characterized by seriously low birth weight, may be due to premature delivery, or to handicapped development *in utero* despite an acceptably normal gestation time. Had Burns's reputedly vigorous coitus, with a possible contributory effect of the seminal prostoglandins, resulted in fatal premature delivery, he was a guilty man. If, on the other hand, Jean had given birth at acceptably normal term, he was innocent, however much his action might attract censure for other reasons. Therefore, the whole judgmental issue centres around what we can deduce about the gestation period.

In a reminiscent letter to Mrs Dunlop, Burns stated 'On my éclatant return to Mauchline, I was made very welcome to visit my girl. The usual consequences began to betray her' (L.254). The date of the 'éclatant return' was 8 or 9 June 1787. To forecast the likely time for a birth, obstetricians regard the normal duration of pregnancy to be 280 days from the start of the previous menstrual cycle. When (as in this case) that date is not known, 15 days are subtracted from the 280 to give an approximation of the term, starting from presumed fertilization. So, if we check back 265 days from 3 March 1788 (the birth date of Jean's twins) we arrive at 11 June 1787 for the approximate date of cell union, lending support to the presumption that intercourse occurred, fruitfully, at the time Burns was made welcome early in the preceding June. This calculation and presumption rule out premature delivery of the infants, and exonerate Burns.

The alternative, pointing to prematurity and guilt, is the possibility that impregnation occurred a month or more later than early June 1787. Burns was back in Mauchline in early July after his trip to West Argyll and remained there to the end of the first week in August (L.118). If the union which initiated the pregnancy happened in that later period, we must infer prematurity and point the accusing finger at Burns. But there are good grounds for rejecting such a thesis. Burns was just not the man to pass up a perfect opportunity for sexual gratification. Such an opportunity was obviously there around 9 June 1787, and the message of the letters is that the opportunity was seized.

On the balance of probabilities we rule out premature birth of the infants and absolve Burns from serious guilt. The alternative causes of infant death within a few weeks from birth at normal term are legion. They include respiratory distress, bowel infection leading to dehydration (tragically common), respiratory tract infection progressing to pneumonia or meningitis, or even simple chilling leading to fatal sclerema. The rather primitive living conditions in that single upstairs room would have been conducive to any of those tragic developments.

Let anyone so inclined censure Burns in retrospect for having *initiated* the pregnancy which, under the circumstances, was to compel Jean Armour to go through a grossly unhappy experience, but any suggestion that Burns's behaviour ten days or so before the birth played any significant part of the neonatal deaths should not be advanced glibly and arbitrarily. There is no positive supporting evidence.

Note: In this Appendix, medical information is largely based on the text of Sir Lance Townsend's *Obstetrics for Students* (Melbourne U.P., 1964), including its important chapter on the newborn contributed by Dame Kate Campbell. Additional information was kindly supplied by Professor N.A. Beischer of Melbourne by personal correspondence.

APPENDIX D: BURNS AND MERCURIAL MEDICATION

1 Published as an Appendix to *Education: Man's Salvation from Crime, Disease and Starvation*, by John Thomson M.D. 1844

Before sending forth these fugitive pages, I am anxious to say that the word 'help-me-up' is no coinage of mine; – that Scotia's immortal poet, Robert Burns, supplied me with that word. Particular circumstances brought me into very intimate intercourse with him during the closing months of his most eventful life. In youth's 'extatic hour' I enjoyed the ineffable happiness and benefit of his society; – for months I met him almost every morning at five o'clock on the banks of the Nith. My opinion and positive belief that 'man shall progress' were there and then often discussed, and the channel of progression here briefly described, he called my Help-me-up.

Reader, permit me to pass from nomenclature to an infinitely more important and holy concern, to vindicate the memory of Robert Burns from the blackest stain which Fame has affixed – diabolically affixed to his splendid scutcheon. Fame prompted by priests, yes, countenanced by friends, has promulgated an untruth, that Robert Burns died – prematurely died dissipation's martyr. From personal correct knowledge, I proclaim that Robert Burns died the doctor's martyr; and as a very few years must sweep away all *living* testimony upon that point, I avail myself of the approaching Festival, and challenge the contradiction of all his living co-temporaries who may there congregate.

The truth stands thus: – The physician of Robert Burns believed that his liver was diseased, and placed him under a course of mercury. In those days, a mercurial course was indeed a dreadful alternative. I know well that his mercurial course was extremely severe. In addition to this severity, his physician believed that sea-bathing was the best tonic after salivation. Thus he was sent to the Breu for sea-bathing. In the course of, I think, three weeks, he returned home from sea-bathing, inflated, black with dropsy, and soon died. Among the last words I ever heard him speak, were, – Well, the doctor has made a finish of it now.

Such I affirm to be the truth; – 'wha then dares battle wi' me?' 'Come forth, thou slanderer'.

[Two further paragraphs on education end the Appendix.]

2 *Hair Analysis*: A modern approach to the solution of the Burns mercury problem was made by Professor J.M.A. Lenihan and Dr Hamilton Smith of the Department of Forensic Medicine, University of Glasgow. (See their letter to the *Lancet* 1971, II, 1030.) A hair sample provided by Mr J.F. Walker of Dundee was subjected to activation analysis. This non-destructive and highly sensitive method gave the figure of 8 parts mercury per million in the hair. That figure is about double the average for the population at large, but well below the levels found in mercury poisoning.

Even accepting the provenance of the hair sample as undoubted, the likelihood that it was collected after death or when Burns was close to death seriously limits the value of any conclusions to be drawn from the analysis. Mercury from the circulating blood is taken up by hair as it is formed in the follicles, but that mercury cannot move along the metabolically inert hair shafts ahead of the region of their formation. As Burns was, allegedly, taking mercury only during his last few months, any tell-tale mercury content would be found only in, or close to, the hair roots. For this reason the sample tested may well have given a misleadingly-low reading.

The result would have been more positively informative had the record shown that mercurial medication had been going on for a year or so prior to death.

The question of lead poisoning, on the other hand, could readily be confirmed or eliminated. Should the day come when aesthetic considerations yield place to historical pragmatism, X-radiography of the skeletal remains would confirm or eliminate severe lead poisoning.

APPENDIX E: A. FOTHERGILL: *ON THE POISON OF LEAD*

Extracts from *Cautions to the Heads of Families*
Essay No. 2: *On the Poison of Lead*, by A. Fothergill F.R.S., M.D., M.R.C.P. Bath. 1790

Lead in every form is unfriendly to animal and vegetable life. The miners who dig the ore, the smelters who reduce it to a metallick state, manufacturers of white lead, painters, plumbers, in a word, all who are much exposed to its effluvia, bear testimony to its pernicious effects. . . . Its various preparations, as litharge, red and white lead, are all poisonous, and their activity is increased by their union with acids. Lead unfortunately being thus liable to be corroded, or even dissolved by almost every species of acid, the dangerous consequences are proportionately increased. For it not only unites with the stronger mineral acids, but also with those of the weaker vegetable kind, as that of wine, beer, cyder, vinegar, verjuice, &c. to which it imparts a manifest sweetness, forming a salt termed sugar of lead. Hence the foundation of that most dangerous abuse of correcting acid wines and cyder with litharge, or other preparations of this metal . . . .

To such an alarming pitch had the dangerous art of adulterating liquors with lead arrived in France, that at length it became necessary to make it a capital offence. I am unwilling to believe that any man would presume to practise this inhuman fraud, were he fully apprized of the poisonous nature of the ingredient. That none of my readers may plead ignorance, I shall briefly mention its principal effects.

This metallick poison then is powerfully styptick, and highly injurious to the nerves, hence it suppresses the natural intestinal discharges, producing obstinate costiveness, and a peculiar species

251

of colick terminating in palsy of the extremities, which generally deprives them of motion, without destroying their sensation. These symptoms, being the genuine effects of lead, seem to mark its specific power, and distinguish it from every other poison.

It moreover occasions a pale sallow countenance, contraction and wasting of the muscles, numbness, tremors, languors, convulsions, epilepsy, and death. These symptoms vary according to the quantity of the poison, the state of the body, the irritability of the system, and other circumstances. Sometimes, without producing spasms or other violent symptoms, it only occasions a slow lingering indisposition, which, however, lasts some years, and at length generally eludes the power of medicine. This well accords with what has been transmitted to us concerning the slow poisons of the ancients, and seems to confirm the suspicion that their basis was no other than a secret calx of lead. – May this fatal calx long rest in oblivion, and never more be revived! [A dissertation on water contamination from lead vessels, guttering and pipes follows.]

Wines: It is worthy observation, that the endemial colick, which formerly was wont to infest the inhabitants of Poitou, so as to become proverbial, is now no longer known, since the practice of adulterating wines has been abolished from that district. In whatever country the liquors are impregnated with lead, either by accident or design, this disease will be found to prevail, as will, I think, more fully appear in the sequel. Hence the colick of Poitou, and of Devonshire, and the dry bellyache of the West Indies, (whatever some may assert to the contrary) are evidently one and the same disease, and may clearly be traced to the same cause, the poison of lead.

Notwithstanding the severity of the laws, the fatal abuse still prevails, particularly in many parts of France and Germany, where their weaker wines, being prone to acidity, are still, in defiance of all laws, human and divine, corrected with litharge, or sweetened with sugar of lead! Nor is this wholly confined to the lower white-wines, such as the Rhenish, and the Moselle, for in a late French publication, intitled *La Maison Rustique*, a large ball of lead is piously directed to be suspended in the cask in order to prevent the wines of *Burgundy* from turning acid! At Paris, the low meagre wines commonly sold to the populace are made to run through a leaden channel, and are distributed to the customers in measures composed of tin, or base pewter containing a large portion of lead. Accordingly, the colick of Poitou is still predominant in Paris. Dr Gadane computes the average number of inhabitants annually afflicted with this disease to amount to five or six hundred. ·M. Senac, late physician to the King of France, adds his testimony concerning the frequency of the disease at Versailles. Dr Warren enumerates thirty instances among the servants and domesticks of an English nobleman, during his residence at Hanover, all occasioned by the same cause. It has been observed with surprize that, at Surinam, the Europeans who drink French wines are extremely liable to this disease, while the natives, who refrain from this beverage, entirely escape.

If we turn our attention to our English *made* wines, I fear they will by no means be found clear of suspicion. In Graham's art of making British wines, are the following choice receipts:

1   To soften green wine
Put in some vinegar wherein *litharge* has been well steeped, and put a quart of it into a tierce, and this will mend it, in summer especially.

2   To hinder wine from turning sour
Put a pound of melted lead in fair water into your cask pretty warm, and stop it close.

From which it appears that William Graham was deep in the mystery of vintners: and his book, having gone through no less than six editions, may be reasonably supposed to have revealed the dangerous secret of those adepts in iniquity, to at least three thousand innocent families, together with their friends and connections! But to estimate the sum total of mischief accruing from the numerous receipt-books of this stamp published within these fifty years past, 'highly necessary (as the editors gravely observe) to *all families*', entirely baffles calculation! For, according to the sage advice of those worthy authors, scarcely any family is now found without one or more of their 'faithful guardians of health, or trusty monitors in every thing relating to food or physick!'

Dr John Hunter, in the year 1781, being stationed with the army at Spanish-town in Jamaica, finding this disease very prevalent among the soldiers who drank new rum, while others who abstained from it remained free, began closely to examine the liquor, and also the implements used in the distillery. The rum, in his experiments, gave evident signs of an impregnation of lead. The worm of the still, consisting of a large proportion of lead, he found corroded. . . .

Distilleries, and even breweries, with all their apparatus, ought to undergo a narrow inspection, as acids, and even their effluvia, are capable of corroding lead. Therefore the leaden worms, spouts, gutters, in a word, every utensil containing that metal, ought to be viewed with a jealous eye. . . .

[Then follow several passages covering Sir George Baker's findings of lead in cider at Devonshire, and warnings of the danger of storing dairy produce, pickles, vinegar etc. in leaden or lead-glazed vessels.]

Tea is imported into this country in chests lined with sheet lead. This, like other vegetables, contains a weak acid, which quality is probably heightened by a latent fermentation which tea undergoes when damaged by moisture. May it not in this state act on the metal? How far the tremors, depression of spirits, and other nervous symptoms generally ascribed to this vegetable, or the hot water in which it is infused, may not, in such instances, with equal probability be attributed to the lead in which it is inclosed, is left for future observation. (It may be of passing interest to note that the biographer of Burns, Dr James Currie, in a footnote to his dissertation on alcohol and opium, groups tea, coffee and tobacco as possibly harmful, and adds a suggestion that 'an inquiry into the particular effects of each on the health, morals and happiness of those who use them, would be curious and helpful. *The Works of R.B.*, vol. I, p. 249)

[Then follow several pages on the dangers of lead in medicines, children's playthings, paints and 'cosmeticks'. Fothergill concludes his *Essay* with some details of chemical tests to indicate the presence of lead.]

APPENDIX F: THE TARNISHED IMAGE OF GEORGE THOMSON

When J.C. Dick, early in the nineteenth century, exposed George Thomson's manipulation of Burns's lyric material and tune specifications for his *Select Collection*, that editor's posthumous career went into a tail-spin. Taking even the smallest liberty with the work of Burns is a heinous offence in the eyes of his ardent admirers. If any defence of Thomson can be raised it can only be that his priority lay in presenting Scotland's *airs*, and that in the way he believed to be suited to the audience he envisaged. Preoccupied with the airs and his overdone accompaniments, he had created musical beds in which the lyrics were in Procrustean peril. It is not a good defence – indeed to many Burnsians it is the core of the offence. But criticism of Thomson should stop there. There is no justice when, after finding a long-dead defendant guilty on one count, writers proceed to pin on him an extra cluster of unproved misdeeds and bad traits.

Without saying why, in 1930 Mrs Carswell wrote that Thomson lacked 'pecuniary decency'. Seeing his chance to build on that assertion, James Barke the Burns novelist wrote off the editor as 'a scrounging hound who never paid a penny for the Bard's immortal songs' (*Bonny Jean* 1959, p. 37). The facts point to the entirely opposite conclusion. Risking – and receiving – a flailing rebuke, Thomson sent Burns five pounds along with a gift copy of the first half-volume of the *Select Collection*. Thereafter, having been told that the collaboration would end if any more money was sent, he dared only send gifts in kind. We know of several: an attractive Indian-style shawl for Jean, a gold-mounted seal engraved with the recipient's own design of arms, costing Thomson twenty-five guineas, and the valuable original of David Allan's painting of *The Cotter's Saturday Night* family group, a gift that gave Burns particular delight. Thomson responded immediately to the poet's appeal for five pounds to help pay off 'a rascal of a haberdasher' who was threatening legal process. Thomson, supporting a family on a modest Civil Service salary, had to borrow that five pounds from an unnamed friend. A short time later he sent a further two pounds in response to the public appeal for funds to aid the distressed family of the deceased Robert Burns. The sums named may seem small today, but to arrive at today's equivalent salary value they must be multiplied by a factor of two or three hundred.

Other unpleasant charges repeatedly levelled at Thomson in recent times include resistance to yielding the copyright of Burns's song lyrics to Dr Currie for inclusion in the biography of 1800, and the suspected editing of his own letters before passing them to that editor. On the copyright issue there is no reason to doubt the observations of Robert Chambers, the first major biographer to mention the matter (1850). Of the lyrics Chambers wrote:

> Of these, only six had as yet been published, for one part or half-volume of Mr Thomson's work had alone appeared. . . . Of course, when a posthumous collection of the poet's writings was designed for the benefit of his destitute family, Mr Thompson at once gave up the songs. As he could not be said to have paid a pecuniary equivalent for them, this conduct was no more than just; but Mr Thomson did all besides which was to be expected from a man superior to sordid considerations. In order that the songs might come out fresh in the posthumous collection, and thus serve the family as far as possible, he interrupted, or at least retarded, the progress of his own work for some considerable time.
>
> (Chambers: vol. IV.)

In the yielding of copyright, Creech's niggardly reaction was in marked contrast. He had already made a handsome profit from the copyright of the 1786 collection, but he needed arm-twisting by Maria Riddell, by Patrick Heron M.P., and by the Lord Advocate before giving in reluctantly.

On the suspected editing by Thomson of his letters to Burns, thirty-one of which were published by Currie, one good question may be posed, and it is this: who would have had no qualms about blindly handing over a substantial set of letters spanning four years? If in fact he did some editing it was hardly a heinous offence. Other correspondents who disallowed publication of *any* of their letters by Currie – Maria Riddell and Agnes M'Lehose – have received little retrospective abuse.

A very damaging charge against Thomson, tediously repeated and overdue for unconditional refutation, is that he was the author of the insensitive and inaccurate obituaries printed soon after the death of Burns. The *Edinburgh Advertiser*, and some other papers, printed the first of these on 26 July 1796, and an expanded version of it appeared in the *London Chronicle* of July 28–30. The accusation that Thomson had written them was promulgated by J. De Lancey Ferguson, a professor whose name ranked high in the Burns world through his important editorship of the Burns *Letters* in 1931. But one ranking high can evidently sink low. In his Notes on Burns's Correspondents, Ferguson had written:

Thomson's sins were visited upon the third generation: his grand-daughter, Catherine Thomas Hogarth, was the unhappy wife of Charles Dickens.

– an example of snide irrelevancy and bad taste. Ferguson's laboured *Obituaries* charge against George Thomson appeared in 1934 (*Modern Philology*, XXXII). His case stands or falls on the interpretation of a brief passage in a letter written from Edinburgh by Alexander Cunningham to John Syme in Dumfries, on the day after Burns died:

Mr T—— has kindly undertaken to announce the Death to the Public. It will appear perhaps tomorrow or Monday, and I dare say from his pen something very elegant will be said. [Full text in Burns Chronicle X, 1935 p. 43]

This is the 'something very elegant':

On the 21st inst., died at Dumfries, after a lingering illness, the celebrated Robert Burns. His poetical compositions, distinguished equally by the force of native humour, and the glowing touches of a descriptive pencil – will remain as a lasting monument of the vigour and versatility of a mind guided only by the Lights of Nature and the inspirations of Genius. The public, to whose amusement he has so largely contributed, will hear with regret that his extraordinary endowments were accompanied with frailties which rendered them useless to himself and his family. The last moments of his short life were spent in sickness and indigence; and his widow, with five infant children, and in hourly expectation of a sixth, is now left without any resource but what she may hope from the regard due to the memory of her husband.

Two more shorter paragraphs follow, the first making an appeal for funds for the family; the second asking for letters and poems to be included in a planned publication.

Neither invocation in Voltaire's aphorism 'One owes respect to the living; but to the dead one owes nothing but the truth' found accord in the Edinburgh death notice. The feelings of relatives and close friends were not too well respected in the passage: 'his exraordinary endowments were accompanied with frailties which rendered them useless to himself and his family'. Furthermore, the

257

statement is untrue. It was not Burns's frailties that made his poetic genius unrewarding. The 1786 and 1787 publications had been financially rewarding, but a firm determination to revert to the status of poetic amateur as an Ellisland farmer and Dumfries exciseman had nothing to do with frailties. He was not without his frailties but the morning of his funeral was hardly the time to publicize them.

If there were statements to slam in the Edinburgh notice, they were mild when set against some in the obituary that was printed a few days later in the *London Chronicle*. As the latter is nearly three times as long as the Edinburgh notice, only some extracts are now quoted, with some concentration on passages that substantially repeat some in the first effusion:

> Burns was literally a ploughman, but neither in that state of servile dependance or degrading ignorance which the situation might bespeak in this country. . . . His early days were occupied in procuring bread from the labour of his own hands, in the honourable task of cultivating the earth; but his nights were devoted to books and the muse, except when they were wasted in those haunts of village festivity, and in the indulgences of the social bowl, to which the poet was but too immoderately attached in every period of his life. . . . A coarse edition of his poems was first published at Dumfries. They were soon noticed by the gentlemen in the neighbourhood. . . . His poems found their way to Edinburgh; some extracts, and an account of the author were inserted in the periodical paper, *The Lounger*, which was at that time in the course of publication. . . . A subscription was set on foot for a new edition of his works, and was forwarded by the exertions of some of the first characters in Scotland . . . Burns was brought to Edinburgh for a few months, every where invited and caressed, and at last one of his patrons procured for him the situation of an Exciseman, and an income somewhat less than 50 1. per annum. We know not whether any steps were taken to better this humble income. Probably he was not qualified to fill a superior station to that which was assigned him. We know that his manners refused to partake the polish of genteel society, that his talents were often obscured and finally impaired by excess, and that his private circumstances were embittered by pecuniary distress. Such, we believe, is the

character of a man, who in his compositons had discovered the force of native humour, the warmth and tenderness of passion, and the glowing touches of a descriptive pencil – a man who was the pupil of nature, the poet of inspiration, and who possessed in an extraordinary degree the powers and failings of genius. Of the former, his works will remain a lasting monument; of the latter, we are afraid that his conduct and his fate afford but too melancholy proofs. Like his predecessor Ferguson, though he died at an early age, his mind was previously exhausted; and the apprehensions of a distempered imagination concurred along with indigence to embitter the last moments of his life. He has left behind a wife, with five infant children, and in the hourly expectation of a sixth, without any resource but what she may hope from the public sympathy, and the regard due to memory of her husband.

As easily-recognizable passages occur in both notices, it appears that the unidentified London journalist used the Edinburgh text, embellishing it with scraps of unbalanced gossip from a Scottish contact and filling it out with the aid of inaccurate presumption. Note the complete silence on any Ayrshire background and on the 300-odd song lyrics sent to Johnson and Thomson. Crediting the publication of the '1786' to a Dumfries printer points to more gross ignorance of the Burns saga. Little more need be said about the London farrago. On the other hand, the need for belated justice calls for a close look at the circumstances surrounding the writing of the Edinburgh notice. There is only one clearly documented clue to give a lead-in – the plain fact that 'Mr T——' had agreed to be the writer. Professor Ferguson obviously began and ended his sleuthing around the name of George Thomson. Ready to hand was a Mr T——, the dog already with a bad name: why not hang him a bit higher? So, the writer of *both* notices just had to be Thomson. Never mind about the other Mr T—— whose name was leaping out from the list of Burns's important Edinburgh associates – that of the lawyer Alexander F. Tytler. The case against Thomson is pitifully weak: the case against Tytler is very convincing. Let us have an orderly listing of the issues.

Against Thomson's authorship:
1 Cunningham would hardly have approached a man who had never met Burns.

2 Thomson's dealings with Burns, spanning four years, were almost entirely about *songs*, and the word 'song' does not occur once in either notice.

3 As to 'frailties', he was not impressed with a possible bad effect of Burns's self-confessed resort to alcohol. His response to one admission was ' . . . drunk or sober, your mind is never muddy' (Letter 25 Feb. 1795).

4 Thomson was by no means unaware of Burns's Ayrshire background. He had written 'I have heard the sad story of your Mary: you always seem inspired when you write of her' (last sentence of Letter VII, Currie IV). It is hard to believe that he did not know the setting of *The Cotter's Saturday Night*, a poem he venerated, and at least the title of the song *Farewell. To the Brethren of St James's Lodge, Tarbolton*, published with *The Cotter* in all editions of the poems up to 1794.

5 Thomson would have been the *last man in Scotland* to write 'Like his predecessor Ferguson . . . his mind was previously exhausted'. In a long succession of letters he praised the excellence of the lyrics received until the final illness brought their cessation.

6 As to 'not qualified to fill a superior station' – recall Thomson's letter to the publisher of Blackie's edition of Burns's works (printed in the Nimmo edition). In it he complimented that publisher on a fair assessment and roasted the Excise for not having found a more senior post for the Bard.

Pointing to Tytler's authorship:

1 A more or less covert personal dislike of Burns by Tytler would have started from his first reading of the lines

    Three lawyers' tongues, turn'd inside out,
    Wi' lies seam'd like a beggar's clout;

– lines that he persuaded Burns to delete from *Tam O' Shanter* – and the dislike would have intensified as Burns's political radicalism became common knowledge in subsequent years. Tytler would have shared the reactionary views of his close friend Creech, a juror at Gerrald's trial for sedition.

2 As to 'his mind was previously exhausted'; Tytler, having accepted the task of appraising for proof-reading all items sent to Creech from 1792 onwards, would have had grounds for

suspecting a drying-up of the poetic fount on reading Burns's letter of 6 December 1792 with its disconcerting advice 'I again trouble you with another, & my last, parcel of Manuscripts'. And, in fact, it was his last. From that time onwards Creech received only some unprintable epigrams and one song – *Behold, My Love* – that arrived long after the last Edinburgh edition had been printed. Tytler would have known little, if anything at all, about the flood of song lyrics that flowed to Johnson and Thomson for a further four years.

3 Alexander Cunningham, himself a lawyer, would have admired the eloquence of his exalted senior at the Bar. He seemed to be just the man to write 'something very elegant'.

4 Tytler visited London as his business required, and was well placed to pass his Edinburgh text to *The Chronicle*, with some hastily-prepared expansions based on gossip. Those extra bits could even have been *viva voce*. For sidelights on his business visits to London, see Tytler's letter to Burns of 27 November 1791 (Currie II, L. CXXV).

Professor Ferguson saw the report of 'a distempered imagination' that embittered 'the last moments of his life' as a convincing proof of Thomson's authorship, Thomson having been the recipient of a frantic appeal for money to pay off 'a rascal of a haberdasher' threatening Burns with legal process. It is by no means a positive proof. In those days before telephones, any intimate group, anxious about the declining health of a mutual friend, would have pooled every scrap of information that came to one of their number by letter. Thomson would certainly have shown the 'panic' letter to Cunningham. We have an example of the exchange process, in the reverse direction, implied in a letter from Cunningham to Burns (L.50 in Currie IV). In approaching Tytler, Cunningham would have seen no reason to suppress that item about the Bard's last days at Brow.

Clutching at every pejorative straw, Professor Ferguson interpreted the absence of any public protest about the notices by Burns's close friends by tendentiously turning that absence against Thomson's character. He postulated the risk of copyright denial – copyright of letters and songs – for the vaguely-planned posthumous publication if Thomson were offended. Such a suppositon is farfetched and very unfair to the memory of a generous man. The friends upset by the notices were John M'Murdo, John Syme, Alexander Cunningham, probably Thomson himself and William Maxwell. There need be no puzzlement about their silence. A father supporting fourteen children and wholly dependant on the salary of a Duke's chamberlain, a Stamps Office clerk, a junior lawyer hoping to become a Writer to the Signet, a clerk to a government Board of Trustees, and a young Revolution-tainted medico building up a practice in a Tory town would never have dared launch a public protest against a Judge Advocate in 1796. A young lady friend named Maria Riddell was bolder in an indirect way, but she took care to use a *nom de plume* – 'Candidior', meaning 'more honest'.

REFERENCES

CHAPTER ONE: SANDS O' LIFE

1 Ferguson, J. De Lancey (ed.), *The Letters of Robert Burns*, (Oxford University Press, 1931).
2 R.B.B., *Isobel Burns: A Memoir*, (Paisley, London, 1894).
3 Brown, R. Lamont (ed.), *Robert Burns' Common Place Book 1783–85*, (Wakefield, 1969).
4 Cromek, R.H., *Reliques of Robert Burns*, (London, 1808) p. 237.
5 Jack, W., 'Burns's Unpublished Common-Place Book', *MacMillan's Magazine*, March–November 1879.
6 Wallace, W., *Robert Burns and Mrs Dunlop: Correspondence Now Published in Full for the First Time*, (London, 1898).
7 The full text of the Ellisland lease is given in Snyder, F.B., *The Life of Robert Burns* (New York, 1932), Appendix C.
8 Paine, Thomas, *The Rights of Man*, (London, 1791–2). Reprinted with Introduction by Seldon, A., London, 1969.
9 *Lives and Trials of the Reformers of 1793–94*, (Glasgow and Edinburgh, 1837). Full transcripts of the trials. The reported views of Henry Dundas are in the Gerrald section, p. 114 n.
10 Lockhart, J.G., *The Life of Robert Burns*, (London, 1828). Hutchinson edn, 1904, p. 165.
11 Chambers, R., revd Wallace, W., *The Life and Works of Robert Burns*, (Edinburgh, London, 1896) vol. III, p. 379.
12 Murray, W.J., 'Poetry and Politics: Burns and Revolution', in Brissenden, R.F. and Eade, J.C. (eds), *Studies in the Eighteenth Century IV*, (Canberra, Australian National University Press, 1979), pp. 57–82.
13 Currie, J., *The Works of Robert Burns*, (Liverpool, 1800), vol. I, pp. 206–213.
14 Thornton, R.D., *James Currie the Entire Stranger and Robert Burns*, (Edinburgh, London, 1963), pp. 296–7.
15 Currie, J., op. cit., vol. IV, pp 1–3.
16 Ibid., p. 7.
17 Chambers, R., revd Wallace, W., op. cit., vol. IV, p. 280.
18 Lockhart, J.G., op. cit., p. 217.

CHAPTER TWO: PROFANE RHYMER

1 Macintyre, R.J. (Rev.), 'The Religion of Robert Burns', in *Burns Chronicle* 1912, pp. 5 ff.
2 Barke, James, *Bonnie Jean*, (London, 1959), p. 129.

3 Mackinnon, J., *The Social and Industrial History of Scotland*, (London, 1921), pp. 36–7.
4 Letter written to Joseph Cooper Walker of Dublin, in Currie, J., *The Works of Robert Burns* (Liverpool 1800), vol. 1, pp.87–98.
5 Chambers, R., revd Wallace, W., *The Life and Works of Robert Burns*, (Edinburgh, London 1896), vol. 1, pp. 455–9.
6 Ibid., pp. 455 ff.
7 For critical analysis of the philosophy of Popper and his successors, see Stove, D., *Popper and After*, (Pergamon, 1982), and O'Hear, Anthony, 'Popper and the philosophy of Science', in *New Scientist*, no. 1470, 22 Aug. 1985, pp. 43–5.
8 Peter Hill's receipts cover plays by Garrick and Cibber only.
9 Smout, T.C., *A History of the Scottish People 1560–1830*, (Glasgow, 1972), Fontana edn, pp. 184–92. A good account of the persecution of alleged witches in Scotland.
10 Mackinnon, J., op. cit., p. 47.
11 Hewat, Kirkwood (Rev.), *In the Olden Times*, (Paisley, London 1898), pp. 282–5.
12 Macintyre, R.J. (Rev.), op. cit., p. 8.
13 Lindsay, Maurice, *Robert Burns: The Man, His Work, the Legend*, (London, New York), 1979 edn p. 69.
14 Douglas, Hugh, *Robert Burns: A Life*, (London: 1976), p. 68.
15 Jamieson, A. Burns, *Burns and Religion*, (Cambridge, 1931), p. 17.
16 Ibid., p. 8 ff.
17 Shairp, Principal, *Robert Burns*, (London, 1879), pp. 18–19.
18 Keith, Christina, *The Russet Coat*, (London, 1956), p. 74.

CHAPTER THREE: DISTANT SHONE, ART'S LOFTY BOAST

1 Currie, James. (ed.), *The Works of Robert Burns*, 4 vols, (Liverpool, 1800), vol. 1, p. 91.
2 Ibid., p. 12.
3 Dick, James C., (ed.), *The Songs of Robert Burns*, (London, Edinburgh, Glasgow, New York 1903); and *Notes on Scottish Song by Robert Burns*, (London, Edinburgh, Glasgow, New York, Toronto, 1908), posthumous, ed. I.M. Dick.
4 Grainger, Percy A., *Music: A Commonsense View of All Types*. A series of lectures given for the Australian Broadcasting Commission in 1934 and published as a pamphlet by the Commission in December 1934, p. 22.
5 Carswell, Catherine, *The Life of Robert Burns*, (London, 1930, 1951), plate VIII.
6 Davie, Cedric Thorpe, 'Robert Burns, Writer of Songs', in *Critical Essays on Robert Burns*, ed. D.A. Low, (Routledge & Kegan Paul, London, Boston 1975), pp. 159–60.
7 Dick, James C., op. cit.
8 Crawford, Thomas, *Burns: A Study of the Poems and Songs*, (Stanford University Press, 1960).

9 Kinsley, James, (ed.), *The Poems and Songs of Robert Burns* (Oxford University Press 1968); and 'The Music of the Heart' in *Critical Essays on Robert Burns*, ed. D.A. Low (Routledge & Kegan Paul, London, Boston 1975), pp. 124–36.

10 Daiches, David, 'Robert Burns and Jacobite Song', in Low, D.A. (ed.), *Critical Essays on Robert Burns*, (Routledge & Kegan Paul, London, Boston, 1975), pp. 137–56.

11 Davie, Cedric Thorpe, op. cit.

12 Two of Allan's watercolour drawings of Leadhills scenes are reproduced in T.C. Smout's *A History of the Scottish People 1560–1830* facing p. 416, (Fontana edn, Glasgow 1979).

13 Allan's drawing for *The Cotter's Saturday Night* is reproduced in Maurice Lindsay's *The Burns Encyclopaedia*, (Hutchinson, London, 1959) facing p. 65.

14 Quoted by Jack Lindsay in *Hogarth: His Art and His World* (London, 1977), p. 146.

15 Pinto, V. De S, 'William Hogarth', in *The Pelican Guide to English Literature 4: From Dryden to Johnson*, (Harmondsworth, 1968), pp. 278–92.

16 Burke, J. and Caldwell, J., *Hogarth: The Complete Engravings*, (London, 1968), note 237.

17 Lindsay, Jack, op. cit., pp. 190–1.

18 Trusler, the Reverend Dr, *Hogarth Moralized* (London, 1841, with additions by John Major), pp. 46–51.

CHAPTER FOUR: RUINOUS BARGAINS

1 Thornton, R.D., *William Maxwell to Robert Burns*, (Edinburgh, 1979), p. 153.

2 For map see Sissons, J.B., *The Evolution of Scotland's Scenery*, 2nd edn, (London, 1947), p. 132.

3 Mitchell, B.D. and Jarvis, R.A., *The Soils of the Country Round Kilmarnock*, (HMSO, Edinburgh, 1956), p. 142.

4 Strawhorn, J., *Ayrshire: The Story of a County* (Ayr, 1975), pp. 5–12.

5 Acts of Parliament of Scotland, vol. II, 499, No. 33 of 1555, repeated in APS III, no. 27 of 1567, 39.

6 Strawhorn, J., Op. cit., p. 49.

7 Handley, J.E., *Scottish Farming in the Eighteenth Century* (London, 1953), pp. 117–9.

8 *The Aberdeen Journal*, 26 Jan. 1767, p. 4.

9 Ibid., 20 April 1767, p. 2.

10 Ibid., 9 Nov. 1767, p. 4.

11 Ibid., 17 Feb. 1772, p. 4; 23 March 1772, p. 3; 4 May 1772, p. 4; 13 July 1772, p. 3; 30 Nov. 1772, p. 3; 25 Jan. 1773, p. 4; 13 Sept. 1773, p. 4.

12 Ibid., 12 Oct. 1772, p. 2.

13 Ibid., 30 May 1774, p. 1.

14 Sheet 14, Soil Survey of Scotland. See also *Annual Report* of the Macaulay Institute for Soil Research, 1959–60.
15 Russell, E.W., *Soil Conditions and Plant Growth* (London), 10th edn, 1973, pp. 658–661.
16 Symon, J.A. *Scottish Farming Past and Present*, (Edinburgh, London, 1959), ch. 25.
17 Cabell, J.B., *Jurgen* (1919, and Penguin Books).
18 Hughes, H., Review of 'Beyond the Jupiter Effect', *New Scientist*, 99, 1374, (1983), p. 704.
19 McVie, J., 'The Lochlie Litigation', *Burns Chronicle* (1935).
20 Sheet 22, Soil Survey of Scotland.
21 Mitchell, B.D. and Jarvis, R.A., op. cit.
22 Ibid., pp. 177–8.
23 McVie, J., op. cit.
24 *Glasgow Mercury*, Jan. 1783, third week.
25 Lockhart, J.G., *The Life of Robert Burns*, (London, 1828), footnote in ch. 2.
26 Brown, Hilton, *There Was a Lad*, (London, 1949).
27 Sheet 14, Soil Survey of Scotland.
28 Mitchell, B.D. and Jarvis, R.A., op. cit.
29 Ramsay, J., *Scotland and Scotsmen in the Eighteenth Century*, 1888, ii, 256n.
30 Lamb, H.H., *Climate, Present, Past and Future* (Methuen, London, 1972).
31 Burroughs, W., 'Cold Spells, Heat Waves and Blocking Anticyclones', *New Scientist* 81, 1142, (1979), p. 492; and Gribbin, J., 'Eighteenth-century Climate May Indicate Future Patterns', *New Scientist*, 83, 1173, (1979), p. 891.
32 Handley, J.E., op. cit., p. 210.
33 Ibid., p. 166.
34 Chambers, R. revd Wallace, W., *The Life and Works of Robert Burns*, (Edinburgh, London 1896), vol. II, p. 17n, and 288.
35 Smout, T.C., *A History of the Scottish People 1560–1830*, Fontana edn (Glasgow, 1979), p. 351.
36 *Dictionary of National Biography* (see Burnett, James).
37 Ferguson, J. De L. *The Letters of Robert Burns*, (Oxford, 1931), p. XXXVI.
38 Cunningham, Allan, *The Works of Robert Burns*, (London, 1834).
39 Beveridge, W.I.B., 'Where Did the Red Flu Come From?', *New Scientist*, 77, 1095, (1978), p. 790.
40 Charlesworth, J.K. 'The Glacial Geology of the Southern Uplands of Scotland, West of Annandale and Upper Clydesdale', *Trans. Roy. Soc. Edin.*, vol. LV, Part 1, (no. 1).
41 Stone, J.C., 'A Description of the Glacial Retreat Features of Mid-Nithsdale', *Scottish Geogr. Mag.*, 75, (1959).
42 Bown, C.J., West of Scotland Agricultural College, personal communication.
43 Chambers-Wallace, op. cit., vol. II, 320n.
44 Bowman, A. Ian, *Symington and the Charlotte Dundas*, (Falkirk

Museums, 1981); and 'Tracing the Charlotte', *Transport History*, (spring 1977 and autumn 1977).
45   Symon, J.A., op. cit., p. 148.
46   Snyder, F.B., *The Life of Robert Burns*, (New York, 1932), Appendix C.
47   Handley, J.E., op. cit., p. 158.
48   Currie, J., *The Works of Robert Burns*, (Liverpool, 1800), vol. I, p. 201.
49   Barke, J., *The Crest of the Broken Wave* (Glasgow, 1975), Fontana, p. 211.
50   Chambers-Wallace, op. cit., vol. III, p. 297n.
51   Ibid., vol. III, p. 440.
52   Cunningham, Allan, op. cit., Part III.
53   Symon, J.A., op. cit., p. 148.
54   Ibid., Appendix III.

CHAPTER FIVE: WHEN 'CATCH THE THIEF!' RESOUNDS ALOUD

1   Lonsdale, Roger, 'Gray and "Allusion": The Poet as Debtor', in *Studies in the Eighteenth Century*, *IV*, R.F. Brissenden and J.C. Eade (eds), (Canberra University Press, 1979), p. 34.
2   Wilford, John Noble, quoting from a letter from Robert Cattley to *Nature*, in *New York Times*, reprinted in *The Age*, (Melbourne), 28 December 1983.
3   Milton, John, *Iconoclastes*, Chapter 23.
4   Eliot, T.S., *Massinger's Debt to Shakespeare*.
5   Henley, W.E., and Henderson, T.F., (eds), *The Poetry of Robert Burns*, 4 vols, (Edinburgh, 1896).
6   Ross, John D., *Henley and Burns*, (Stirling, 1901).
7   Rolfe, Patricia, *The Journalistic Javelin*, (Sydney, 1979), Wildcat Press.
8   Serle, Percival, *Dictionary of Australian Biography*, (Sydney, London, 1949), Angus and Robertson, entry on A.G. Stephens.
9   *Australian Dictionary of Biography*, vol. 8, 1891–1939, (Melbourne University Press, 1981), entry on James Edmond, by Sylvia Lawson.
10   'MacParritch', letter to *The Bulletin*, (Sydney), 8 January 1898, p. 26.
11   Black, George, letters to *The Bulletin*, (Sydney), 5 February, 19 February, 12 March, 26 March 1898, Red Page.
12   'Tom Collins' (Joseph Furphy), letter to *The Bulletin* (Sydney), 12 March 1898, Red Page.
13   Black, George, *In Defence of Robert Burns: The Charge of Plagiarism Confuted*, (W. Dymock, Sydney, 1901).

CHAPTER SIX: THE LOVELY DEARS

1   Hughes, J.L., *The Real Robert Burns*, (Edinburgh, 1922).
2   Currie, J., *The Works of Robert Burns*, (Liverpool, 1800), vol. I, p. 221.
3   Lockhart, J.G., *The Life of Robert Burns*, (London, 1828).
4   Dent, Alan, *Burns in His Time*, (London, 1966), p. 109.

5 Rowbotham, Sheila, *Women, Resistance and Revolution*, (Harmondsworth, 1972), p. 46.
6 Graham, Harvey, *Eternal Eve*, (Altrincham, 1950), p. 369.
7 Browne, O'D.T.D., *The Rotunda Hospital 1745–1945*, (Edinburgh, 1947).
8 Simpson, K.G., 'The Impulse of Wit: Sterne and Burns's Letters' in *The Art of Robert Burns*, R.D.S. Jack and Andrew Noble (eds), (London and Totawa, NJ. 1982).
9 Cromek, R.H., *Reliques of Robert Burns*, (London, 1808), p. 237.
10 Snyder, F.B., *The Life of Robert Burns*, (New York, 1932).
11 Lindsay, Maurice, *Robert Burns: The Man, His Work, the Legend*, (London, 1976), pp. 111–14.
12 Ferguson, J. De L., (ed.), *The Letters of Robert Burns*, (Oxford University Press, 1931) vol. II, p. 336.
13 Chambers, R., revd Wallace, W., *The Life and Works of Robert Burns*, (Edinburgh, London, 1896), vol. II, p. 121.
14 Ibid., p. 145.
15 Fitzhugh, R.T., *Robert Burns: The Man and the Poet*, (Boston, 1970), p. 154.
16 Kinsley, J., *The Poems and Songs of Robert Burns*, (Oxford University Press, 1968), vol. III, p. 1438.
17 Chambers, R. revd Wallace, W., Op. cit., vol. III, p. 300.
18 McNaught, J.P., *The Truth About Burns*, (Glasgow, 1921) p. 174.
19 Angellier, A., *Robert Burns: La Vie, Les Oeuvres*, (Paris, 1893).
20 Brown, Hilton, *There Was a Lad*, (London, 1949), p. 103.
21 Keith, Christina, *The Russet Coat*, (London, 1956), p. 147.
22 Ford, R., *The Heroines of Burns*, (Paisley 1906), pp. 133–150.
23 Jack, R.D.S., 'Burns and Bawdy', in *The Art of Robert Burns*, R.D.S. Jack and Andrew Noble, (eds), (London, Totawa NJ., 1982).
24 The text is from Currie, J., Op. cit., p. 253 ff., widely reprinted.
25 Murray, W.J., 'The Women in Burns's Poems and Songs: the Poet as Liberationist', *Burns Chronicle*, 1982.
26 Smout, T.C., *A History of the Scottish People 1560–1830*, (Glasgow 1972, Fontana edn), plate adj. to p. 416.
27 R.B.B., *Isobel Burns: A Memoir*, (Paisley, 1894), p. 123.
28 Haynes, D.K., 'Our Guest Tonight Is . . . ', *Burns Chronicle*, 1977, p. 29.
29 Norman, John, *Cases of Conscience Practically Resolved*, (London, 1673).

CHAPTER SEVEN: BUT WHY O' DEATH BEGIN A TALE?

1 *Burns Chronicle*, 1981, p. 14.
2 The Heron *Memoir* is reprinted in Lindsay, M., *The Burns Encyclopaedia*, (London, 1959).
3 McCutcheon, G.B., *Anderson Crow Detective*, (New York, 1920) pp. 45–6.
4 Estling, R., 'The Trouble with Thinking Backwards', *New Scientist*, vol. 98, (1983) p. 619.
5 Fitzhugh, R.T., *Robert Burns: the Man and the Poet*, (Boston, 1970).

6   Anderson, H.B., 'Robert Burns, His Medical Friends, Attendants and Biographer', *Ann. Med. Hist.*, March 1928, pp. 47–58.

7   Wells, W.C., 'On Rheumatism of the Heart', *Trans. Soc. Improv. Med. Chir. Knowl.*, 3 (London, 1812), pp. 373–424.

8   Thornton, R.D., *William Maxwell to Robert Burns*, (Edinburgh, 1979), p. 99.

9   Ferguson, J. De L., (ed.), *The Letters of Robert Burns*, (London, 1931), p. XXXVII.

10 Stollerman, G.H. *Rheumatic Fever and Streptococcal Infection*, (New York, London, 1975).

11 Diamond, S. 'Masks of Depression', *Mod. Med. Australia*, 9, no. 7, March 28, 1966, pp. 97–8.

12 R.B.B., *Isobel Burns: A Memoir*, (Paisley, London, 1894), p. 9.

13 Reed, Christopher, *The Age*, (Melbourne), 13 Oct. 1984.

14 Gilchrist, R.S., 'Robert Burns: What Ailed Him?', *Burns Chronicle* 1979, pp. 81–4.

15 Hart, F.D. (ed.), *French's Index of Differential Diagnosis*, (Bristol, 1979), 11th edn, p. 362.

16 Harvey, Johns, Owens, Ross, *The Principles and Practice of Medicine*, (New York, 1972), 18th edn, p. 1383.

17 Stollerman, G.H., op. cit.

18 Harvey, Johns, Owens, Ross, op. cit., p. 205.

19 Harries, E.H.R. and Mitman, M., *Clinical Practice in Infectious Diseases*, (Edinburgh, 1951), 4th edn, p. 187ff.

20 Chambers, R. revd Wallace, W., *The Life and Works of Robert Burns*, (Edinburgh, London, 1896), vol. IV, p. 247.

21 Smith, S. Watson, 'The Disease that Killed Robert Burns', *Burns Chronicle* 1946, pp. 4–5.

22 Bardwell, S., in Fitzhugh, R.T., op. cit., App. B.

23 Hart, F.D., (ed.), op. cit., p. 464.

24 Anderson, T., in *Chambers Encyclopaedia* 1969, vol. 14, p. 68.

25 Lawrence, J., *General Treatise on Cattle: The Ox, the Sheep and the Swine*, (London, 1805).

26 Fleming, G., *Textbook of Veterinary Obstetrics*, (London, 1878).

27 Harries, E.H.R. and Mitman, M., op. cit., p. 548ff.

28 Harvey, Johns, Owens, Ross, op. cit., p. 675ff.

29 Thornton, R.D., *James Currie the Entire Stranger and Robert Burns*, (Edinburgh, London, 1963), p. 168.

30 Thornton, R.D., *William Maxwell to Robert Burns*, op. cit., p. 207.

31 Ibid., p. 188.

32 Drummond, J.C. and Wilbraham, A., *The Englishman's Food*, (London, 1939).

33 Waldron, H.A. and Stofen, D., *Sub-clinical Lead Poisoning*, (London, 1974).

34 Nye, L.J.J., *Chronic Nephritis and Lead Poisoning*, (Sydney, 1933).

35 Nelson, W.E., *Textbook of Pediatrics*, (Philadelphia, London), 8th edn, 1964, p. 1557.

36 Sodeman, W.A. and Sodeman W.A. Jnr, *Pathologic Physiology* (Philadelphia, London), 4th edn, 1967.

REFERENCES

37 Canterow, A. and Trumper, M., *Lead Poisoning*, (Baltimore, 1944).
38 Nelson, W.E., op. cit., p. 1559.
39 Ferguson, J. De L., op. cit., p. XXXVII.
40 Thornton, R.D., *William Maxwell to Robert Burns*, op. cit., pp. 163–8.

INDEX

271